George Meredith
A Bibliography

George Meredith
A Bibliography

Michael Collie

Dawsons of Pall Mall

ISBN 0 7129 0636 3
LC 73-85962

First published by Wm. Dawson & Sons Ltd. 1974
© University of Toronto Press
Toronto and Buffalo

Printed in Canada
by University of Toronto Press
For Wm. Dawson & Sons Ltd. Cannon House,
Folkestone, Kent, England.

Lc

Contents

Acknowledgements

Many people have assisted me during the last five years. I am extremely grateful for their help.

It is a pleasure to have this opportunity to thank Elizabeth Sweetnam, Irene Bennell, Sam Asein, Maurice Elliott, Gisela Argyle, and Jonathan Udoeyop for the help they gave me while the bibliography was being prepared. I am also grateful for the help I received during visits to American research libraries which have Meredith holdings, particularly:

The Beinecke Rare Book and Manuscript Library, Yale University
The Berg Collection of the New York Public Library
The Fales Collection of the New York University Library
The Henry E. Huntington Library, San Marino, California
The Pierpont Morgan Library, New York
The Miriam Lutcher Stark Library, University of Texas, Austin
The Harry Elkins Widener Collection, Harvard College Library.

The members of staff at each of these libraries have made my visits both useful and enjoyable and I am most grateful for their assistance. For permission to quote from Meredith's correspondence, manuscripts, and contracts I am grateful to Yale University Library, the Pierpont Morgan Library, and the Humanities Research Center, The University of Texas at Austin.

Finally, I thank Margaret Bowman most warmly for her constant help and encouragement.

This book has been published with the help of grants from the Humanities Research Council, using funds provided by the Canada Council, and from the Publications Fund of the University of Toronto Press.

Abbreviations

Beinecke
The Beinecke Rare Book and Manuscript Library, Yale University, New Haven, Connecticut

Berg
The Berg Collection of the New York Public Library, New York

Carter
John Carter, *Binding Variants in English Printing*, 1820–1900, London, Constable 1932

Fales
The Fales Collection, New York University Library

Forman
M. Buxton Forman, *A Bibliography of the Writings in Prose and Verse of George Meredith*, Edinburgh 1922
M. Buxton Forman, *Meredithiana: Being a Supplement to the Bibliography of Meredith*, Edinburgh 1924

Huntington
The Henry E. Huntington Library, San Marino, California

Letters
C.L. Cline, *The Letters of George Meredith*, Oxford University Press, London 1970

Morgan
The Pierpont Morgan Library, New York

Stark
The Miriam Lutcher Stark Library, University of Texas, Austin, Texas

Stevenson
Lionel Stevenson, *The Ordeal of George Meredith*, Charles Scribner's Sons, New York 1953

Widener
The Harry Elkins Widener Collection, Harvard College Library, Cambridge, Massachusetts

George Meredith
A Bibliography

Introduction

After his death in 1909, Meredith went out of fashion. The first world war brought an end to the era in which he at first struggled and then flourished – the era of the three-decker novel and the Olympian author. Since then Meredith's papers and manuscripts have gradually become available and there have been valuable, detailed studies of his work, so that a critical evaluation is possible that was not possible at all before, say, 1945. The present bibliography aspires to be a description of Meredith's writing life which is dependable for practical purposes and which takes into account work that has been done during the last fifty years.

Though Meredith's first novel was published in 1856, some thirty years were to pass before he had any real success as a writer. During this period he wrote continuously, dabbled in journalism to keep himself alive, married twice, worked as a reader for Chapman and Hall, and travelled extensively, mostly on foot. Even the better novels of the early period passed unnoticed by the majority of readers. *The Egoist* (1879) and *The Tragic Comedians* (1880) were the first sign of a greater compatibility between writer and public, but the real change occurred in 1885. *Diana of the Crossways*, published that year, was an instant success and was re-issued twice. Just as important was the first collected edition of Meredith's work, published by Chapman and Hall in 1885, since the ordinary reader could from this point on buy a single novel for a fifth and very soon for a tenth of the original price. It was through this first collected edition that Meredith for the first time reached a wider public.

From 1885 to his death in 1909 Meredith enjoyed immense popularity and prestige. He published three more novels. His work sold well in North America. He enjoyed two further collected editions of his work. And, perhaps regrettably, he was encouraged to pontificate on every subject under the sun in the daily press. The Order of Merit was the public recognition of a major author, who in retrospect was seen to have written boldly on a number of contemporary issues: marriage, divorce, and problems of sexual freedom; the question of the status of women; problems of class and the Radical conscience; and so on. Because his critique of society, albeit an implied critique, was solidly within the nineteenth-century English tradition stemming in part from Mill, it could be accepted more readily than a more strident revolutionary writing would have been, and thus, wise after the event, people came to see that Meredith had anticipated their own concerns and encased them in stories which, though abrasive and difficult in parts, were not unpalatable as a whole. The ending of *Diana of the Crossways* had more meaning for them than it has for us.

Meredith's popularity was short-lived but it gave rise to a spate of critical and bibliographical writing constituting the ancestry of this present work. The interest, indeed zeal, with which people talked about Meredith between 1896 (the date of Constable's first collected edition) and 1924 (the date of *Meredithiana*, a book that must have seemed a final compilation) resulted both in a spate of minor publication and in the first serious attempts to review Meredith's career. The existence of these minor publications extends Meredith's writing life, for the purposes of this bibliography, to 1924, fifteen years after his death, since by that time most of the ephemera had been collected and republished.

The attempts to review his career must be mentioned, since they in part determine the structure of this present work and since anyone who writes about Meredith must be deeply indebted to them. Early lists of Meredith's work were made in John Lane's bibliographical appendix to Richard Le Gallienne's *George Meredith: Some Characteristics* (1900), in Wm. Dallam Armes' *The Principal Works of George Meredith: A Brief Bibliography* (1898), Arundell Esdaile's *Bibliography of the Writings in Prose and Verse of George Meredith O.M.* (1907), and Dodd and Livingston's *First Editions of George Meredith* (1912). Though these works were prepared at much too early a date for them to have been accurate and comprehensive, they have a charm which derives from their closeness to their subject. M. Buxton Forman absorbed all of them, together with the bibliographical parts of the Memorial Edition, into his *A Bibliography of the Writings in Prose and Verse of George Meredith* (1922) and into the supplement *Meredithiana*, which followed in 1924. All that could be done so soon after Meredith's death, Forman did: photographic reprints of both books are currently available. The need for a new bibliography arises not so much from Forman's deficiencies, though he was weak on the collected editions and the identification of copy text, but from the fact that much more is known about Meredith's work now than it was possible to know then. A brief review will make the matter clear.

In the years following Meredith's death, the manuscripts of his work, notably those left as bequests to his gardener and to his nurse, reached the sale room and eventually found their way to American research libraries. Many American libraries built up substantial collections of manuscripts and books, including the important publications of Meredith's work in the United States, and these collections provide the basis for the present study. Amongst these libraries, special mention must be made of Yale, where the Altschul Collection provided the nucleus for a major and comprehensive Meredith collection: the mecca of all Meredith scholars. The catalogue of the original collection – *A Catalogue of the Altschul Collection of George Meredith in the Yale University Library* (1931) – is the second indispensable guide to anyone interested in Meredith's work, even though the collection has continued to grow. (A fact which is noted in part in two articles in the *Yale University Library Gazette:* 'The Altschul Collection of George

Meredith,' vol. 6, 1931, and 'The Altschul Collection of George Meredith Seventeen Years Later,' vol. 22, 1948.) In all these collections, the manuscripts are only a part, albeit an important part: equally important is the array of printed books, proof-sheets, annotated copies, letters, publisher's notes, contracts, and notebooks, very little of which was available to Buxton Forman in 1922. Thus, though the debt to Forman is considerable, the present bibliography is much wider in scope. In particular it attempts authoritative statements on the development of Meredith as a writer; on the circumstances in which individual books were written; on the relationship of the manuscripts where they exist to first editions; on the evolution of a text through various editions during Meredith's lifetime; on the significance of publications in the United States; and on the central place in Meredith's writing life of the collected editions.

Because of these extensive and varied aims, the bibliography is not arranged chronologically. Instead, under the main heading entry of the first edition, there is a listing of the serial, of subsequent editions in the author's lifetime and of the manuscript or manuscripts, and a brief discussion of the circumstances of publication and of the development of the text from the manuscript onwards. This can be done because there are very few editions of Meredith's work after the first: it is the collected editions that mark the important points in Meredith's career, and these are described in Part IV. Thus a reader will find everything that relates to a particular work under the main entry as indicated in the table of contents. As mentioned above, the effective terminal date for the bibliography is 1924: the main entries contain references to editions and re-issues that appeared before that. Re-issues that have appeared since 1924 have not been enumerated; such publications are mentioned only when they have bibliographical or textual interest. In passing, it is worth mentioning that there have been only two or three serious twentieth-century attempts to edit single novels by Meredith properly. Such work remains to be done and one can only regret, as ever, the re-issuing of unedited books – a practice which hampers study of several nineteenth-century novelists. Within the time span of the bibliography as a whole, a chronological list of Meredith's work is, however, given as an appendix, while the index supplements the system of cross-reference in an all-inclusive way.

Though the emphasis in a bibliography is necessarily on printed books, supplementary information about work that appeared in magazines and journals is given in additional listings in both Part II (Other Prose) and Part III (The Poems). The only part of the bibliography that does not aspire to completely comprehensive coverage is Part V: Translations. The listing is, of course, accurate within the period covered by the bibliography, but one would be taking one's courage in both hands if one claimed it to be complete. In passing, it must be stated that there is no instance of Meredith's returning to his manuscript after first publication in book form; no instance of the serial being textually more important than the first edition; and no revision by Meredith of individual works after 1885, though he did engage in a second general revision for the collected edition by Constable that first appeared in 1896. This means that each work has a compact history that can be treated without distortion in the way described above.

The final structure of the bibliography is influenced by Professor Cline's recent edition of Meredith's letters (*The Letters of George Meredith* edited by C.L. Cline, Oxford University Press 1970) and by the impending edition of the poems by Phyllis Bartlett to be published by Yale University Press. It seemed reasonable to attempt a work that complemented, rather than duplicated, the work that had been done already, particularly in the case of the poetry, where a detailed statement of individual uncollected poems would have been superfluous.

A TECHNICAL NOTE

Meredith's work provides an example of late nineteenth-century publishing and printing practice in one of its simple commercial forms. In the case of the novels, plainly designed three- or two-volume first editions are followed by cheaper, single-volume reprints, for the most part by the same publisher. In the case of the poems, plain and for the most part uniform first editions are followed by reprints, also in single-volume form, by a different publisher. Because Meredith's chief publishing contact was for many years the firm of Chapman and Hall for whom he worked, because his work did not sell until late in the century, and because he had little interest in 'fine' or 'limited' editions, most of the books described in the present bibliography have economical, trade exteriors.

On the other hand, there are important textual differences between the first editions of the novels and the two principal collected editions, those begun by Chapman & Hall in 1885 and by Constable in 1895. As mentioned in the introduction, it was not for subsequent single-volume editions but for the collected editions that Meredith for the most part revised his work. Consequently, in the arrangement adopted in this bibliography as a whole, Part IV on the Collected Editions is an important complement to Parts I and II, in that the various stages of revision lead in every case to the establishment of the definitive text in a volume in one of the collected editions. Whereas there is relatively little in Meredith to interest someone looking for elegant limited editions or splendid bindings, the evolution of the text under the guise of conventional nineteenth-century trade exteriors is fascinating. This fact has determined the balance of the bibliography and in particular the emphasis upon the evolution of the text as part of the descriptive process.

Throughout the bibliography, the words 'edition' and 'issue' or 're-issue' are used in an orthodox way. The distinction is doubly important with Meredith, as it is with some other authors, because he took every opportunity to revise his work. A new printing, if he knew about it, meant further revision to the text. On the other hand, it is not necessary to distinguish between single copies of particular editions or issues. The instances where there is disturbance of any kind *within* an edition or issue are recorded, but there are only a few such instances.

For the reasons given above normal procedures have been very slightly adapted to the special problems presented by Meredith's works. It is hoped that by this means the information which follows will be accessible both to bibliographer and bibliophiles on the one hand and to a wide range of literary people on the other. The list which follows corresponds to the order in which the details of a printed book are given throughout the bibliography and might therefore be read in conjunction with a sample description.

DATES The date of publication only appears in the main entry if it is known from the direct, physical evidence of the book or books being described. The entries in each part of the bibliography are in chronological order, while the appendix provides the chronology of Meredith's work as a whole. The absence of a date in a main description may mean, in the strict sense, that the date is not known.

TITLES The title of the main entry is identical to that on the titlepage and will not correspond in all cases to the title on the spine or the title by which the book is popularly known.

COLLATION Information under the sub-heading '*Collation*' is given in the following order: (a) the signatures of gatherings or an indication of actual gatherings when there are no signatures; (b) the number of leaves; (c) the measurement in centimetres of the largest leaf in the book examined, the height being given first; (d) an abbreviated summary of the pagination which distinguishes between the text and the prelims, included for convenience though it is, in effect, identical to what follows immediately under '*Contents*.' Because it may happen that a reader has in his hands one volume only of a three-volume edition, the '*Collation*' and '*Contents*' are given for each volume separately.

CONTENTS Information given under the sub-heading '*Contents*' is to be distinguished from 'table of contents' and constitutes the minimum transcription of those pages in a book which permit identification of it. It is a minimum description in a double sense. First, in transcribing the prelims one customarily moves closer to facsimile reproduction when the difficulty of distinguishing between one copy of a book and another is greatest. Second, except where it is essential, there is no detailed transcription of chapter headings, blank pages, and running titles in the body of the book described, because in the large number of copies examined no variations have been discovered.

Thus the transcription of the contents is a type of pseudo-facsimile. Of course all transcription might be termed pseudo-facsimile, since only the facsimile itself reproduces exactly what is on the page. What matters from case to case is the degree of faithfulness to the object being described necessary to the purpose in hand. There is no point in devising an elaborate procedure for inessential detail. In the case of Meredith, the watermark, the type-face used in the prelims, and the colour of individual printed words, for example on a titlepage printed in different colours, are never essential. For this reason they are not given. Meredith's books are far from being ornate. When someone comes forward with two copies of the first edition of *Evan Harrington* which can only be distinguished by the colouring of the lettering on the titlepage, or a further version of *A Reading of Life* only to be identified by the 'gothic' type on the titlepage, a method one or two degrees more complex may have to be adopted. For the time being simplicity has been preferred, although all known variants have been recorded.

Contents in Detail

So that a transcription under '*Contents*' can be read easily and accurately, a number of minor points have to be made.

a Puctuation, except for the punctuation of what is transcribed, is reduced to the minimum.

b A colon invariably divides the *statement* about what is there on the page from the details of the *transcription* itself. (Thus: '[i] halftitle: THE SHAVING OF SHAGPAT.')

c To avoid clutter and to reduce the possibility of error the page number is used as the punctuation between items. (Thus: '[i] halftitle: THE SHAVING OF SHAGPAT. [ii] blank [iii] titlepage.') Any punctuation that falls between colons is transcribed from a copy of the book being described, except in the very rare case where the colon is part of what is being transcribed.

d The pagination of prelims where there are no numbers on the page derives from a backward count from the first numbered page of text, instances of the backward count not coinciding with the gathering or the actual numbers on some of the pages being duly noted.

e In works of more than one volume, items that are repeated are not re-transcribed. Thus, if the printer's imprint is to be found on the final page of each volume of a three-volume novel, it is transcribed in full under the sub-heading '*Contents*' for Volume I, the word 'imprint' in the relevant place indicating that what is printed in Volume II and III is in every respect identical.

ƒ The existence of a table of contents is indicated simply by the word 'contents.' This means no more than that there is a page or more in the prelims in which a table of contents is given. Where the full transcription of the table of contents serves a purpose, as it does in the case of some volumes of poems, it is given as a separate item which reports the prelim pages accurately, not the titles and page numbers of the text itself. The chapter headings in the content tables of the novels are, in the case of Meredith, without either bibliographical or critical interest: they are not therefore included.

BINDING VARIANTS Of books published during Meredith's lifetime, books which therefore have a main entry in this bibliography, there are few genuine examples of variant bindings. One or two issues of the earlier novels may be distinguished principally by the binding but, even here, as in the case of *The Shaving of Shagpat*, the variant is likely to be a remainder binding.

Variant bindings of a few copies or of a single copy, and these indeed exist, come into a special category. Sometimes a trial binding was rejected in preference for something sturdier, as may have happened with the first edition of *Farina*. Sometimes the author's presentation copies, usually six, were separately bound, as is conjectured must have been the case with *One of Our Conquerors*. Sometimes a contemporary rebinding of a book for its owner causes a search for a variant where in fact none exists. Such variants as exist are of course interesting in their own right and those that have been seen are described.

THE POEMS Special mention must be made of the poems. Phyllis Bartlett's edition of them, based in part on a thorough study of the manuscripts, is in the press. Consequently to describe the manuscripts of the poems in the present book seems unnecessary. Before the bibliography appears her variorum edition of the poems will have been published. It is for this reason that the description of the volumes of poetry in Part III is supplemented by a census of poems, in alphabetical order according to the first line, giving the title, its serial publication, and its first appearance in book form. By this means the reader will be able to identify single poems even if he does not know in which volume they were published.

THE MANUSCRIPTS There are more than a thousand Meredith manuscripts in existence, all but a handful of them enjoying the excellent care of American research libraries. They do not, however, receive equal treatment m the present bibliography and this note is to explain why. For convenience they can be considered in main categories: the letters, the poems, notebooks and contracts, and the novels. There is no need to describe the manuscripts of the letters since a precise statement about each of them is included in Cline's edition of the letters.

The same applies to the poems, though here the decision to exclude a description of at least some manuscripts was more difficult. Even when the work for the bibliography was begun, it was seen that manuscripts which gave variants of individual poems would have to await an editor, not a bibliographer, yet it would have been consistent to have included a description of the more substantial MSS, such as those of *Modern Love* (in the Beinecke) and *The Empty Purse* (in the Huntington). Because of Phyllis Bartlett's edition of the poems to be published by Yale University Press, the poetry manuscripts have not been included. As for the manuscripts of Meredith's contracts with publishers, though they have been referred to usefully in the occasional article, they have not been used in a systematic way before to provide or illustrate the structure of his life as a writer. Their inclusion, either by reference or by transcription, has therefore been judged essential.

The more extensive description of the manuscripts of Meredith's novels is provided for a variety of reasons. Firstly, we are still without a good edition of Meredith's novels. Secondly, though there are only one or two instances where the MS version of a novel or story might be preferred to the first printed version, it seemed consistent in what for most novels is the first attempt to trace the evolution of the work from edition to edition, and issue to issue, to include the first stage in the process. Thirdly, the fact that the surviving manuscripts are scattered has in practice made it difficult for students to use them or even, in the early stages of work, to be aware that they all exist. To relate the various manuscripts of *The Amazing Marriage* or of *Diana of the Crossways* to each when they are as far apart as San Marino and New Haven has been beyond the powers of impecunious research students. Consequently, because they have proved difficult to use, a minimal description is included of each manuscript of each novel and story, the pagination in most cases being given in full so that the reader can speculate or calculate for himself about possible relationships and so that such manuscripts as may later turn up can quickly be related to what is known already.

PART I

Novels

Short Stories

I a

THE SHAVING OF SHAGPAT

FIRST EDITION

THE / SHAVING OF SHAGPAT. / AN ARABIAN ENTERTAINMENT. / BY GEORGE MEREDITH. / [crinkly short rule] / LONDON: / CHAPMAN AND HALL, 193, PICCADILLY. / 1856. / [*The Author reserves the right of translating this Work.*]

Collation [A]⁴B–R¹² 196 leaves (19.7 x 12.4) [i–vii] viii [1]–384

Contents [i] halftitle: THE / SHAVING OF SHAGPAT. [ii] blank [iii] titlepage [iv] imprint: PRINTED BY / JOHN EDWARD TAYLOR, LITTLE QUEEN STREET, / LINCOLN'S INN FIELDS. [v] author's note: It has seemed to me that the only way to tell / an Arabian Story was by imitating the style and / manner of the Oriental Story-tellers. But such an / attempt, whether successful or not, may read like a / translation: I therefore think it better to prelude / this Entertainment by an avowal that it springs from / no Eastern source, and is in every respect an original / Work. / G.M. / *December* 8, 1855. [vi] blank [vii]-viii contents [1]–384 text, on 384 at centre: THE END. and at foot: JOHN EDWARD TAYLOR, PRINTER, / LITTLE QUEEN STREET, LINCOLN'S INN FIELDS.

Binding Spine, and boards at front and back, covered in deep red cloth. Primrose endpapers.

Front cover Within a blind-stamped rectangle slightly smaller than book size and with ornamental devices in its corners, and in the centre at the top, in gilt: THE / SHAVING / OF / SHAGPAT

Spine Between blind-stamped rules, an arabesque ornament filling the space not needed for the words: THE SHAVING / OF / SHAGPAT / [rule] / G. MEREDITH. / CHAPMAN & HALL

Back cover Similar to front cover but with a blind-stamped device in place of the words.

Variant bindings (a) The binding of the second issue of *The Shaving of Shagpat* is in the same deep red cloth as the copy described above, though with white endpapers. The leaves measure 18.7 x 12.0; it is a slightly smaller book, though printed from the same plates.

Front cover Blind-stamped frame of three lines, the inner two of which are brought in at the corners. Within this frame a very simple blind-stamped design. The title of the book does not appear.

Spine In gilt, between horizontal lines at top and bottom: THE / SHAVING / OF / SHAGPAT. / [short rule] / MEREDITH. / [floral device] / 10/6 / LONDON / CHAPMAN & HALL

Back cover Identical to front cover.

(*b*) A further variant binding has a two-lined rectangular border at front and back, but without the blind-stamped design inside it.

These three would appear to correspond to Carter's A, C, and D copies (John Carter, *Binding Variants in English Printing, 1820–1900*, London, Constable and Co. Ltd. 1932, pp. 136–7). His B binding, which in title at least sounds like a re-binding, has not been seen. Sadleir, however, noted a further variant: 'dark blue-green (also medium-light green, also dark purple-brown) coarse-morocco cloth, blocked in blind on front and back with (*a*) a $\frac{1}{4}$ in. frame, (*b*) a single line frame, (*c*) a five-framed panel, of which frames 1 and 4 are $\frac{1}{16}$ in. and the other three single-liners, (*d*) a central lozenge-shaped ornament; on spine, blind-blocked into four panels (each divided by a double decorated rule, and all, save the second from the top, subdivided by a double plain rule with ornamentation above and below) and gold-lettered in the second panel: THE SHAVING / OF / SHAGPAT / [short rule] / G. MEREDITH (no stop and no imprint at foot). Primrose end-papers; top edges uncut, fore-edges and tail trimmed.

'The front covers measure $4\frac{15}{16} \times 7\frac{15}{16}$ in., i.e. they are as broad as the first binding (Carter A in *Binding Variants*, p. 136) and $\frac{1}{8}$ in. shorter. The sheets measure $4\frac{7}{8} \times 7\frac{5}{8}$ in., i.e. as broad as Carter A and $\frac{1}{16}$ in shorter. The spine lettering of the title (except 'OF') is $\frac{3}{16}$ in. tall and, I think, blocked from type, although carefully and sharply done. The book, as seen by me, has all the appearance of an issue of the late fifties or very early sixties' (Sadleir p. 261).

I b

SECOND EDITION

THE / SHAVING OF SHAGPAT/AN ARABIAN ENTERTAINMENT./BY/GEORGE MEREDITH. / A NEW EDITION. / LONDON: / CHAPMAN AND HALL, 193, PICCADILLY. / 1865. / [*The right of Translation is reserved.*]

Collation [A]⁴B-s⁸T⁶ 146 leaves (19.0 × 12.5) [i]-viii [1]-283 [284]

Contents [i] titlepage [ii] imprint: LONDON: / PRINTED BY C. WHITING, BEAUFORT HOUSE, STRAND. [iii] inscription: AFFECTIONATELY INSCRIBED / TO / WILLIAM HARDMAN, / OF / NORBITON HALL. [iv] blank [v] prefatory statement [vi] blank

[vii]-viii contents [1]-283 text, on 283: THE END. [284]imprint: LONDON / PRINTED BY C. WHITING, BEAUFORT HOUSE, STRAND. Bound in at the front is an engraved frontispiece by F. Sandys entitled: BHANAVAR AMONG THE SERPENTS OF LAKE KARATIS.

Binding Spine, and boards at front and back, covered in rough-surfaced red cloth. Cream endpapers.

Front cover Blind-stamped with a two-lined rectangular margin within which is a second rectangular design with ornamental breaks in the lines and in each corner a fan-like device. At centre a roughly circular device, within which is the publisher's monogram and around the outer ring of which is: STANDARD EDITIONS OF POPULAR AUTHORS.

Spine Stamped in gilt, horizontal lines at top and bottom with diagonal bars, between which: The / Shaving / of / Shagpat / [short rule] / G. MEREDITH / [device] / 1865

Back cover Identical to front cover.

THE RELATIONSHIP OF THE FIRST EDITION TO THE SECOND

There were only two editions of *The Shaving of Shagpat* before Chapman and Hall's Collected Edition of 1885. Little is known about the early years of Meredith's first marriage, but it is likely that this novel was written in the two years which followed the birth of his son, Arthur, in June 1853. It was published on 19 December 1855, although 1856 appears on the titlepage. The manuscript did not survive.

The second edition was published in 1865 as part of Chapman and Hall's Standard Edition of Popular Authors. Though the different type allowed it to be reduced in size by about a hundred pages, there were no significant changes in the text. Meredith was not responsible for the minor editorial changes that were made.

The plates of this second edition of 1865 were not used again.

II a

FARINA

FIRST EDITION

FARINA: / A LEGEND OF COLOGNE. / BY / GEORGE MEREDITH, /AUTHOR OF "THE SHAVING OF SHAGPAT." / LONDON: / SMITH, ELDER, & CO., 65 CORNHILL. / 1857.

Collation [π]²A-P⁸Q² 124 leaves (19.2 × 12.2) [i-iv] [1]-244

Contents [i] titlepage [ii] imprint: EDINBURGH: / PRINTED BY OLIVER AND BOYD, / TWEEDDALE COURT. [iii] contents [vi] blank [1]-244 text, on 244: THE END. / EDINBURGH: / PRINTED BY OLIVER AND BOYD, / TWEEDDALE COURT. Some copies of the first edition have, bound in, sixteen separately numbered pages ([1]-16) advertising other works published by Smith, Elder and Co. One such copy is in the Berg.

Binding Spine, and boards at front and back, covered with a ribbed apple-green cloth. Cream endpapers.

Front cover Blind-stamped with complicated design similar to that used for the first edition of *The Shaving of Shagpat*.

Spine Stamped in gilt, three horizontal lines at top and bottom, below and above which is an ornament. Between these devices: FARINA / A LEGEND / OF / COLOGNE / [short rule] / MEREDITH. / [ornament] / LONDON / SMITH, ELDER & CO.

Back cover Identical to front cover.

Variant binding Sadleir noted a variant binding to the first edition, which has not been seen. He himself had only seen his own copy, to be distinguished by its dark olive-green pebble-grain cloth and the design on the front and back cover. 'The blind blocking on front and back is quite different on the two copies. That on Copy I has elaborate foliage corner decorations and a complicated central ornament; that on Copy II consists of a handsome but more or less rectangular frame with a plain centre. The spine lettering is identical on both copies, but the decorative bands top and bottom and the ornament under MEREDITH are more ambitious on Copy I than on Copy II. This is the only specimen of Copy II I have ever seen' (Sadleir 1696).

II b

SECOND EDITION

FARINA / Legend of Cologne [device] By George Meredith / [illustration by W[alter] C[rane] engraved by W.J. Linton] / Smith. Elder. & Co. 65 Cornhill. / 1865.

Collation $1-7^{16}8^{12}$ 124 leaves (16.8 x 10.5) [i-iv] [5]-248

Contents [i] titlepage [ii] blank [iii] contents [iv] blank [5]-248 text, on 248 at centre: THE END. and at foot: [rule] / London: SMITH, ELDER & CO., Little Green Arbour Court, Old Bailey, E.C.

Binding Spine, and two centimetres of front and back, covered in a coarse-textured red cloth. Boards at front and back otherwise covered with green paper. Towards the top of the spine a gummed label: FARINA.

The second edition of *Farina* was based on the first, but was printed from new plates. Though there are minor textual and typographical differences between them, there is no evidence that Meredith participated in the preparation of the second edition. He was probably unaware of it.

VARIANT OF SECOND EDITION

FARINA / A Legend of Cologne [device] By George Meredith / [engraving by Linton] / Smith, Elder, & Co. 65 Cornhill. / 1865 [The titlepage of this edition is enclosed within a thin rule frame.]

Collation $[1]^{16}2\text{-}8^{16}$ 128 leaves (17.4 x 10.9) [1-5] 6-248 [249-56]

Contents [1] titlepage [2] blank [3] contents [4] blank [5]-248 text, on 248: THE END and at the foot of 248: [rule] / London: SMITH, ELDER & CO., Little Green Arbour Court, Old Bailey, E.C. [249]OPINIONS OF THE PRESS / ON / "FARINA." / [rule] / [A number of press opinions are reprinted on this page] / [rule] / LONDON: SMITH, ELDER AND CO., 65, CORNHILL. [250-6]advertisements for works published by Smith, Elder and Co.

Binding Stiff orange paper.

Front cover The titlepage, without its date, is reproduced on the front cover within frame roughly of page size, and is surrounded by an ornamental frame measuring 16.1 x 10.1. Above the reproduced titlepage at top: MONTHLY VOLUME OF / STANDARD AUTHORS. Above this the number: 28 [and the number of the volume in the monthly series]. Beneath the reproduced titlepage: ONE SHILLING.

Spine Three ornamental panels each containing: ONE / SHILLING / FARINA / SMITH / ELDER & CO

Back cover Within a frame similar to that on the front cover an advertisement for: FORTHCOMING VOLUMES / IN / THE ILLUSTRATED SERIES [*Farina* is listed as a volume already published.]

II c

THIRD EDITION

FARINA: / A LEGEND OF COLOGNE. / BY / GEORGE MEREDITH, / AUTHOR OF "THE SHAVING OF SHAGPAT," "EVAN HARRINGTON," / "ORDEAL OF RICHARD FEVEREL." / THIRD EDITION. / LONDON: / CHAPMAN AND HALL, 193, PICCADILLY. / 1868.

Collation [π]²A–P⁸Q² 128 leaves (17.4 × 11.2) [i–iv] [1]–244

Contents [i] titlepage [ii] blank [iii] contents [iv] blank [1]–244 text, on 244: THE END and at foot of 244: EDINBURGH: / PRINTED BY OLIVER AND BOYD, / TWEEDDALE COURT. [245]blank [246]advertisement for: STANDARD AUTHORS. / ONE SHILLING. [247–52]separately numbered 1-6, detailed advertisements for thirty-one novels in the series, mention of *Farina* appearing on p. 4.

Binding Pale yellow paper. Printed in lilac on front endpapers: advertisement for THE SELECT LIBRARY OF FICTION.

Front cover The same design as on the front cover of the 1865 paperback edition, except that this one is coloured red and blue. Within a frame slightly smaller than the cover: STANDARD AUTHORS. / FARINA / A Legend of Cologne [device] By George Meredith / [engraving] / ONE SHILLING. In the copy examined, at top right, within a separately stamped circle: REDUCED PRICE 6d

Spine In indigo lettering within frame, from top to foot: STANDARD / AUTHORS FARINA [device] 1/–

Back cover Full page indigo advertisement of the works of Charles Lever.

III a

THE ORDEAL OF RICHARD FEVEREL

FIRST EDITION

THE ORDEAL / OF / RICHARD FEVEREL. / A History of Father and Son. BY / GEORGE MEREDITH. / IN THREE VOLUMES. / VOL. I. / LONDON: CHAPMAN AND HALL, 193, PICCADILLY. / 1859. / [*The Right of Translation is reserved.*]

VOLUME I

Collation [A]²B–U⁸ 154 leaves (19.5 × 12.0) [i–iii] iv [1]–303 [304]

Contents [i] titlepage [ii] imprint: PRINTED BY / JOHN EDWARD TAYLOR, LITTLE QUEEN STREET, / LINCOLN'S INN FIELDS, LONDON. [iii]–iv contents [1]–303 text [304] imprint: PRINTED BY / JOHN EDWARD TAYLOR, LITTLE QUEEN STREET, / LINCOLN'S INN FIELDS.

VOLUME II

Collation [A]²B–Y⁸Z⁶ 176 leaves (20.0 × 12.3) [i–iii] iv [1]–348

Contents (i) titlepage [ii] imprint [iii]–iv contents [1]–348 text, on 348: END

OF VOLUME II. / JOHN EDWARD TAYLOR, PRINTER, / LITTLE QUEEN STREET, LINCOLN'S INN FIELDS.

VOLUME III

Collation [A]²B–Z⁸2A–2B⁸2C⁶ 198 leaves (19.9 x 12.2) [i–iii] iv [1]–395 [396]

Contents [i] titlepage [ii] imprint [iii]–iv contents [1]–395 text, on 395: THE END. / JOHN EDWARD TAYLOR, PRINTER, / LITTLE QUEEN STREET, LINCOLN'S INN FIELDS.

Binding Spine, and boards at front and back, covered in greenish-brown cloth. Glazed primrose endpapers.

Front cover Centrepiece and plain double lined border, blind-stamped.

Spine Stamped in gilt: [double rule] / THE / ORDEAL / OF / RICHARD / FEVEREL / [short rule] / G. MEREDITH / VOL. I. / CHAPMAN & HALL

Back cover Identical to front cover.

Some copies of the first edition of Volume III have 16 pages of advertisements at the end, dated 1 July 1859. One such copy is in the Berg.

Variant bindings (*a*) Reddish-brown cloth, with a blind-stamped variant decoration on the front and back covers and without the publisher's name at the foot of the spine. (*b*) Grey cloth (Forman 19).

THE RELATIONSHIP OF THE FIRST TO THE SECOND EDITION

Meredith wrote *The Ordeal of Richard Feverel* between August 1857 and June 1859 while living in Hobury Street in London. Probably the greater part of the work was done in 1858. The novel was published by Chapman and Hall on 20 June 1859 but never appeared in a magazine or journal during the author's lifetime, except in French.

When the novel failed, Meredith at first blamed Mudie, who had ordered copies for his library but had quickly decided not to circulate them. Occasional references in later years make clear that Meredith never forgave Mudie, who epitomized for Meredith as for others the worst type of prurience. But in addition, the reviewers had their effect. 'The quaint sarcastic style of the book makes it enticing,' exclaimed the reviewer in *John Bull and Britannia*, who went on to say: 'Indeed, though we are no advocates for the sickly doctrine which would ignore the facts of life and society, we are bound to say that Mr. Meredith has here and there overstepped the legitimate boundaries of what is known by the adjective "proper".' This opinion was echoed by the *Literary Churchman* on 1

September 1859: ... were it not for the forbidden ground on which it treads, and the extreme licence the author allows to his pen, it would probably make a greater sensation than any work that has appeared this season.' Perhaps, however, it was in *The Athenaeum* of 9 July 1859 that the Victorian reader's perplexity was expressed most pithily: 'The only comfort the reader can find on closing the book is – that it is not true. I hope the author will use his great ability to produce something pleasanter next time.'

Though the British reading public either did not react favourably to *The Ordeal of Richard Feverel* or was not given a chance to do so, the fact that it went through a number of foreign editions must have kept the novel in Meredith's mind. A severely compressed translation into French appeared in *La Revue des Deux Mondes* on 15 April, 1 May, and 15 May 1865. (It appeared as *L'Epreuve de Richard Feverel, Roman de la vie anglaise* and the page numbers in the three issues are: 911–50, 137–75, and 315–56.) A two-volume translation into Italian was published by Emilio Croci in 1873. And Meredith may have had preliminary negotiations with an American publisher, for there is a letter dated 29 July 1874 in which he says: 'My copy of *The Ordeal of R[ichar]d Feverel* has been lent to some friend. It is possible that Chapman & Hall have one, and if they have, I will request them to forward it to Holt & Co. Supposing the latter to be desirous to publish it in America, I should be of opinion that it would be as well for me to cut the opening chapters short, and correct here and there the lumpy style' (*Letters* I 487). He had already protested to Jessopp that when he opened a copy of the book he felt 'a sharp distaste. The lumpy style is offensive' (8 April 1873: *Letters* I 478).

Meredith did in fact revise the novel for Tauchnitz soon afterwards and it appeared the next year, 1875, as volumes 1508 and 1509 in his 'Collection of British Authors.'

It may be observed in passing that when Meredith revised *The Ordeal of Richard Feverel* he did not delete or change those parts of the story previously judged to be offensive to the British matron. The changes, which were the beginning of a longish process of emendation, were structural and stylistic. They involved the condensing of the first four chapters and innumerable minor shifts of emphasis, but not the deletion of chapter XIX, which did not occur until 1885. The second English edition published by Kegan Paul and described below, is identical, except in insignificant detail, to Tauchnitz, but it is printed from new plates. In a typewritten agreement (in the Berg) between Kegan Paul and Meredith, dated 3 November 1877, the publisher agreed to purchase the copyright of the novel for seven years from 1 December 1878 and to sell the book in one volume at 6s., Meredith to receive 1s. 6d. a copy after the first 750 sold.

III b

SECOND EDITION

THE ORDEAL / OF / RICHARD FEVEREL. / A HISTORY OF FATHER AND
SON. / BY / GEORGE MEREDITH. / LONDON: / C. KEGAN PAUL & CO.,
I PATERNOSTER SQUARE. / 1878.

Collation $[\pi]^2$A–Z^{8}2A–2G^{8}2H^2 210 leaves (18.5 x 12.4) [i–iii] iv [1]–384 [1]–32

Contents Frontispiece designed by C.O. Murray, with illustration on verso (i)
titlepage [ii] [*The Rights of Translation and of Reproduction are reserved.*] [iii]–iv
contents [1]–383 text, on 384: THE END. / [short rule] / PRINTED BY BALLANTYNE,
HANSON AND CO. / EDINBURGH AND LONDON [1]–32 with separate signatures, 32
pages of advertisements.

Binding Spine, and boards at front and back, covered in green cloth. Endpapers
black, but white on verso of free endpaper.

Front cover Stamped in black: at top and bottom a horizontal continuous line; at
top and bottom a horizontal broken line. In the middle, from top to bottom, a
spray of flowers stamped in gilt. At centre, between two horizontal lines, a book
with, on its open pages: THE PILGRIM'S SCRIP and THE ORDEAL OF / RICHARD
FEVEREL.

Spine Lines and spray as on front cover, but stamped in black. Stamped in gilt:
THE / ORDEAL / OF / RICHARD / FEVEREL / [short rule] / GEORGE / MEREDITH / C.
KEGAN PAUL & CO.

Back cover Stamped in black. Lines as on front and spine. At centre, publisher's
monogram.

In the Beinecke, there is a copy of the second edition with some half-dozen corrections to the text in Meredith's handwriting.

When Chapman and Hall published *The Ordeal of Richard Feverel* in the Collected Edition of 1885, it was again revised, though not substantially. Several
corrected copies of the second edition have survived – there is one in the Houghton
Library – but it is not clear that any one of them was used as the basis of the new
edition. A more substantial revision, including the excision of chapter XIX, was
made for Constable's first edition in the mid-nineties, so that as with some other
novels, the de luxe, though not the most interesting, has to be regarded as the
most authoritative version of the novel. The pocket 'revised edition' published

in 1899 by George Newnes 'By arrangement with Messrs. ARCHIBALD CONSTABLE & CO.' of course came after Meredith's final revision and is therefore without textual interest.

IV a

EVAN HARRINGTON

FIRST EDITION

EVAN HARRINGTON; / OR, / HE WOULD BE A GENTLEMAN. / BY / GEORGE MEREDITH. / NEW YORK: / HARPER & BROTHERS, PUBLISHERS, / FRANKLIN SQUARE. / 1860.

Collation $[\pi]^3[\text{A}]^{12}\text{B}–\text{U}^{12}\text{X}^6$ 260 leaves (19.25 × 12.5) [i–ix] x (misnumbered **iv**) [5]–491 [492]

Contents (i–vi] blank [vii] titlepage [viii] blank [ix]–x (misnumbered iv) contents [5]–491 text [492] blank [493–504] publishers' advertisements [505–10] blank

Binding Spine, and boards at front and back, covered in rough-grained black cloth. Light brown endpapers.

Front cover Blind-stamped border with publisher's monogram at centre.

Spine Blind-stamped border continued at top and bottom. Stamped in gilt: EVAN / HARRINGTON; / OR, / HE WOULD BE A / GENTLEMAN. / BY / GEORGE MEREDITH. / [device with five leaves] / HARPER & BROTHERS.

Back cover Identical to front cover.

Variant bindings Forman (p. 23) gives a terse account of the remainder bindings. 'Mr. Livingston in his *First Editions of George Meredith* says that "this edition of Harper's evidently had a small sale. Almost all copies are of a remainder, turned out twenty years or more after publication and bound in plain binder's cloth. The present copy is of the original issue in stamped black cloth." My own view is that blue cloth and black cloth copies are both of the original issue while those in brown cloth and red cloth came on the market later. Internally the four varieties differ only in size. The leaves of the blue and black cloth copies measure $7\frac{5}{8} \times 4\frac{7}{8}$ inches; those of the brown cloth copies $7\frac{1}{2} \times 4\frac{7}{8}$; and those of the red $7\frac{1}{4} \times 4\frac{15}{16}$ inches. The brown cloth is fine grained with blind stamping on the recto and verso, and on the back gilt lettering similar to that on the black and blue copies save that *Harper & Brothers* is in slightly smaller lettering; the end papers are white. The red cloth copies are lettered on the back *Evan / Harrington* between two rules and there are double lines at the top and bottom; the end papers are salmon coloured.'

IV b

EVAN HARRINGTON

FIRST ENGLISH EDITION

EVAN HARRINGTON. / BY / GEORGE MEREDITH, / AUTHOR OF "THE ORDEAL OF RICHARD FEVEREL," / "THE SHAVING OF SHAGPAT," ETC. / IN THREE VOLUMES. / VOL. I. / LONDON: / BRADBURY & EVANS, II, BOUVERIE STREET. / 1861. / [*The Right of Translation is reserved.*]

VOLUME I

Collation [A]²B–U⁸ 154 leaves (19.8 x 12.2) [i–iii] iv [1]–302 [303–4]

Contents [i] titlepage (ii) imprint: LONDON: / BRADBURY AND EVANS, PRINTERS, WHITEFRIARS. [iii]–iv contents [1]–302 text, on 302: END OF VOL. I. / BRADBURY AND EVANS, PRINTERS, WHITEFRIARS. [303–4] blank

VOLUME II

Collation [A]⁴B–S⁸T⁴ 142 leaves (19.7 x 12.2) [i–iii] iv [1]–279 [280]

Contents [i] titlepage [ii] imprint [iii]–iv contents [1]–279 text, on 279: END OF VOL. II. / imprint

VOLUME III

Collation [A]⁴B–S⁸T⁶ 152 leaves (19.2 x 12.2) [i–vi] vii [viii] [1]–282 [283–4] [1]–12

Contents [i–ii] blank [iii] titlepage [iv] imprint [v]–vii contents [viii] blank [1]–282 text, on 282: THE END. / imprint [1]–12 publishers' advertisements

Binding Spine, and boards at front and back, covered in reddish-brown cloth. Primrose endpapers.

Front cover A fairly elaborate blind-stamped design on a cloth the surface of which is rough-textured. The design itself consists of a large, ornamental oval surrounded by five pointed leaves, the whole contained in a double border.

Spine At top and bottom, the same border as on the front cover. Adjacent to the border at top and bottom, three leaves identical in shape to those on the front cover. At centre, blind-stamped, a double circle suspended from which are three leaves. Within these two circles, stamped in gilt: VOL. I.
Above the circle, also stamped in gilt: EVAN / HARRINGTON / [short rule] / GEO. MEREDITH

Back cover Identical to front cover.

IV b

SECOND EDITION

EVAN HARRINGTON. / BY GEORGE MEREDITH, / AUTHOR OF "THE ORDEAL OF RICHARD FEVEREL," / "THE SHAVING OF SHAGPAT," ETC. / LONDON: / BRADBURY, EVANS, AND CO., 11 BOUVERIE STREET. / 1866. / [*The Right of Translation is reserved.*]

Collation [A]⁴B–Z⁸AA–KK⁸LL⁴ 264 leaves (19.8 x 12.2) [i–viii] [1]–519 [520]

Contents [i–iii] blank [iv] engraving illustrating p. 192 [v] titlepage [vi] imprint: LONDON: / BRADBURY, EVANS, AND CO., PRINTERS, WHITEFRIARS. [vii–viii (viii misnumbered iv)] contents [1]–519 text, on 519 at centre: THE END. and at foot: BRADBURY, EVANS, AND CO., PRINTERS, WHITEFRIARS. [520] blank

Binding Spine, and boards at front and back covered in dark green cloth. Endpapers pale primrose.

Front cover Plain.

Spine In gilt: [double rule] / MEREDITH / [short rule] / EVAN / HARRINGTON / [double rule]

Back cover Plain.

SERIAL PUBLICATION

Evan Harrington was written for publication in *Once a Week*. Meredith had settled at Copsham Cottage, Esher, in the late summer of 1859, but had not yet started to work as reader for Chapman and Hall. Despite a slow start, the novel was written relatively quickly during the winter of 1859-60.

Stevenson (pp. 76–84) gives a good account of the writing of the novel, though with a stress on the autobiographical elements. *Evan Harrington* is the only novel that Meredith wrote primarily for magazine publication and his correspondence with Evans and with Lucas of *Once a Week* is evidence of some of the difficulties he encountered. The serial was typeset as Meredith wrote, both the American and the English first editions being set from the serial sheets.

Reade's *Good Fight* (the first version of *The Cloister and the Hearth*) was withdrawn from *Once a Week* before it had ended. This meant that the magazine badly needed a serial story. Even so, Meredith had to give himself time. He told Lucas: 'I think I must say definitely, that I can't begin the serial before February. I am in doubt about the title. Lewes don't like it; and his judgement is worth something. Besides it binds me too much to a positive course, and tempts to extravagance in the unfolding of situations' (December 1859: *Letters* 1 47). He did begin it almost immediately, however, for later in the month he wrote to Lucas about the length of the serial parts. 'Try and allow my 3rd number to occupy $7\frac{1}{2}$ or 8 pages. "On the Road" is rather long. I will leave it at the office on Friday. Read and let me have your opinion. It develops the character of the hero partly: the incidents subsequently affect him. But I wish to know how you take it. It does not much move the tale. But do not yet insist on that entirely, at present' (*Letters* 1 49). By the end of December he had corrected the proofs of the first three chapters, but when he sent them to Lucas he said: 'Copy you shall have very shortly. But try and spur me on without giving me the sense that I am absolutely due; for then I feel hunted, and may take strange leaps. I think we shall do, but I am in a sort of a knot just now. The endings of the numbers bother me. I can work out my idea; but shall I lead on the reader? That's my difficulty, till I get into the thick of it. After the first 4 numbers, the game will be clear' (*Letters* 1 50).

Alas, this was not the case. Meredith continued to have difficulties. 'To invent probabilities in modern daily life is difficult,' he announced in his next letter to Lucas (*Letters* 1 51). The correspondence about practical details and about the likelihood of the novel having popular appeal continues for some months: it is sufficient to mention here that Meredith only just managed to keep up with the serial issue. At the same time, when he had written only a few chapters, he began to think about the sale of the American rights. Before going to see Evans to arrange the details of publication in book form in England, he asked Lucas to arrange for possible American publication. 'One thing I want you to ask him *now*. That is, to give me the permission to dispose (if in his gift, and not mine) of the first sheets to an American publisher. I'm horridly poor and £30 or £40 is a windfall' (*Letters* 1 52). Publication by Harper was eventually arranged, though it was Evans who kept Meredith alive throughout 1860. Meredith sent Lucas the last pages of the manuscript on 27 September 1860. By that time, as C.L. Cline noted (*Letters* 1 62), Bradbury and Evans had advanced £310 of the £400 purchase price.

Meredith made heavy weather of the writing of *Evan Harrington* and when it was finished said that it disgusted him. When the time came for publication in book form, he was not prepared to do much more work on it. 'I wish I could have done more for Ev[an] Harrington, for both our sakes: but I should have had to cut him to pieces, put strange herbs to him, and boil him up again – a tortuous and a doubtful process: so I let him go much as Once a Week exhibited him' (Letters I 71).

The serial appeared in volume II of Once a Week, on 11 February 1860, pp. 133–42 of no. 33; 18 February, pp. 155–60, no. 34; 25 February, pp. 177–84, no. 35; 3 March, pp. 199–204, no. 36; 10 March, pp. 221–6, no. 37; 17 March, pp. 243–7, no 38; 24 March, pp. 265–70, no. 39; 31 March, pp. 287–97, no. 40; 7 April, pp. 309–16, no. 41; 14 April, pp. 331–5, no. 42; 21 April, pp. 353–6, no. 43; 28 April, pp. 375–9, no. 44; 5 May, pp. 403–8, no. 45; 12 May, pp. 431–8, no. 46; 19 May, pp. 459–64, no. 47; 26 May, pp. 487–94, no. 48; 2 June, pp. 515–18, no. 49; 9 June, pp. 543–7, no. 50; 16 June, pp. 571–7, no. 51; 23 June, pp. 599–604, no. 52; and in volume III, 30 June, pp. 1–5, no. 53; 7 July, pp. 29–33, no. 54; 14 July, pp. 57–63, no. 55; 21 July, pp. 85–91, no. 56; 28 July, pp. 113–18, no. 57; 4 August, pp. 141–6, no. 58; 11 August, pp. 169–74, no. 59; 18 August, pp. 197–221, no. 60; 25 August, pp. 225–32, no. 61; 1 September, pp. 253–8, no. 62; 8 September, pp. 281–5, no. 63; 15 September, pp. 309–12, no. 64; 22 September, pp. 337–41, no. 65; 29 September, pp. 365–70, no. 66; 6 October, pp. 393–6, no. 67; 13 October, pp. 421–5, no. 68.

V

EMILIA IN ENGLAND

FIRST EDITION

EMILIA IN ENGLAND / BY / GEORGE MEREDITH / AUTHOR OF "EVAN HARRINGTON" "THE ORDEAL OF RICHARD FEVEREL" / "THE SHAVING OF SHAGPAT" / IN THREE VOLUMES / VOL. I. / LONDON: / CHAPMAN & HALL, 193, PICCADILLY. / 1864. / [The right of Translation is reserved.]

VOLUME I

Collation [A]²B–U⁸X¹ 146 leaves (19.5 × 12.4) [i–iii] iv [1]–306

Contents [i] titlepage [ii] imprint at centre: LONDON: / BRADBURY AND EVANS, PRINTERS, WHITEFRIARS. [iii]–iv contents [1]–306 text, on 306 at centre: END OF VOL. I. and at foot: BRADBURY AND EVANS, PRINTERS, WHITEFRIARS.

VOLUME II

Collation [A]²B–T⁸ 154 leaves (19.5 × 12.2) [i–iii] iv [1]–59 [60] 61 [62]–285 [286–8]

Contents [i] titlepage [ii] imprint [iii]–iv contents [1]–285 text, on 285: END
OF VOL. II. / LONDON: BRADBURY AND EVANS, PRINTERS, WHITEFRIARS. [286–8]
blank

VOLUME III

Collation [A]²B–Y⁸Z¹ 171 leaves (19.5 × 12.5) [i–iii] iv [1]–338

Contents [i] titlepage [ii] imprint [iii]–iv contents [1]–338 text, on 338 at
centre: *This is the ending of* "EMILIA IN ENGLAND" and at foot: BRADBURY AND
E[V]ANS, PRINTERS, WHITEFRIARS.

Binding Boards at front and back covered in violet cloth with vertical ribbing
and a diagonal bead-grain pattern. The endpapers inside and out have a pale,
greenish-yellow coating.

Front cover Blind-stamped, a five-line border the inner rectangle of which en-
closes a design made up of two horseshoe shapes joined at the centre by an obtuse
angle, this design surrounded by stylized leaves, vines, and flowers.

Spine Between gold bands at top and bottom, stamped in gilt: EMILIA / IN /
ENGLAND / BY / GEORGE MEREDITH / VOL. I. / CHAPMAN & HALL.

Back cover Identical to the front cover.

Variant binding Carter has noted another version in violet faint-ribbed cloth,
with a blind-stamped ornament on both covers, no imprint, and abbreviated
author's name on the spine, but regarded it as 'secondary.' No such copy has
been seen.

PUBLICATION

Emilia in England was published in April 1864 and was not reissued in England
until the 1885 Collected Edition by Chapman and Hall. At that time, the title
was changed to *Sandra Belloni*, though the old title was retained on each verso.
The novel had, however, been translated into French and appeared in a 'condensed' version in the *Revue des Deux Mondes* in three parts: 15 November 1864,
pp. 444–82; 1 December 1864, pp. 550–98; 15 December 1864, pp. 908–47. In
1886 this version was published in book form by Hachette.

Meredith had begun *Emilia in England* at least as early as 1861, for on 17 May
of that year he wrote to Janet Ross about it. 'I have three works in hand. The
most advanced is *Emilia Belloni*; of which I have read some chapters to your
mother, and gained her strong approval. Emilia is a feminine musical genius. I

gave you once, sitting on the mound over Copsham, an outline of the real story
it is taken from. Of course one does not follow out real stories; and this has
simply suggested Emilia to me' (*Letters* I 80–1). Though it was the most advanced, the novel did not proceed very quickly. 'I have left Emilia Belloni un-
touched for months,' he told Janet Ross on 19 November 1861, 'and my novel
is where it was. *En revanche*, I am busy on Poems. I think it possible I shall publish a small volume in the winter, after Christmas' (*Letters* I 116). He returned to
the novel in 1862, revised it in part and rewrote in part, and then made a final
attempt to finish it satisfactorily in 1863. 'I am overwhelmed with disgust at
Emilia. Am hurrying her on like ye deuce. She will do. But, ahem! – she must
pay. I have taken some trouble with her and really shall begin to think her character weak in this respect, if she don't hand me what I think due, speedily. I'm
afraid, considering hopes of cash, house to build, linen to buy, that *Once a Week*
will hold me from St. B. and the Blue Medi T.' (to Hardman, 20 March 1863:
Letters I 195).

Eventually he was obliged, with Chapman's consent, to publish the novel at
his own expense, apprehensive about what 'the British P. [will] say to a Finis
that holds aloft no nuptial torch.' His apprehensions were justified.

VI

RHODA FLEMING

FIRST EDITION

RHODA FLEMING. / *A Story*. / BY / GEORGE MEREDITH, / AUTHOR OF /
"THE ORDEAL OF RICHARD FEVEREL," "EVAN HARRINGTON,"
ETC. ETC. / IN THREE VOLUMES. / VOL. I. / LONDON: / TINSLEY
BROTHERS, CATHERINE STREET, STRAND. / 1865. / [*All rights of
Translation and Reproduction are reserved.*]

VOLUME I

Collation [π]³1–20⁸21³ 166 leaves (18.4 × 12.3) [i–v] vi [7]–331 [332]

Contents [i] halftitle: RHODA FLEMING / [short rule] / VOL. I. [ii] blank [iii]
titlepage [iv] imprint at centre: LONDON: / SAVILL AND EDWARDS, PRINTERS,
CHANDOS STREET, / COVENT GARDEN. [v]–vi contents [7]–331 text, on 331 at
foot: END OF VOL. I. [332] imprint: LONDON: / SAVILL AND EDWARDS, PRINTERS,
CHANDOS STREET, / COVENT GARDEN.

VOLUME II

Collation [π]³1–17⁸18⁷ 146 leaves (18.4 × 12.3) [i–v] vi [7]–291 [292]

Contents [i–ii] blank [iii] titlepage [iv] imprint [v]–vi contents [7]–291 text, on 291 at centre: END OF VOL. II. [292] imprint

VOLUME III

Collation [π]³1–15⁸16⁵ 128 leaves (18.4 x 12.3) (i–v) vi [7]–256

Contents [i–ii] blank [iii] titlepage [iv] imprint [v]–vi contents [7]–256 text, on 256 at bottom: THE END.

Binding Spine, and boards at front and back, covered in dark olive cloth with a sandy pattern. Endpapers a yellowish-white with a slightly dark yellow coating on the lining papers.

Front cover Front cover has a three-line border blind-stamped around the edge of the cover, the centre line being 1.5 mm. in width, and the other two each .5 mm. in width. Blind-stamped in the centre is a scalloped lozenge-shaped ornament filled with an arabesque pattern.

Spine The spine has a decorative border stamped in gilt at the top and bottom, consisting of two lines with a scroll border between them and, stamped in gilt: *Rhoda / Fleming / by / George / Meredith /* [an engrailed line and an invected line each with hooks at the ends, and below these a vesica-shaped ornament] / VOL. I. / LONDON / TINSLEY. BRO^S

Back cover Identical to front cover.

PUBLICATION

The business arrangements for *Rhoda Fleming* were completed with remarkably little fuss. Meredith wrote to Edward Tinsley from 18 Catherine Street on 11 August 1865: 'I place my novel *Rhoda Fleming* in your hands to publish for me; you to receive one fourth of the profits in return for your expenditure of labour etc: – the profits accruing from American and foreign issues and sales to belong to me solely' (*Letters* 1 314). On the same piece of paper Tinsley replied: 'We agree to the terms contained in the note on the flyleaf of this respecting the publication of your novel entitled "Rhoda Fleming".' If Meredith did expect Tinsley to offer £400, as he said in his letter to Jessopp dated 24 April [1865], he must have been bitterly disappointed and perhaps even kept to himself the arrangement that he had in fact been obliged to make. To publish a novel was of vital importance to him at this stage in his career; he had just married, was in debt, and no doubt had to demonstrate that he could make a living by his writing alone. Meredith's letter to Jessopp of 30 January 1865 makes fairly clear that *Rhoda Fleming*, though conceived in 1863, was written hurriedly in Ploverfield during a prolonged honeymoon. 'But, hear! the man went and got married: it was well for him: he bought linen, he bought plate, disbursed early and eke late: the fat end of his purse did set flowing towards his fireside, and the lean was to them that did accredit him. So. And meantime, in prospect of the needful, he put aside *Vittoria* (which contains points of grandeur and epical interest), to "finish off" *Rhoda Fleming* in one volume, now swollen to two – and Oh, will it be three? – But this is my Dd. Dd. Dd. uncertain workmanship. You see, I am three days in town, and I am hustled with moving and can't get my shoulders into a place, but the toe of Fate takes me somewhat lower and away I go; and this is not favourable to composition, though my dear wife does all that she can for me, and would hush the elements, bidding them know me pen in hand. However I hope in six weeks to be clear of Miss Rhoda, into whose history I have put more work than she deserves. Ere that time, I will remit to you a portion of the due. I wrote in saddish spirits, rare with me. Stomach, my friend. I am not in the bracing air which befits me. But, in future I will be punctual. By degrees I will reduce the portentous OO's. And I thank you with all my heart for the friendly peace-breathing letter. It's precious balm to read' (*Letters* I 302–3).

Rhoda Fleming, which Lionel Stevenson has suggested grew out of the story 'The Parish Clerk's Story' published in *Once a Week* in February 1861, was finished in July 1865 and was published in book form in October of the same year. It was not republished until Chapman and Hall's Collected Edition of 1885.

VII

VITTORIA

FIRST EDITION

VITTORIA / BY / GEORGE MEREDITH. / IN THREE VOLUMES. / VOLUME I. / LONDON: / CHAPMAN & HALL, 193, PICCADILLY. / MDCCCLXVII. / [*Legal rights reserved.*]

VOLUME I

Collation [A]³B–U⁸X⁷ 162 leaves (19.8 × 12.4) [i–v] vi [1]–317 [318]

Contents [i] halftitle: VITTORIA. / VOLUME I. [ii] blank [iii] titlepage [iv] imprint at foot: [short rule] / PRINTED BY WILLIAM CLOWES AND SONS, STAMFORD

STREET, / AND CHARING CROSS [v]–vi (misnumbered iv) contents [1]–317 text, on 317 at centre: END OF VOLUME I. and at foot: [short rule] / PRINTED BY W. CLOWES AND SONS, DUKE STREET, STAMFORD STREET, / AND CHARING CROSS. [318] blank

VOLUME II

Collation [A]²B–Y⁸ 170 leaves (19.7 x 12.5) [i–iii] iv [1]–333 [334–6]

Contents [i] titlepage [ii] imprint [iii]–iv contents [1]–333 text, on 333 at centre: END OF VOL. II. and at foot: [short rule] / LONDON: PRINTED BY W. CLOWES AND SONS, STAMFORD STREET, / AND CHARING CROSS. [334–6] blank

VOLUME III

Collation [A]²B–T⁸ 146 leaves (19.8 x 12.5) [i–iii] iv [1]–288

Contents [i] titlepage [ii] imprint [iii]–iv contents [1]–288 text, on 288 at centre: THE END and at foot: [short rule] / LONDON: PRINTED BY W. CLOWES AND SONS, STAMFORD STREET, / AND CHARING CROSS.

Binding Spine, and boards at front and back, covered in a deep purplish-red patterned cloth. Endpapers pale yellow.

Front cover Entirely blind-stamped, an outer double border and an inner four-line border containing at each corner a three-lobed leaf and at centre a double-line vesica-shaped ornament, within which is a two-line circle. Above and below this circle is a decorative cross within a small circle, which has five small tri-foliate leaves spaced around it, and is flanked on each side by a stylized leaf.

Spine Stamped in gilt: [two-line border] / VITTORIA / [short rule] / G. MEREDITH / [stylized triangular design] / VOL. I. / [inverted triangular design] / CHAPMAN & HALL. / [two-lined border, as above]

Back cover Identical to front cover.

SERIAL PUBLICATION

The serial, published as forty-six chapters, appeared in the *Fortnightly Review* in 1866.

Chapters 1–3 of the serial appeared in the issue of 15 January, vol. 3, pp. 539–58; 4–7 in 1 February, vol. 3, pp. 679–704; 8–9 in 15 February, vol. 4, pp. 32–48; 10–11 in 1 March, vol. 4, pp. 163–83; 12–13 in 15 March, vol. 4, pp. 301–16; 14–15 in 1 April, vol. 4, pp. 437–58; 16–18 in 15 April, vol. 4, pp. 589–606; 19–20 in 1 May, vol. 4, pp. 710–28; 21–2 in 15 May, vol. 5, pp. 76–90; 23–4 in 1 June, vol. 5, pp. 184–99; 25–6 in 15 June, vol. 5, pp. 321–42; 27 in 1 July, vol. 5, pp. 480–96; 28–9 in 15 July, vol. 5, pp. 560–86; 30–1 in 1 August, vol. 5, pp. 685–704; 32 in 15 August, vol. 6, pp. 47–70; 33–4 in 1 September, vol. 6, pp. 229–42; 35–6 in 15 September, vol. 6, pp. 311–26; 37–8 in 1 October, vol. 6, pp. 455–73; 39–40 in 15 October, vol. 6, pp. 579–604; 41–4 in 1 November, vol. 6, pp. 688–713; 45–6 and epilogue in 1 December, vol. 6, pp. 857–77. In the Stark Library there are corrected serial page proofs (pp. [1]–6, 9–16) consisting of parts of chapters XXI, XXII, and XXIII. The corrections on these particular pages are of no great critical consequence.

PUBLICATION

Vittoria was written by fits and starts. Though it was started before *Rhoda Fleming* Meredith put it aside because of the financial pressures experienced at the time of his second marriage in September 1864. *Rhoda Fleming* was the pot-boiler that would allow him to pay his debts, settle at the new house in Copsham, and convince his father-in-law that he was a successful novelist. *Vittoria*, on the other hand, was to be a serious work involving a study of people during the course of significant political events. Marie Vulliamy had in fact been helping Meredith by copying chapters of *Vittoria* during the summer of 1864; it was only after their wedding that he began to concentrate on *Rhoda Fleming*.

By the summer of 1865, it was settled that *Vittoria* would appear in *The Fortnightly Review*. Meredith had come to an arrangement with George Lewes, who at that time was the editor. His son, William, was born on 26 July 1865 and *Rhoda Fleming* was published in October. Things were going well for him and he remained confident that *Vittoria* would be a good book. This confidence shows in the letters he wrote in the latter part of 1865: 'I am very hot upon *Vittoria*. Lewes says it must be a success ... I fancy I begin in the *Fortnightly* in February. Perhaps I have given it too historical a character to please the brooding mind of Fred. But, we shall see. I think one must almost love Italy to care for it and the heroine. There are scenes that will hold you; much adventure to entertain you; delicate bits and fiery handling. But there is no tender dissection, and the softer emotions are not kept at half gasp upon slowly-moving telescopic objects, with their hearts seen beating in their frames' (*Letters* I 320).

In retrospect, it can be seen clearly enough that *Vittoria* anticipated those later novels in which Meredith bound together the political, social, and personal or psychological aspects of a situation. *Vittoria* is as ambitious a novel as those later books, but while writing it Meredith was still feeling his way. Progress was therefore very slow indeed.

The serialization of *Vittoria* began on 15 January 1866, Meredith having sold the serial rights to Lewes for £250 (*Letters* I 320). Even then, however, the novel had not been completed. He was still having difficulties as he explained to Lewes. 'I shall be glad to make over to you the use of the copyright of my novel *Vittoria* for issue in the *Fortnightly Review*, in consideration of the sum of £250: all subsequent rights to the use of it being reserved by myself. Your saying "write to me" did not seem to imply "write immediately or there will be no contract". In fact, I supposed you were careless about any stipulation until more of my work had been submitted to you. I am hard at it, and as carefully as possible. Pardon me, if my apparent negligence shall have put you out. I thank you very much for your foregoing letter, which quite solves my difficulty, and settles the matter justly. – If my progress seems to you slow, remember that I am on foreign ground and have to walk warily. I read a good deal of the novel to Mdme Venturi the other day, who says that the Italian colouring is correct' (*Letters* I 320–1). Indeed, it is only on 18 May 1866 that Meredith wrote to Jessopp: 'I am rapidly finishing *Vittoria*' (*Letters* I 337).

The novel was finally published in book form on 20 December 1866. It was not republished until the first Collected Edition of 1885 by Chapman and Hall.

VIIII a

THE ADVENTURES OF HARRY RICHMOND

FIRST EDITION

THE ADVENTURES / OF / HARRY RICHMOND. / BY / GEORGE MEREDITH. / IN THREE VOLS. / VOL. I. / LONDON: / SMITH, ELDER & CO., / 15 WATERLOO PLACE. / 1871. / [ALL RIGHTS RESERVED.]

VOLUME I

Collation $[\pi]^2 1-20^8$ 162 leaves (20.0 x 12.5) [i–iii] iv [1]–319 [320]

Contents [i] titlepage [ii] blank [iii]–iv contents [1]–318 text, on 318 at centre: END OF VOL. I. [319] imprint: LONDON: / PRINTED BY SMITH, ELDER AND CO., / OLD BAILEY, E.C. [320] blank

VOLUME II

Collation $[\pi]^2 21-40^8 41^4$ 166 leaves (20.0 x 12.5) [i–iii] iv [1]–325 [326–8]

Contents [i] titlepage [ii] blank [iii]–iv contents [1]–325 text, on 325 at foot: END OF VOL. II. [326] imprint [327–8] blank

VOLUME III

Collation [π]²4²–59⁸60⁶ 152 leaves (18.9 × 12.5) [i–iii] iv [1]–298 [299–300]

Contents [i] titlepage [ii] blank [iii]–iv contents [1]–298 text, on 298 at foot: THE END. [299] imprint [300] blank

Binding Spine, and boards at front and back, covered in deep red cloth. End-papers beige: white on insides.

Front cover Stamped in black, a single line border to all four edges. Within it a smaller rectangle the lines of which extend beyond the corners and expand into ornament. Within this rectangle, also stamped in black: THE ADVENTURES / OF / HARRY RICHMOND. / [rule] and at the bottom: [rule] / BY / GEORGE MEREDITH.

Spine Stamped in black: [ornament] [rule] in gilt: THE / ADVENTURES / OF / HARRY / RICHMOND in black: [rule-ornament-rule] in gilt: BY / GEORGE / MEREDITH / [short rule] / VOL. I. in black: [rule-ornament] in gilt: SMITH, ELDER & CO.

Back cover Identical to front cover in design, but without the lettering.

VIII b

SECOND EDITION

The second 'edition' was reprinted from the same setting and re-issued on 11 December 1871 with a new titlepage. Meredith had written to Smith on 14 November 1871: 'I am told that W. H. Smith's Library gives the bound-up copies of the "Cornhill" containing "Richmond" in the place of the 3 volumes' (*Letters* I 456). It is possible that this letter was part of the correspondence about the relative sales success of the novel.

THE MANUSCRIPT

The manuscript of *The Adventures of Harry Richmond* is in the Beinecke and is divided into two separately numbered volumes, as follows: Volume I; 1–24, 24a, 25–48, 49–63, (64–71 = a single page), 72–91, 92–131, 132–52, 153–80, 181–95, 195a, 196–219, 220–9, 230–43, 244–60, 260a, 261–85, 286–305, 306–22, 323–9, 329–46, 347–62, 363–5, 365a–b–c, 366–73, 373a, 374–95, 396–414, 415–36, 437a, 437–49, 450–61, 462–72, 473–95, 495a–b–c, 496–505, 506–19, 520–40, 541–64, 565–80, 581–92, 593–616, 617–28, 629–59, 660–82, 682–705, 706, 706a–32, 733–48.

Volume II; 1–25, 25–49, 50–88, 88–117, 117a–b–c, 118–27, 127–58, 159–88, 189–209, 212–21, 222–45, 245–50, 250a–b, 251–71, 272–85, 286–304, 304–34, 335–59, 359–68, 369–410, 411–55, 456–89, 490–3, 493–530, 531–47, 548–67, 568–85, 586–99, 600–33, 1–25.

THE RELATIONSHIP OF THE MANUSCRIPT TO THE FIRST EDITION

The Adventures of Harry Richmond occupied Meredith for at least six years, for as early as 1864, as Forman noted, Meredith wrote to Jessopp to tell him he had 'in hand an Autobiography. *The Adventures of Richmond Roy, and his friend Contrivance Jack: Being the History of Two Rising Men*: – and to be a spanking bid for popularity on the part of this writer' (18 May 1864: *Letters* I 255). Meredith had evidently encountered the problem that was to preoccupy him as a novelist to the end of his career. He was about to marry and wished to make a 'bid for popularity'; at the same time his real or first interest was in personality. The movement towards the later psychological novels had begun but he had also to earn his living. 'I fear I am evolving his personality too closely for the public, but a man must work by the light of his conscience if he's to do anything worth reading' (27 January 1870: *Letters* I 415).

A letter to Hardman dated 6 July 1870 makes it clear that he had finished the novel by the end of June (*Letters* I 420) while in a later letter to Smith he confirmed that he had in fact finished work by the time the serial began: 'What I did was to rewrite a large portion of the work before it appeared in the *Cornhill*: so as to make it an almost entirely different thing from what you read in MS. It has been touched subsequently, but not enough to make mention of it and trip the practice of the library people' (19 November 1871: *Letters* I 457). This means that a novel that was conceived as far back as 1864 was revised at least once before first being published.

The letters give hints of Meredith's concern. To Jessopp, just after the beginning of the serial, he confirmed that despite his attempt to write a popular adventure story, his concern had been predominantly psychological. 'Consider first my scheme as a workman. It is to show you the action of minds as well as of fortunes – and here and there men and women vitally animated by their brains at different periods of their lives – and of men and women with something of a look-out upon the world and its destinies: – the mortal ones: the divine I leave to Doctors of D' (4 October 1871: *Letters* I 451). Forman was of course quite correct in printing part of Meredith's letter to Hardman in the same vein, since it indicates clearly that Meredith's sense of what he could do, at this stage in his career, was affected by his notion of public response. 'I resisted every temptation to produce great and startling effects (after the scene of the

Statue, which was permissible in art, as coming from a boy and coloured by a boy's wonder). Note as you read, the gradual changes of the growing Harry, in his manner of regarding his father and the world. I have carried it so far as to make him perhaps dull towards adolescence and young manhood, except to one *studying* the narrative – as in the scenes with Dr. Julius. Such effects are deadly when appearing in a serial issue. I was here and there hand-tied, too, by gentlemanly feeling in relation to the royal reigning House, sweet, Tory Tuck! or I should (and did on paper) have launched out. The Speech at the City banquet would have satisfied a Communist Red, originally' (2 November 1871: *Letters* I 453–4).

A discussion of whether or not Meredith's attempt to integrate the picaresque and the psychological was successful, or whether or not the repression or suppression of political comment improved the novel, would be out of place here. A Meredith reader interested in critical questions of this kind will wish to consult at the outset L.T. Hergenhan's edition of *The Adventures of Harry Richmond* and in particular Appendix A, A Note on the Text, pp. 547–72, as well as Appendix B, Revisions of the Original Printed Text, pp. 573–609.

The manuscript carries the names of the compositors, has the printer's name – Hales & Co. – on a number of pages, and has the continuous pagination associated with final copy, despite many corrections and renumberings. In the same holder in the Beinecke are a number of corrected page proofs for the serial, confirming that it was printed from the manuscript and that Meredith himself corrected proof. In correcting and emending *The Adventures of Harry Richmond*, Meredith followed his normal practice, which is simply the practice you would expect of someone who has to write everything himself in longhand. Where he could retain pages from the earlier version he did; some of these pages are, however, heavily corrected.Where pages had to be replaced or where the correction was too heavy for rewriting to be avoided, the ink and the handwriting sometimes reveal the break. At some points in this manuscript there was evidently a second stage revision, if one is to judge by the change in ink.

Since Meredith was taking up the manuscript of a novel he had written some years before, and since he would not likely give himself the labour of unnecessary changes, any alteration in the page numbering presumably indicates the points, among others, at which substantial revision occurred. To demonstrate this a full collation would be necessary. Though only an outline can be given here, however, at least it will indicate the nature of the problem. Evidence of rewriting, then, is as follows:

a Pages that, because of their numbers, must have been added later: MS Vol. I 24a, 195a, 365a–b–c, 373a, 437a, 706a; Vol. II 117a–b–c.

b Suppressed passages where the paging ought to be continuous and is not: e.g. MS Vol. I 65–71 (a passage in the middle of chapter 4).

c Very heavy deletions and corrections: e.g. MS Vol. I 65–71.

d Chapters that to judge by the handwriting have been entirely rewritten: e.g. MS Vol. I chapter 19 'Our Return Homeward.'

e Passages, written in black ink, perhaps at another time: e.g. MS Vol. I 468–70, 495.

f Chapters in which the page numbers have been altered: e.g. MS Vol. I chapter 32.

g Chapters whose numbers have been altered: e.g. MS Vol. I chapters 30–2 become in the first edition one chapter, i.e. volume II chapter IX. Deleted was a clandestine meeting between Richmond and Ottilia in the forest.

h At the beginning of MS Vol. II 18 was previously numbered 17, 19 was 774, 20 was 775, 21 was 776, 22 was 777, 23 was 778 and 24 was 779. Since volume I ends at 748, presumably some six or seven pages have been deleted.

i Meredith himself divided up the novel for the *Cornhill*. On MS Vol. II 272, for example, he wrote 'Part 12 – August.' This means that although the novel had been finished in June, the process of revision continued.

i The new page numbers make it clear that the final chapter was an afterthought.

In summary, one can say that the novel was begun in 1864 or thereabouts, that a more or less complete but no doubt corrected version existed by 1866 or so, that when Meredith returned to the novel in 1869 or 1870 he made substantial changes which can be seen fairly clearly in the manuscript itself, and that as he prepared the final manuscript for the *Cornhill* he made further emendations. The *Cornhill* was copy for the first edition. Meredith doe not appear to have done further work on *The Adventures of Harry Richmond* until he revised it for the Collected Edition of Chapman and Hall in 1885.

IX

BEAUCHAMP'S CAREER

FIRST EDITION

BEAUCHAMP'S CAREER / BY GEORGE MEREDITH, / AUTHOR OF "THE SHAVING OF SHAGPAT", "THE ORDEAL OF RICHARD / FEVEREL", ETC., ETC. / IN THREE VOLUMES. / VOL. I. / LONDON: / CHAPMAN AND HALL, 193, PICCADILLY. / 1876. / [*All rights reserved.*]

VOLUME I

Collation [A]⁴B–U⁸X⁴ 160 leaves (18.5 x 12.5) [i–v] vi–vii [viii] [1]–312

Contents [i] halftitle: BEAUCHAMP'S CAREER / [short rule] / VOL. I. [ii] blank [iii] titlepage [iv] imprint at centre: LONDON: / PRINTED BY VIRTUE AND CO., LIMITED. / CITY ROAD. [v]–vii contents [viii] blank [1]–312 text, on 312 at centre: END OF VOL. I. and at foot: [rule] / PRINTED BY VIRTUE AND CO., LIMITED CITY ROAD, LONDON.

VOLUME II

Collation [A]⁴B–X⁸ 164 leaves [18.5 × 12.4) [i–v] vi–vii (viii] [1]–318 [319–20]

Contents [i] halftitle [ii] blank [iii] titlepage [iv] imprint [v]–vii contents [viii] blank [1]–318 text, on 318: END OF VOL. II. / [imprint] [319–20] blank

VOLUME III

Collation [A]⁴B–Y⁸Z² 174 leaves (18.5 × 12.4) [i–vi] vii [viii] [1]–339 [340]

Contents [i] halftitle [ii] blank [iii] titlepage [iv] imprint [v]–vii contents [viii] blank [1]–339 text, on 339: THE END / [imprint] [340] blank

Binding Spine, and boards at front and back, covered in dark yellowish-green cloth with diagonal stripe. Endpapers yellowish-white with a greenish-yellow coating.

Front cover Stamped in black, within a two-lined border, a rectangular design of two lines within two other lines the margin between having a die of five spots at each corner and ten rosettes spaced evenly. At the top and bottom of the whole is a stylized fleur-de-lys.

Spine The spine has a double border, at the top and bottom, consisting of an outer black-line and an inner decorative border of four-lobed flowers and heart-shaped leaves between two lines. Between these borders at top and bottom, stamped in gilt: [wide rule] / BEAUCHAMP'S / CAREER / GEORGE MEREDITH in black: [small three-leafed ornament]
in gilt: VOL. I.
in black: [stylized branch with four leaves] / [wide rule]
in gilt: CHAPMAN & HALL / [wide rule]

Back cover Identical to front cover.

Some copies of *Beauchamp's Career* have a cancel at pp. 217–18 of Volume III.

SERIAL PUBLICATION

The serial of *Beauchamp's Career* appeared in the *Fortinghtly Review*, beginning August 1874, and ending in December 1875. Chapters 1–3 appeared in the August issue of volume 22, pp. 249–72; chapters 4–8 in September, pp. 377–404;

chapters 9-11 in October, pp. 537-54; chapters 12-14 in November, pp. 676-700; chapters 15-17 in December, pp. 836-56; chapters 18-19 in volume 23, January 1875, pp. 132-49; chapters 20-2 in February, pp. 271-94; chapters 23-5 in March, pp. 438-64; chapters 26-8 in April, pp. 590-612; chapters 29-30 in May, pp. 739-62; chapters 32-4 in June, pp. 876-98; chapters 35-7 in volume 24, July, pp. 123-48; chapters 38-40 in August, pp. 267-90; chapters 41-3 in September, pp. 407-28; chapters 44-6 in October, pp. 551-78; chapters 47-51 in November, pp. 699-730; and chapters 52-6 in December, pp. 869-902.

Though Meredith for a time expected *Beauchamp's Career* to be published by Smith, Elder, John Morley seems to have had some connection with the novel from the beginning. Meredith respected his friend Morley as a man of affairs and it was natural for him to write about his new book because of its special nature: 'He advises me in these serious times "to take to political writing". I reply that it demands special study. He insists that I have only to give my genuine convictions.' In retrospect one can see that there is an undercurrent of political commitment in the greater part of Meredith's work and that *Beauchamp's Career* was only one attempt of many at the writing of a political novel. While he was writing the novel, however, for reasons not connected with it, he became estranged from Morley and arranged to have it published in the *Cornhill*.

Meredith experienced some difficulty in completing the book. It became too long. He was incapable of writing a simple political novel; the characters rebelled. 'I am due to you this month,' he wrote to Smith on 11 February 1873, 'but am all behindhand, and want an extension of time – till May fully' (*Letters* I 476). His letter to Jessopp on 18 April indicates in part the nature of the difficulty: 'But I am at present too busy on *Beauchamp's Career* to spend a day in town. I was bound to send it to the publisher not later than the end of May, but it will run on with me through June. And it is already full to bursting – it and I. "The world is too much with me" when I write. I cannot go on with a story and not feel that to treat of flesh and blood is to touch the sacredest; and so it usually ends in my putting the destinies of the world about it – like an atmosphere, out of which it cannot subsist. So my work fails. I see it. But the pressure is on me with every new work. I fear that *Beauchamp* is worse than the foregoing in this respect. The central idea catches hold of the ring of the universe; the dialogues are the delivery of creatures of this world, and the writing goodish. But altogether it will only appeal (so I fear) to them that have a taste for me; it won't catch the gudgeon World, and I, though I never write for money, want it – and there's a state of stultification for you' (*Letters* I 477-8). Political motive, by itself, was never enough for Meredith. The political, the social, and the personal had always to be seen together.

Smith must have been sent the complete manuscript towards the end of the summer of 1873. He turned it down. Through the good offices of Maxse and Greenwood, however, Meredith was reconciled with Morley, who agreed to published it in the *Fortnightly Review* if its length could be reduced.

Once again Meredith was faced with the problem of altering his work in order to have it published. Once again he could find the inner resource to acknowledge the need for *some* change and yet once again he felt that the pressure exerted by the publisher represented society's inability to understand his purposes. A miserable year passed in which he tried to patch the book up for *The Fortnightly Review*. Eventually he abandoned the task and rewrote a good part of it.

The way in which Meredith thought about the need for revision is intrinsically interesting, even though in this case no manuscript survives to permit a study of the process. At first he told Morley that he would do his utmost to reduce the length of the novel. 'It strikes me that the parts to lop will be the letters, a portion of the Visit to Normandy, the heavier of the electioneering passages, introductory paragraphs to chapters, and dialogues passim that may be considered not vital to the central idea. That, which may be stated to be the personal abnegation coming, in spite of errors here and there (and as it were in spite of the man himself), of a noble devotion to politics from the roots up, I think I can retain uninjured – possibly improved by the exclusion of a host of my own reflections.' That was in May. More time was to pass, however, before he tackled the task of revision. He said that he feared his main character would seem dull 'save by those who can enter into his idea of the advancement of Humanity and his passion for it' and thought that the book could not be popular because it was 'philosophical – political, with no powerful stream of adventure' (*Letters* I 485). In July he still hesitated. 'The central portion, I fear, must be cut to pieces, condensed, re-written,' he said, when assuring Morley that the work would in fact be done (*Letters* I 486).

Meanwhile, Morley had evidently come to his own understanding with Chapman, and the two men, the Editor and the Publisher, simply waited in London until the author sent them the revised copy. There was a correspondence about whether Meredith might condense a 'host of his own reflections' into a preface but he eventually decided that it would be too difficult to write such a preface 'for a piece of fiction having a serious aim, and before a public that scorns the serious in fiction, and whose wits are chiefly trained to detect pretension' (*Letters* I 486–7). There may have been further discussion after this, for several more months passed before Meredith acknowledged to himself that it was impossible to patch the book up just by making changes here and there. 'Absolute re-writing I find to be my lamentable task for the whole of it!' he told Morley on 19 November 1873 (*Letters* I 496). The revised version of the novel must therefore have been written during the next seven or eight months, for in August 1874 *Beauchamp's Career* began to appear in *The Fortnightly Review* and Meredith signed the contract for the publication of the novel in three volumes.

There is no way of telling whether Meredith improved or marred the novel by rewriting it to Morley's specifications. Clearly he only agreed to rewrite the book because he needed to publish it, both for the money and for the sake of his career as a novelist. On the other hand, Morley may have been right in thinking that the unrevised book was too unwieldy to be a commercial success. Not until the publication of *Diana of the Crossways* did Meredith completely free himself from the pressures of editors and publishers, and perhaps only in that novel did he achieve an adequate integration of political and psychological thematic material. At all events he survived this harrowing period.

Meredith's agreement with Chapman and Hall for the publication of *Beauchamp's Career* is in the Widener Collection and is dated 14 August 1874. Meredith sold the copyright for ten years for £420, 50 guineas to be paid immediately, 150 guineas on 15 September 1875, 100 guineas on 1 March 1875, and 100 guineas on completion of the serial in the *Fortnightly Review*. The novel was published by Chapman and Hall in November 1875.

X a

THE EGOIST

THE EGOIST / *A COMEDY IN NARRATIVE* / BY / GEORGE MEREDITH / IN THREE VOLUMES / VOL. I. / LONDON / C. KEGAN PAUL & CO., I, PATERNOSTER SQUARE / 1879

VOLUME I

Collation [A]²B–Y⁸Z¹[e]¹ 172 leaves (19.0 × 12.5) [i–iv (misnumbered v)] [1]–337 [338–40]

Contents [i] titlepage [ii] imprint at centre: *Ballantyne Press* / BALLANTYNE AND HANSON, EDINBURGH / CHANDOS STREET, LONDON and at foot: [*The right of translation and of reproduction is reserved.*] [iii–iv) contents [1]–337 text, on 337: END OF VOL. I. [338] blank [339–40] advertisement of Kegan Paul's publications pasted in.

VOLUME II

Collation [A]²B–X⁸[e]¹⁶ 178 leaves (19.0 × 12.5) [i–iii] iv [1]–320 [1]–32

Contents [i] titlepage [ii] imprint [iii]–iv contents [1]–320 text, on 320: END OF VOL. II. [1]–32 advertisements

VOLUME III

Collation [A]²B–Z⁸AA¹ 179 leaves (19.0 × 12.5) [i–iii] iv [1]–353 [354]

Contents [i] titlepage [ii] imprint [iii]–iv contents [1]–353 text, on 353: THE END [354] blank

Binding Spine, and boards at front and back, covered in olive-brown cloth. Endpapers black.

Front cover Stamped in black, a two-line border, the inner line being thicker than the outer.

Spine Stamped in black, at top and bottom, lines the same thickness as those on the front cover. In gilt: THE / EGOIST / [short rule] / GEORGE / MEREDITH / VOL. I. / C. KEGAN PAUL & CO.

Back cover Identical to front cover.

In the copy of *The Egoist* in the Widener Collection, Meredith wrote: 'Errata innumerable, incredible, a printer's carnival.' The corrections Meredith made in this copy were all, however, to the first volume.

X b

SECOND EDITION

THE EGOIST / *A COMEDY IN NARRATIVE* / BY / GEORGE MEREDITH / LONDON / C. KEGAN PAUL & CO., I, PATERNOSTER SQUARE / 1880

Collation [A]⁴B–2N⁸2M⁴ 288 leaves (18.2 × 12.1) [i–v] vi [vii–viii] [1]–535 [536] [1]–32

Contents [i] halftitle [ii] advertisement in a rectangular panel: THE EGOIST. / [rule] / *EXTRACTS FROM PRESS NOTICES OF THE FIRST EDITION.* / [press notices] / [rule] / BY THE SAME AUTHOR. / THE ORDEAL OF RICHARD FEVEREL. A / History of Father and Son. In one vol., with Frontispiece. / Crown 8vo. Cloth, price 6s. / [rule] / LONDON: C. KEGAN PAUL AND CO., I, PATERNOSTER SQUARE. [iii] titlepage [iv] at foot: (*The rights of translation and of reproduction are reserved.*) [v] vi [vii] contents [viii] blank [1]–535 text, on 535: THE END. / [rule] / *Printed by William Clowes and Sons, Limited, London and Beccles.* [536] blank

Between [ii] and [iii] has been inserted an illustration of p. 414 by H.M.P. with the inscription: 'I offer you my hand and name.' In some copies and separately numbered [1]-32: publisher's advertisements.

Binding Spine, and boards at front and back, covered in coarse grained royal blue cloth. Endpapers a glazed chocolate colour.

Front cover Stamped in black, an ornamental border at top and bottom. In between, but nearer the top than the bottom and stamped in gilt, at left a peacock design and at right: THE EGOIST / GEORGE MEREDITH

Spine The ornamental border is continued to the spine, but with an additional gilt line. Between the borders: THE / EGOIST / [rule] / GEORGE / MEREDITH / C. KEGAN PAUL & CO.

SERIAL PUBLICATION

Meredith completed *The Egoist* during the winter of 1877-8. On 4 June 1878 he told Stevenson: 'My *Egoist* is on the way to a conclusion. Of pot-boilers let none speak. Jove hangs them upon necks that could soar above his heights but for the accursed weight' (*Letters* II 560). He continued to work at the novel during the following winter, however, and no doubt it was during this second spell of work that he produced the only existing manuscript, which is largely a fair copy. Presumably he referred to the rewriting or copying of the novel when he told Cotter Morrison that 'At present I have the Devil behind me slave-driving' (*Letters* II 565). Yet Meredith continued to regard the novel, if not as a pot-boiler, as a work that had been unnatural to him. He wrote to Stevenson on 14 January 1879: '*The Egoist* is not yet out of my hands, and when it is I doubt that those who care for my work will take to it. How much better it is always to work in the groove. From not doing so, I find myself shunning the day of publication: the old dream of pleasure in it has long gone by' (*Letters* II 568). Meredith must have finished the novel, in its final version, in February 1879 because, on 16 April 1879, he wrote to Stevenson again: 'My *Egoist* has been out of my hands for a couple of months, but Kegan Paul does not wish to publish it before October. I don't think you will like it; I doubt if those who care for my work will take to it at all. And for this reason, after doing my best with it, I am in no hurry to see it appear. It is a Comedy, with only half of me in it, unlikely, therefore, to take either the public or my friends' (*Letters* II 569).

The novel was published in October 1879, but Kegan Peul, without Meredith's knowing, had sold the serial rights to the *Glasgow Weekly Herald*, according to Forman, for £100. In the *Herald* it appeared with the title *Sir Willoughby Patterne The Egoist*, much to Meredith's disgust. 'The diplomatic Kegan has delt me a stroke. Without a word to me, he sold the right of issue of the *Egoist* to the *Glasgow Herald*, and allowed them to be guilty of a perversion of my title. I wrote to him in my incredulous astonishment' (*Letters* II 577). This letter is dated 26 July 1879, but the serialization in the *Glasgow Weekly Herald* had begun in June; it ran in weekly numbers from 21 June 1879 to 10 January 1880. Forman's statement (p. 236) that it was 'Reprinted in three volumes and published in 1879 by Messrs. C. Kegan Paul and Company' is thus a little misleading: the novel was not reprinted from the serial at all.

DRAMATIZATION

Meredith collaborated with Alfred Sutro in 1898 to prepare a stage version of *The Egoist* apparently at the instigation of Forbes Robertson. It was never performed. The typescript original, with a large number of manuscript corrections and additions, is in the Beinecke.

A version of the play was printed privately in 1899.

THE EGOIST / From the Novel by / GEORGE MEREDITH / Arranged for the stage by / GEORGE MEREDITH / AND / ALFRED SUTRO / LONDON: PRIVATELY PRINTED BY CLEMENT SHORTER / DECEMBER 1899

Contents [1] halftitle: THE EGOIST [2] blank [3] titlepage [4] publisher's note: Of this book thirty copies / have been privately printed / by Clement Shorter. [5] the characters of the play [6] blank [7]-8 introduction 9-134 text [135] imprint: [short rule] / *Eyre & Spottiswoode, Ltd., East Harding Street, E.C.4*

A copy of this limited edition is in the British Museum. Though Meredith collaborated with Alfred Sutro, it is unlikely that he was party to Clement Shorter's publication.

MANUSCRIPT

The manuscript of *The Egoist* is in the Beinecke and is a fair copy prepared for and used in the press. The pagination, which is continuous, reveals that Meredith revised certain parts of the novel after the fair copy has been prepared. The most substantial of these revisions is towards the beginning of the novel in chapters IV-VI. The few passages that have been deleted from the manuscript have to do with feminine hypocrisy.

XI a

THE TRAGIC COMEDIANS

FIRST EDITION

THE TRAGIC COMEDIANS. / *A Study in a well-known story.* / (ENLARGED
FROM THE FORTNIGHTLY REVIEW.) / BY / GEORGE MEREDITH. / IN TWO
VOLUMES. / VOL. I. / LONDON: / CHAPMAN AND HALL, LIMITED, 193,
PICCADILLY. / 1880. / (*All Rights Reserved.*)

VOLUME I

Collation [A]²B–N⁸O⁴ 102 leaves (17.8 x 12.0) [i–iv] [1]–199 [200]

Contents [i] halftitle: THE TRAGIC COMEDIANS. [ii] blank [iii] titlepage [iv]
imprint at centre: LONDON: / R. CLAY, SONS, & TAYLOR, / BREAD STREET HILL.
[1]–199 text, on 199: END OF VOL. I. [200] imprint at centre: LONDON: / R.
CLAY, SONS, AND TAYLOR, / BREAD STREET HILL.

VOLUME II

Collation [A]²B–M⁸N⁴ 108 leaves (17.8 x 12.0) [i–iv] [1]–181 [182–4] [1–3]
4–27 [28]

Contents [i] halftitle [ii] blank [iii] titlepage [iv] imprint [1]–181 text, on
181: THE END [182] imprint [1–3] 4–27 [28] publishers' advertisements.

Binding Spine, and boards at front and back, covered in dark olive cloth with
a faint horizontal ribbing.

Front cover Stamped in black, a two-lined border on all four sides, the inner
line being thicker than the outer.

Spine At top and bottom, stamped in black, a two-lined border, as on the
front cover. Between these borders, stamped in gilt: THE / TRAGIC / COMEDIANS
/ [short rule] / GEORGE / MEREDITH / VOL. I. / CHAPMAN / & HALL

Back cover Identical to front cover but blind-stamped.

SERIAL PUBLICATION

The serial of *The Tragic Comedians* appeared in the *Fortnightly Review* in
volumes 34 and 35. Chapters 1–4 appeared in the October 1880 issue, pp.
510–32; chapters 5–7, November, pp. 653–80; chapters 8–9, December, pp.

785–803; chapters 10–11 in January 1881, pp. 103–18; chapters 12–15, February, pp. 244–60.

ONE VOLUME VERSION OF FIRST EDITION

The first edition of *The Tragic Comedians* was published on 15 December 1880. Early in the new year cancel title leaves were inserted with no change except the date 1881. What amounts to a third version of the first edition was also created. Copies of the 1881 first edition were later bound as one volume, no further changes being made There is a copy of the first edition in one volume in the Widener Collection.

The binding of the one-volume first edition is different from that of the two-volume version. The spine, and boards at front and back, are covered with a light chocolate brown cloth. Endpapers are primrose, but white on the inside.

Front cover Stamped in black, a conventional floral design, left of centre.

Spine Between three lines at the top and bottom, and stamped in gilt: THE / TRAGIC / COMEDIANS / [ornament] / G. MEREDITH. / CHAPMAN & HALL

Back cover Blind-stamped, the same design as on front cover.

REPRINTING OF THE FIRST EDITION

Meredith had sold the copyright of *The Tragic Comedians* to Chapman and Hall in an agreement dated 24 September 1880 by which he was to receive £250, £150 on the signing of the agreement and £100 on the day of publication. The agreement was without term (Widener Collection).

Forman (p. 64) states, however, that Ward, Lock & Bowden acquired the plates of the first edition in 1881. A copy of this 1881 paperback re-issue is in the British Museum.

THE TRAGIC COMEDIANS. / A Study in a well-known Story. / *(ENLARGED FROM THE FORTNIGHTLY REVIEW.)* / BY / GEORGE MEREDITH. / London: / WARD, LOCK AND CO., WARWICK HOUSE, / SALISBURY SQUARE, E.C. / [*All rights reserved.*]

Collation [B]^{8}C–X^8 160 leaves (17.6 x 11.3) [i–iv] [1]–309 [310–16]

Contents [i] halftitle: THE TRAGIC COMEDIANS [ii] blank [iii] titlepage [iv] blank [1]–309 text, on 309: THE END and at foot: [rule] / London: SWIFT & CO., Newton Street, High Holborn, w.c. [310] blank [311–16] advertisements

Binding Spine and boards covered in pale blue paper.

Front cover At the top, on a brick-red ground, the title lettered in blue and the author's name in black: THE / TRAGIC COMEDIANS / BY / GEORGE MEREDITH and at the bottom: LONDON: WARD, LOCK AND CO.

Back cover An advertisement for FRY'S COCOA.

XI b

THE EDITION OF 1892

Ward, Lock and Bowden published *The Tragic Comedians* in 1892 in the same format as the Chapman and Hall Collected Edition of 1885, except for the titlepage and the prelims. According to a statement made on the verso of the titlepage of the 1892 reissue, the 6s. version was published in January 1892 and was reissued in June, with slight alterations to the Introduction, while the 3s. 6d. version appeared in July and was reissued in December.

Meredith made minor revisions and corrections in the proof stage. The description of this revised edition is as follows:

THE TRAGIC COMEDIANS. / A Study in a well-known Story. / BY / GEORGE MEREDITH. / REVISED AND CORRECTED BY THE AUTHOR. / With an Introductory Note on Ferdinand Lassalle, by / CLEMENT SHORTER. / WARD, LOCK, BOWDEN & CO., / LONDON, NEW YORK, AND MELBOURNE. / 1892. / (*All rights reserved.*)

Collation [a]⁴b–c⁸B–R⁸S⁸¹ 148 leaves (19.0 x 12.4) [i–xxxviii] [1]–258

Contents [i] halftitle: THE TRAGIC COMEDIANS. [ii] blank [iii] blank [iv] photograph [v] titlepage [vi] THE TRAGIC COMEDIANS. / [short rule] / Published in a compressed form as a serial in the *Fortnightly Review*, / October, 1880, to February, 1881. / [short rule] / [details of editions] [vi (misnumbered v)] bibliography [viii] blank [ix–xxvii (misnumbered vii–xxxv)] introduction [xxxviii] blank [1]–258 text, on 258: THE END

MANUSCRIPT

The manuscript of *The Tragic Comedians* was given to Miss Nicholls and was sold at Sotheby's on 1 December 1910. It is now in the Beinecke. The compositors' names are on various pages, but though it was evidently used as copy by the printer, Meredith had followed his usual practice of introducing the chapter divisions at a late stage. As usual, also, the process of final revision can be followed by the rearrangement of chapters and the renumbering of pages. This revision occurred after Meredith had first submitted it to Chapman and Hall, as one can tell for example from MS 184 on which Meredith has written, as he invariably did when sending folios to the printers one batch at a time: 'Chapters XI–XII–XIII / From George Meredith / Box Hill, Dorking'. But these chapters do not precisely coincide with the final version, while chapter

XIII has been fairly extensively revised. The division between chapter I and the pages which precede it must have been made at the proof stage.

The manuscript is numbered as follows: 1–16, 16a–26, 26–30, 32–55, (56–7 is one page, the other having been removed in the process of revision), 58–73, 74–86, 86–106, 107–35, 135–45, 145–7, 147a–b, 148–52, 152–70, 170–83, 184–185a–b–c–d, 186–186a–187–91, 191–205, 205–16, 216–26, 227–37, 237–56, 256–9.

XI c

AN EARLY AMERICAN EDITION

Because of the rapid growth of Meredith's reputation in North America during the last two decades, it is interesting to note an American edition of *The Tragic Comedians* which antedates the collected editions of Chapman and Hall and Roberts Brothers. Meredith was not read widely on this side of the Atlantic until 1885 when these collected editions became available. The titlepage, which is also the cover, of this perhaps pirated edition reads as follows:

THE / Seaside Library / THE TRAGIC COMEDIANS. / BY GEORGE MEREDITH. / This Number contains a Complete Story, Unchanged and Unabridged. / Vol. XLVI. / SINGLE   GEORGE MUNRO, PUBLISHER,
    NUMBER.   NOS. 17 to 27 VANDEWATER STREET, NEW YORK.
PRICE / 10 CENTS. / No. 939 / Copyrighted 1881. by GEORGE MUNRO. – Entered at the Post Office of New York at Second Class Rates. – February 18, 1881. / The Tragic Comedians. / A STUDY IN AN OLD STORY. / BY GEORGE MEREDITH. / [short rule] / advertisement / [short rule] / NEW YORK: / GEORGE MUNRO. PUBLISHER / 17 TO 27 VANDEWATER STREET.

XII

DIANA OF THE CROSSWAYS

FIRST EDITION

DIANA OF THE CROSSWAYS / *A Novel* / BY / GEORGE MEREDITH / CONSIDERABLY ENLARGED FROM "THE FORTNIGHTLY REVIEW" / IN THREE VOLUMES / VOL. I. / LONDON: CHAPMAN AND HALL / LIMITED / 1885 / [*All rights reserved.*]

VOLUME I

Collation [A]⁴B–Y⁸Z⁴ 176 leaves (18.8 x 12.3) [i–vii] viii [1]–344

Contents [i] halftitle: DIANA OF THE CROSSWAYS / [short rule] / VOL. I [ii] blank [iii] titlepage [iv] imprint at centre: LONDON: / PRINTED BY J.S. VIRTUE AND CO., LIMITED, / CITY ROAD. [v] dedication: INSCRIBED / TO / FREDERICK POLLOCK. [vi] blank [vii]–viii contents [1]–344 text, on 344 at foot: END OF VOL. I. / [rule] / PRINTED BY J.S. VIRTUE AND CO., LIMITED, CITY ROAD, LONDON. [Note that 1–28 of Volume I are printed in small pica, twenty-eight lines to a page, while the rest of the novel is printed in pica, twenty-one lines to a page.]

VOLUME II

Collation [A]^{3}B–Y^8 171 leaves (18.8 x 12.3) [i–v] vi [1]–335 [336]

Contents [i] halftitle: DIANA OF THE CROSSWAYS / [short rule] / VOL. II. [ii] blank [iii] titlepage [iv] imprint [v]–vi contents [1]–335 text, on 335 at foot: END OF VOL. II. / [rule] / PRINTED BY J.S. VIRTUE AND CO., LIMITED, CITY ROAD, LONDON. [336] blank

VOLUME III

Collation [A]^{3}B–X^{8}Y^5 168 leaves (18.8 x 12.3) [i–v] vi [1]–330

Contents [i] halftitle: DIANA OF THE CROSSWAYS / [short rule] / VOL. III. [ii] blank [iii] titlepage [iv] imprint [v]–vi contents [1]–330 text, on 330 at foot: THE END. / [rule] / PRINTED BY J.S. VIRTUE AND CO., LIMITED, CITY ROAD, LONDON.

Binding Spine, and boards at front and back, covered in reddish-brown cloth with a fine horizontal and vertical grain. Yellowish-white endpapers.

Front cover At top and bottom, stamped in black, a horizontal floral scroll between two sets of double lines.

Spine At top and bottom, stamped in gilt, a horizontal floral scroll between two sets of dooble lines. Between them, stamped in gilt: DIANA / OF THE / CROSSWAYS / [short rule] / GEORGE MEREDITH / [short rule] / VOL. I [II III] / CHAPMAN & HALL

Back cover At centre, stamped in black, Chapman and Hall's monogram.

The first edition of *Diana of the Crossways* was reissued at least twice during 1885, no other change being made in the process of reprinting and binding than the addition of '*Second Edition*' and '*Third Edition*' to the titlepage of all three volumes.

SERIAL PUBLICATION

The serial, published in six instalments during the second part of 1884 in the *Fortnightly Review*, is a truncated version of the first version of the first edition.

Meredith worked at *Diana of the Crossways* during the winter of 1883–4. On 16 January 1884 he wrote to Raffalovich: 'My present novel is for *The Fortnightly*, and it begins in March or April. It is partly based on a real instance; if my health holds out I shall have done my part of the task with the publication of the first number' (*Letters* II 723). To Admiral Maxse he wrote on 18 February 1884: 'I am besides heavily weighted with work, and must get as near to the close of a Novel for the *Fortnightly*, that appears in April or May, as I can' (*Letters* II 726). A little more than a month later he told Stevenson, in a letter dated 24 March 1884, that he was still having difficulties: 'I have developed a spinal malady and can walk not much more than a mile. On the other hand I can work passably well, and am just finishing at a great pace a two-volume novel, to be called *Diana of the Crossways* – partly modelled upon Mrs. Norton. But this is between ourselves. I have had to endow her with brains and make them evidence to the discerning. I think she lives. She appears by instalments in the *Fortnightly Review*, commencing May or June. I hope to have done with her – have her out of me – in April' (*Letters* II 730–1).

While he worked, he was no doubt negotiating with Chapman and Hall for the publication of the novel in book form, and in fact on 21 April 1884 he wrote to Frederic Chapman: 'Pray do not fail to bring the matter of my book before the Directors instantly – or the publication in the *Fortnightly* will have to be retarded. I bring up the first half of the book to town on Thursday for printers, and will be with you about noon' (*Letters* II 733).

From these excerpts it may be gathered that the novel was shaping itself as it was written. The serial publication in fact began in June, and *Diana of the Crossways* had by that time become a three-volume novel. Meredith's contract with Chapman and Hall for the publication of *Diana of the Crossways* was signed on 21 July 1884 (Morgan). For £500, the firm purchased the copyright for five years, £200 to be paid on signing and £100 on 31 October, 30 November, and 31 December. 'The purchase shall include the right to the said company to first publish the said novel in the *Fortnightly Review* and shall also include the right to publish the said book in America.' As neither party anticipated that *Diana of the Crossways* would go to a third edition within three months of publication, Meredith accepted Chapman and Hall's promise of a further £25 if the book turned out to be successful. Later, on 10 October 1884, Meredith wrote again to Stevenson: 'My *Diana* is out of hand, leaving her mother rather inanimate. Should you see the *Fortnightly*, avoid the section under her title. Escott gives me but 18 pages in 8 numbers – for a 3 volume novel; so the poor girl has had to be mutilated horribly, and one foresees the "much to her advantage" of reviewers, who care less than the honest public for the consecutive in concrete matter' (*Letters* II 747—8).

The novel did not in fact run for eight numbers. It began in the last number of volume 41 of the *Fortnightly Review* and continued through the whole of volume 42, that is until December 1884. Chapters 1–3 of the serial appeared in the June issue, pp. 763–80; 4–7 in July, pp. 108–25; 8–11 in September, pp. 345–62; 12–14 in October, pp. 484–501; 15–18 in November, pp. 657–74; 19–26 in December, pp. 738–67. When the serialization was 'abruptly terminated' (to retain the midwifery image), Meredith added the very unsatisfactory note: 'Thus was the erratic woman stricken; and those who care for more of Diana of the Crossways will find it in the extended chronicle.' Though, in his letter to Stevenson, he had been critical of Escott, the editor of the *Fortnightly*, Meredith himself had evidently become dissatisfied with his own story and was, while the serial was appearing, already rewriting it for publication by Chapman and Hall. The titlepage of the first edition says that the novel was 'Considerably enlarged from "The Fortnightly Review",' but critical interest is not so much in the relation of the serial to the first edition as in the relation of both to the two manuscripts. The serial version of *Diana of the Crossways* was published by Munro in New York as part of his 'Seaside Library.'

MANUSCRIPTS

There are three fragments and one complete MS of *Diana of the Crossways*.

A In the Morgan, in two volumes, 987 leaves, numbered as follows: pp. 1–40, 41–66, 66–87, 88–92, 92a, 93–117, 118–42, 143–60, 160a, 161–3, 163–84, 185–216, 217–34, 235–43, 243–59, 260–74, 275–95, 296–323, 324–43, 343a, 343b, 343c, 343d, 344–6, 347–81, 382–405, 406, 406a–28, 429–51, 452–5 (one page), 456–74, 475–82, 482–6 (one page, additional to the previous 482), 487–507, 508–31, 432–56, 556–70, 570–93, 594–623, 624–60, 661–72a, 672b, 672c, 673–86, 687–722, 723–47, 748–63, 764–79, 731–43, 744–58, 759–77, 778–800, 801–27, 828–42, 843, 845–8, 848a, 849–71, 872–99, 900–24, 925–52, 952a–54, 955–87. (Note: where the same number appears on either side of the comma the chapter division occurs mid-page.)

On the back of 954 Meredith wrote: 'From George Meredith / Box Hill, Dorking / To Messrs. Virtue & Co. / 294 City Road E.C. London.' In other words, this was at one point the end of the novel. The MS was sold by Cole to J. Pierpont Morgan (Forman p. 75).

B In the Huntington, 95 leaves, numbered as follows: pp. 324-9, 335-43, 405, 692-707, 707-12, 715, 730, 823-7, 845-50, 858-66, 867-95, 900-2, 919-[920]. This MS was sold by Miss Nicholls at Sotheby's on 1 December 1910. John Quinn resold it to Henry E. Huntington in 1914.

C In the Beinecke, 50 leaves numbered as follows: pp. 480, 661-91, 958-74, 976.

D In the Fales Collection of the New York University Library, 3 leaves numbered as follows: pp. 956, 975, 977.

RELATIONSHIP OF THE MANUSCRIPTS TO THE FIRST EDITION

Meredith had been unwell for several years so that *Diana of the Crossways*, when it at length seized his mind, came as something of a surprise. He had, so it seems, derived little satisfaction from his own work during this period. Of *The Egoist* he gave G.W. Foote a melancholy account in a letter dated 30 May 1879: 'I have been away from home, rather unwell, as I grieve to hear it is the case with Mr. Thomson. I finished a 3 volume work rapidly, and as it comes mainly from the head and has nothing to kindle imagination, I thirsted to be rid of it soon after conception, and it became a struggle in which health suffered, and my unfailing specific of hard exercise was long in restoring me' (*Letters* II 572). Stevenson says (p. 243) that Meredith had two novels in hand in 1881. Perhaps during these years (1879-83) he made a number of starts: *Celt and Saxon* dates from this period; so does the first manuscript of *The Amazing Marriage*. Moreover, he had promised a novel to the *Cornhill* which in the end he was unable to write.

All in all he was at a low ebb. In 1881 he spent some time in convalescence in Brighton. In 1882 he travelled, restlessly, in France, Switzerland, and Italy. 'I begin to have a touch of despair,' he wrote in a letter dated 5 August 1881; 'my work gets on so slowly, and I must hand in a certain quantity by the end of October' (*Letters* II 635). But in December, he was still 'in harness to my novel' (*Letters* II 646); in February 1882 he told Chapman he had been 'rather upset, bothered by a wrestle with my work at a difficult point' (*Letters* II 653); while months later, on 28 September 1882, he had to confess to Leslie Stephen: 'If things go well I shall have the story ready by the Spring, but I dare not forecast very hopefully' (*Letters* II 675). A combination of ill-health and waning imaginative vitality seems to have brought him to a standstill: 'I am stagnant and can't write,' he told Admiral Maxse on 16 August 1883 (*Letters* II 708). It is not certain that any of these remarks refer to *Diana of the Crossways*; what is certain is the fact that the novel derives from this long period of despair, in which he described himself as 'passing from the pathetic obscurity into the ludicrous, for who can help laughing to see an old fellow stitching books that nobody buys' (Beinecke: 23 June 1882 to Mrs. Wise).

In the autumn of 1883 Meredith recovered some of his old energy. He told Cotter Morrison: 'Ever since I took to your prescription in diet – from the first day miraculously – I sprang to the pen, and am producing rapidly' (*Letters* II 719: 30 October 1883). He recovered his spirits as well as his energy. He must have worked steadily on his first draft throughout the winter of 1883–4, no doubt finishing it shortly after the beginning of the serial. In March, he told Mrs. Leslie Stephen: 'I am now working daily very hard, and though the work flows to its end in full view, my health at present is of a kind hardly to bear the strain ... Meanwhile I hope to finish with the delivery of the terrible woman afflicting me (a positive hereoine with brains, with real blood, and demanding utterance of the former, tender direction of the latter) by the end of April' (*Letters* II 731–2: 24 March 1884). As he worked, however, and as the characters took over, the 'real instance' became less and less important. Even in the first manuscript version of the novel it is not important to know that Diana is partly based on Mrs. Norton. Likewise, though he claimed that 'the work flows to its end in full view,' many difficulties remained. He had to reconcile the central concern of the novel, as it then appeared to him, with the need to resolve the psychological crux created by the behaviour of his main character. In the Morgan MS there is a deleted passage on a page saved from the first version which perhaps indicates the way in which Meredith thought about the book during the first six months of 1884: 'And the woman had already been "compromised." Her passions have broken out again. No wonder she refuses to go back to the long-suffering husband who for morality's precious sake is ready to be a sacrifice to his vows, that he may take her, guide, control her, defend her from the world & from herself' (Morgan 482–6). The novel, one has to suppose, was much more simply 'about marriage,' and that was no doubt Meredith's reason for saying: 'I have a fear that it is too didactic for modern readers, though it says things that should be thought of.'

Meanwhile he had difficulty with Diana herself. Meredith seemed to recover his power as a novelist as he wrote and as he thought his way into Diana's situation. 'Diana of the Crossways keeps me still on her sad last way to wedlock. I could have killed her merrily, with my compliments to the public; and that was my intention. But the marrying of her, sets me traversing feminine labyrinths, and you know that the why of it never can be accounted for' (*Letters* II 737: 19 May 1884). Had Diana been killed, nothing would have been resolved: the novel would have been left at the romance level of *Celt and Saxon*. Meredith must have become aware of this during the summer of 1884 since he did not manage to complete the book by the time the serial began. 'My *Diana* still holds me; only by the last chapter; but the coupling of such a woman and her man is a delicate business. She has no puppet-pliancy. The truth being, that she is a mother of Experience, and gives that dreadful baby suck to brains. I have therefore a feeble hold of her; none of the novelist's winding-up arts avail; it is she who leads me. But the delay of the conclusion is owing to my inability to write of late' (*Letters* II 743). As he later wrote to an American critic, he found it impossible to have his characters 'boxed in a plot.' On the other hand, as he explored Diana's predicament – the predicament created by the involvement of passion with politics – he discovered for himself a type of psychological novel, the formal or structural features of which had to be markedly different from anything he had written before.

Between August 1884 and the premature end of the serial in December 1884, he therefore decided to rewrite the novel. Since *Diana of the Crossways* was published on 16 February 1885, he probably began the process of revision in November or early December 1884. Broadly speaking one can say that in the winter of 1883–4 Meredith wrote a novel about a woman who compromises herself with a cabinet member, a novel in which Meredith could raise topical questions about marriage. In 1884–5, he rewrote the book, reducing the importance of the topical allusions to the repeal of the Corn Laws and reducing the emphasis on the moral dilemma of the woman compromised by her lack of social conformity, but increasing the psychological interest by not resorting to a facile conclusion such as in this instance a death would have been. This account is unavoidably sketchy: but it is necessary, if the mechanical description of the way the manuscripts relate to each other is to have any point. As it happens, one can be reasonably certain about the process of rewriting.

Meredith became dissatisfied with the course of the novel at least by the time that the serial had reached chapter XXVI. To understand what happened it is easiest to begin at this point. As noted already, by the end of August Meredith had one complete manuscript of the novel, the first version. The manuscripts in the Beinecke and in the Huntington are fragments of this first version. The three manuscript leaves in the Fales Collection may also be part of it. The manuscript that Meredith had used for the final publication of the novel in book form is in the Morgan. This copy prepared for and used by the printers is a fabrication: it consists of pages incorporated from the first version with little change, fair copy which would indicate that parts of the first version had been entirely rewritten, new material that did not correspond to anything in the first version, and heavily corrected leaves from the first version the marginal additions to which almost make them new material. When Meredith reconstructed the novel, and rewrote part of it, the fact that he incorporated pages from the first version allows one to reconstruct in part what must have happened. In addition, because in the nature of the case he had to work quickly he changed as little as possible. The renumbering of the pages and chapters in the Morgan copy is a clue to the extent of the rearrangement. An important feature of the Morgan copy is the heavy marginal writing at various points: an entirely new manuscript leaf may in fact, though recognizably the second version, be a rewriting of something quite similar or even identical in the first version; a manuscript leaf that has been heavily corrected as a result of the rewriting may, because the process is visible on the one page, be better evidence of its actual nature.

Because the leaves of these manuscripts are scattered and because it is possible that others may turn up, a fairly detailed tracing of the process of emendation seems justified. Meredith, then, rewrote in the winter of 1884–5 parts of the novel that concerned Diana's relationships with Redworth and Dacier, toning down the Dacier episodes and rewriting some of the early Redworth parts to make Diana's marriage to him credible. The rewriting started at chapter XXVIII. This is an entirely new chapter, with no equivalent in the Beinecke and Huntington fragments. The interpolation of this new chapter XXVIII had three results.

Firstly, Meredith had to renumber and correct the preceding chapters, a process that took him back at least to chapter XIX where three pages were omitted from the Morgan MS. Chapter XXVII had previously been chapter XXV; chapter XXVI had previously been chapter XXIV; and chapters XXV, XXIV, and XXIII (i.e. pages 532–93 in the Morgan MS) had previously been chapter XXIII. This was a fairly gentle process of remodelling: no major changes were introduced between chapter XIX and chapter XXVII and the Morgan MS which corresponds to these chapters in fact consists of sections taken completely from the first MS.

Secondly, Meredith had to rewrite the chapters that followed his new chapter XXVIII. Beinecke MS 661–74 was the old chapter XXVI: that is, in the first version it had followed directly the present chapter XXVII and is therefore the end of the serial version. Beinecke MS 675–91 was the old chapter XXVII. Meredith reconstructed and rewrote these two Beinecke chapters to create the new chapter XXIX; the changes in page numbers in the Morgan MS suggest that there were more than one draft of the rewriting. Next he rewrote chapter XXX. Huntington MS 692–707 was the old chapter XXVIII, and Huntington 707–[13] the old chapter XXIX; these two chapters in the first version were entirely rewritten and greatly expanded to make the present chapter XXX. A certain amount of reconstruction and remodelling was necessary to the end of chapter XXXII, at which point Meredith was able to return to using the pages of the first version. When he did that he marked on the page 779 = 731, giving a rough indication of how many additional pages had been introduced in the course of the rewriting.

Thirdly, Meredith had to cast back in order to reconsider the early episodes in which Dacier appeared so that his handling of them would be consistent with the rewriting of Diana's relationship with Redworth. Chapters I–XIV in the Morgan MS are fair copy and no earlier version exists; whether or not rewriting was necessary, and if so how much, is impossible to tell. Chapter xv, however, was largely rewritten. Huntington MS 324–9 was part of the old chapter XIV: the renumbering of the first fourteen chapters was a consequence of the rewriting of the present chapter xv. Four new leaves were introduced. These were Morgan MS 330 and 331–3, formerly 231–3 and therefore part of a rejected early version. (The four interpolated leaves correspond to Morgan MS 164–7.) Huntington MS 335–43 corresponds to the rewritten Morgan MS 339–43 (roughly M 168–9). In brief, only the last four MS pages (i.e. 344–6 which correspond roughly to M 172–3) were not reconsidered and rewritten.

There were thus three phases to the rewriting of the first part of the novel in the winter of 1884–5. Meredith also had difficulty with the second part. He had to reconsider chapters XXXIV to XLI, introducing a small amount of new material and rewriting sections that correspond to the rejected Huntington fragments. (Note that the page numbers of the Huntington fragments do *not* correspond to those of the Morgan MS.) Finally, he made several attempts to end the novel. Chapter XLII is a chapter that has been rewritten, though at what stage in the process is not so clear. Chapter XLIII was completely rewritten. Beinecke MS 958–74, 976 and NYUL MS 956, 975, and 977 together constitute a recognizable but weakly written version of the actual conclusion, including a final page (NYUL 977). But the final chapter XLIII is a greatly expanded rendering of the episodes sketched in rather a feeble way in the first version represented by the Beinecke and NYUL fragments.

RECONSTRUCTION OF REJECTED VERSION and ANALYSIS OF FINAL COPY

I	II
Rejected MS fragments in the Huntington, Beinecke, and Fales Collection at NYUL	Final MS Copy in the Morgan used in setting up the First Edition. Parts definitely rewritten and without an earlier version are in italic

I	I–XIV 1–92 92a 93–160 160a, 161–320, 321–3 (retained from I)

These first fourteen chapters are a fair copy. It is difficult to tell when the fair copy was made, except that the redivision into chapters must have preceded the rewriting of Morgan xv.

2 Huntington 324–9 (previously chapter XIV)	XV [324]–29, 330, 331–3 (previously numbered 231–3), 334–7 (previously numbered 330–3), 338 (previously numbered 334)

Huntington 335–43	*339–43* (339–40 = Memorial 168–9), *343a–b–c–d* (previously 343, 343a–b–c), 344–6 (= Memorial 172–3)

This chapter is where the rewriting began. To retain continuity Meredith had to write the last lines of 332 in the margin. This means that Morgan 333 is probably the old 329. The four leaves introduced into Morgan xv are Morgan 330, a new page, and Morgan 331–3, formerly 231–3 and therefore a fragment from the rejected first version of the novel. The only parts of this chapter not rewritten are Morgan 334–7 and 344–6.

3		XVI 347–81
4		XVII 382–405
5	Huntington 405 The old final page of chapter XVII	These chapters appear to have been retained from the early version.

6	XVIII 406–28

To judge by the muddle at the beginning of the chapter (i.e. at Morgan 405–6), it seems likely that it was largely incorporated from the early version.

7	XIX *429–51 452/455*

At the bottom of 451, 4 lines are crossed out which presumably connected with the old 452–4.

8	Beinecke 480	XX 456–74 XXI 475–507 XXII 508–31 XXIII 532–56 XXIV 556–70 XXV 570–93 (532–93 were together the old chapter XXIII)
9		XXVI 594–623 (previously chapter XXIV
10		XXVII 624–60 (previously chapter XXV)

Chapters XX–XXVII are incorporated from 1, but heavily corrected. Some pages are completely rewritten.

11	XXVIII *661–72, 672a–b–c, 673–86*

An entirely new chapter without a direct equivalent in the first version. (Beinecke 673 and Morgan 682–4 = Memorial 333–4).

12 Beinecke 661–74 (old chapter XXVI)
   Note that Beinecke 661–74 corresponds
   to the end of the serial, being the old
   chapter XXVI. Chapter XXVI in the
   Morgan and in the first edition is *not* the
   equivalent of the end of the serial.
   Beinecke 675–91 (old chapter XXVII)   XXIX
                                            687–722
   Meredith reconstructed and rewrote Beinecke 661–91 to make an entirely new
   Morgan XXIX, though Morgan 687–9 were formerly 681–3.

13 Huntington 692–707 (old chapter   XXX
   XXVIII   723–47
   On Huntington 692 at top left is
   written 'Chapters XXX–XXXI–XXXII.'
   Chapter XXXI began on Huntington 707.
   Huntington 707–[13] (old chapter XXIX
   On Huntington 7[13] is the end of
   chapter XXXI ('They parted for the night,
   simply squeezing hands, if warmly.') and
   the beginning of XXXII, the chapter
   number and title being written in the
   margin.
   Note that Huntington 692–707 was at a
   second stage marked chapter XXX and
   707–[13] marked chapter XXXI.
   This indicates that they were at first
   retained by Meredith after he had
   written Morgan XXVIII, but that later –
   not much later – he realized they also
   had to be changed.
   Huntington 692–[13] was entirely rewritten and greatly expanded as Morgan 723–47.
   Nevertheless the gist of the chapter has been retained.

14   XXXI
                                            748–60, 761–2 (previously numbered
                                            714–15), 763

15 Huntington 730   XXXII
                                            764, 765–78 (previously numbered
                                            716–29), 779
16   XXXIII
                                            731–43
                                            XXXIV
                                            744–58
                                            XXXV
                                            759–71
                                            XXXVI
                                            778–800
   On 731 Meredith wrote 779 = 731. In other words he returned to the first version
   since the major revision (Morgan XXVIII–XXXII) was over.

17 Huntington 823–7	XXXVII
	801–27
	XXXVIII
	828–42
18 Huntington 845–50	XXXIX
	843–8
Huntington 858–66	848a–71

The Huntington pages that were abandoned include the visit of Emma and Diana to Crossways, a different version of the cricket match, and an episode between Diana and Arthur Rhodes.

Though these chapters have been largely retained from the first version, parts have been rewritten and parts heavily edited.

---

19 Huntington 867–95	XL
	872–99

Morgan 872 is roughly equivalent to 867. Five pages were therefore added in the rewriting of Morgan XXXVIII and XXXIX.

---

20 Huntington 900–2	XLI
Huntington 919–20	900–17, 918–24 (previously numbered
	919–25)
Morgan 900–2 are new.	
21	XLII
	925–52, 952a–54

---

22 NYUL 956	XLIII
Beinecke 958–74	955–87
NYUL 975	
Beinecke 976	
NYUL 977	

The last chapter was rewritten. Beinecke and NYUL constitute a recognizable but pallid and incomplete version of the end of the novel. The actual ending is a greatly expanded version of the first draft. 975–7 are renumbered but exceptionally difficult to decipher. It looks as though 975 was previously 797.

XIII

ONE OF OUR CONQUERORS

FIRST EDITION

ONE OF OUR CONQUERORS. / BY / GEORGE MEREDITH. / IN THREE VOLUMES. / VOL. I. / LONDON: CHAPMAN AND HALL, LIMITED. / 1891. / [ALL RIGHTS RESERVED.]

VOLUME I

Collation [A]²B–U⁸ 154 leaves (19.5 × 12.8) [i–iv] [1]–302 [303–4]

Contents [i] titlepage [ii] blank [iii] contents [iv] blank [1]–302 text, on 302: END OF VOL. I. / [short rule] / PRINTED BY WILLIAM CLOWES AND SONS, LIMITED, / LONDON AND BECCLES. [303] blank [304] blank

VOLUME II

Collation [A]²B–X⁸ 162 leaves (19.3 x 12.8) [i–iii] iv [1]–320

Contents [i] titlpage [ii] blank [iii]–iv contents [1]–320 text, on 320: END OF VOL. II with imprint at foot.

VOLUME III

Collation [A]²B–U⁸X² 156 leaves (19.2 x 12.6) [i–iii] iv [1]–307 [308]

Contents [i] titlepage [ii] blank [iii]–iv contents [1]–307 text, on 307: END OF VOL. III with imprint at foot [308] blank

Binding Spine, and boards at front and back, covered in deep blue cloth with regular morocco grain. Yellowish-white endpapers with pale yellow coating, on the recto of the front free endpaper and the verso of the back free endpaper. On the verso of the front free endpaper is a publisher's advertisement, enclosed by a black border, listing Meredith's works: GEORGE MEREDITH'S WORKS / [short rule] / *Each Novel complete in One Volume, price 3s. 6d.* / [short rule] / DIANA OF THE CROSSWAYS. / EVAN HARRINGTON. / THE ORDEAL OF RICHARD FEVEREL. / THE ADVENTURES OF HARRY RICHMOND. / SANDRA BELLONI. / VITTORIA. / RHODA FLEMING. / BEAUCHAMP'S CAREER. / THE EGOIST. / THE SHAVING OF SHAGPAT, and FARINA.

Front cover A three-lined border stamped in black at top. Beneath this, another line stamped in black with a crook at each end. Beneath this, a curving triangular-shaped ornament stamped in black so that the blue cloth forms the pattern of a blossom flanked by two fronds. The design, inverted, is repeated at the bottom of the front cover.

Spine A two-lined border stamped in gilt at top and bottom, and, stamped in gilt: ONE / OF OUR / CONQUERORS / [short rule] / GEORGE / MEREDITH / VOL. I / CHAPMAN & HALL.

Back cover Publisher's monogram blind-stamped at centre.

Variant bindings A number of variant bindings have been noted, including biscuit coloured smooth cloth, green cloth, cherry red smooth cloth, powder blue cloth with a very fine sand grain, and coffee coloured smooth cloth. In all these the verso of the front endpaper is blank. Since most, and perhaps all, of these examples were complimentary copies given to friends, it is possible that the six copies due to Meredith were made up in a variety of bindings after the lettering brasses had been cut, and that they were thus not a variant issue in the real sense.

SERIAL PUBLICATION

In a letter to Chapman in May, Meredith suggested that the serial could begin in November. On 5 July he wrote to Chapman again: 'Expect me on Monday at the Office about Midday. There seems no reason why we should not come to terms.' (He had already been approached by American publishers.) He did in fact come to terms and indeed signed a contract with Chapman and Hall, of which a clerk's copy is in the Beinecke.

'Memorandum of Agreement made this 10th day of July, 1890 Between Chapman & Hall Limited of 11 Henrietta Street, Covent Garden, London WC. Publishers hereinafter called the Company of the one part and George Meredith of Flint House, Mickleham in the County of Surrey, Esquire, hereinafter called the Author of the other part Whereby the Author agrees to sell, and the Company agrees to buy the Copyright for a period of six years from the date of publication in three volume form of a work written by the Author and called "One of Our Conquerors." The Company to pay the Author for such six years the right of publication the sum of One thousand pounds payable as follows: – £500 on 15th November next and the remaining £500 on 15th March 1891. The above sum of One thousand pounds not to include any foreign rights all of which the author reserves to himself. The Company to have the right to publish the said work in the Fortnightly Review and the Author undertakes to reduce the same so that it can be passed through the said Review in not more than seven monthly issues. George Meredith.'

On 24 August, he wrote from Scotland: 'Send no more. I will give you MS. on my return. But I have still to write the 2 final chapters. These are clear and current in the head ...' In the same letter: 'Please at the beginning of next week, forward to Box Hill two sets of the revised 2 first volumes, that I may prepare them for the *Fortnightly*' (*Letters* II 1003). Evidently the first two volumes had been set before Meredith had completed the third. Though he had contracted to reduce *One of Our Conquerors* for serial purposes to the equivalent of seven issues, he in fact told Chapman on 19 November: 'The Proofs here sent may be divided for the further Serial ... according to the number of the months you decide that it shall run before publication in the volumes' (*Letters* II 1012).

The novel was actually published in eight instalments during the winter and spring of 1890–1 in the *Fortnightly Review*. The eight issues were numbered 286–94 consecutively and were divided as follows: magazine chapters I–VI in October, pp. 614–40; chapters VII–X in November, pp. 795–816; chapters XI–XIV in December, pp. 859–992; chapters XV–XIX in January, pp. 143–72; chapters XX–XXII in February, pp. 324–44; chapters XXIII–XXVI in March, pp. 485–512; chapters XXVII–XXIX in April, pp. 656–80; chapters XXX–XXXI in May, pp. 834–56.

MANUSCRIPTS

There are two MSS of *One of Our Conquerors*, both in the Beinecke, and one fragment, a single leaf of no significance, which is in the Huntington.

MS A

The shorter of the two manuscripts was sold with Miss Nicholls' collection at Sotheby's on 1 December 1910. This MS is divided into batches of leaves, some of which have chapter numbers and titles. The chapter divisions are not the same as in the first edition. In the listing of these batches of papers that follows, the figure at the left is for convenience: it does not appear on the MS itself.

1 CHAPTER I
'Across London Bridge,' pp. 1–24 (equivalent, with small changes, to Memorial I and II).

2 CHAPTER II
'Old Veuve,' pp. 25–50 (equivalent of Memorial III and IV, the break occurring at MS 37).

3 CHAPTER III
'The London Walk Westward,' pp. 51–78 (equivalent to Memorial V and VI, the break occuring at MS 67).

4 CHAPTER IV
'Between a General Man of the World and a Professional,' pp. 79–97 (equivalent to Memorial VII).

5 CHAPTER V
'A Visit to Lakelands,' pp. 98–128 (equivalent to Memorial VIII and IX, the break occurring roughly at MS 115).

6 CHAPTER VI
'Skepsey in Motion,' pp. 129–55 (equivalent to Memorial X).

7 CHAPTER VII
'Wherein the Couple Justified by Love have sighted their Scourge,' pp. 156–87.

8 A SECOND VERSION OF CHAPTER VII
'Wherein We Behold the Couple justified of Love Having Sight of their Scourge,' pp. 156–74 (these two versions of chapter VII roughtly equivalent to Memorial XI). In 8 there are four additional leaves. Of these p. 164 does

not belong but is rather an alternative to p. 164 in 7. It must be a rejected alternative since 7 reads continuously. The same is the case with the additional pp. 165, 166, and 167 in 8. It follows that the Beinecke note at the beginning of 8 – 'Second draft of Chapter VII' – is not correct. Pp. 164 and 165, 166 and 167 in 8 which are variants of 164, 165, 166, and 167 in 7 are quite different from 7 which is printer's copy. 7 is significantly different from Memorial XI. In particular, the passage of analysis at Memorial 118–19 is quite different at MS 174–81 (see discussion below). The verbal parallel between 7 and Memorial XI resumes at MS 181/Memorial 119, 'They had evil to no one as yet.'

9 CHAPTER VIII

'Of the Dumbness Possible with Members of a Household Having One Heart,' pp. 188–200 (continuing from MS 187 in 7, and corresponding roughly to Memorial XIII). The treatment here is different from the final printed version chiefly in that the abstract analysis of the relationship between Victor and Nataly is omitted, e.g. at MS 196.

10 CHAPTER IX

'Later News of Mrs. Burman,' pp. 200a–35 (the 'a' appears to be in Meredith's hand). This group of leaves actually includes both chapter IX (roughly the equivalent of Memorial XIII) and Chapter X, entitled 'Dr. Themison.' P. 217 is missing. Not much of MS chapter X is retained in the printed version: it is a theoretical account of Victor's appreciation of the problem, and of his side of his relationship with Nataly. Victor's episode with Themison is shortened in Memorial to pp. 142–5.

11 CHAPTER XI

'Slow Movement: With Something of Nesta and Touches upon Many of the Characters,' pp. 236–73 (roughly equivalent to Memorial XIV beginning halfway down Memorial 144). In the MS, the description of the trip to France tails off into an abstract analysis of Victor's character, e.g. at MS 270–3.

12 CHAPTER XII

'A Patriot Abroad' and chapter XIII 'Accounts for Skepsey's Misconduct, showing How it Affected Nataly,' pp. 274–305. MS chapter XII is the equivalent of Memorial chapter XV though a few sections are omitted in the printed version, and MS XIII coincides with Memorial XVI as far as Skepsey is concerned. But the account of Victor breaking the news to Nataly is less brutal in the final version (c.f. MS 299, 'We must think of ourselves, dear girl').

13 CHAPTER XIV

'Chiefly on the Theme of a Young Maid's Imaginations,' pp. 306–31 (equivalent to Memorial XVII). This group of MS leaves consists of several variants, as follows:

a pp. 306–10

b pp. 306–7

c pp. 306–7

d pp. 306–9

e p. 305 (this number is in pencil and not in Meredith's hand)

f pp. 311–29

The first and the last, i.e. 'a' and 'f,' are continuous, and therefore presumably make up the final version. The discarded variants are of little interest. 13 also contains one and a half pages of MS chapter XV, i.e. pp. 330–1.

14 CHAPTER XV

pp. 330–55 (roughly equivalent to Memorial XVIII) in the treatment of the two suitors, but continuing to a theoretical description of the relationship between Nesta and Sowerby that is not in Memorial at all.

15 This final group is a miscellany, as follows:

a pp. 338, 339, 340, 341, 342 (alternatives to pages with the same numbers in 14), p. 343 (not continuing from p. 342 in Memorial 13, but an alternative to p. 343 in 14), 344, 345, 346 (in pencil), 347. These pages seem to have been rejected during the rewriting of MS XV.

b chapter XVI, pp. 356–74. The p. 356 which follows p. 347 is the beginning of the first version of MS XVI which begins again at p. 356.

c chapter XIX, pp. 433–60. In this group p. 434 is missing but there is a second p. 459 out of place.

d chapter XIX, pp. 433–68. If this is the complete MS XIX of which 'e' is an earlier version, maybe pp. 459–60 in 'e' really belong to 'd.'

e pp. 473, 683, 687, 688, and two unnumbered pages in different inks.

MS B

The longer MS was deposited in the British Museum in March 1910 by W.M. Meredith. It was subsequently removed and sold at Christie's on 20 July 1960, by the estate of Mrs. M.E. Sturgis. The MS consists of a total of 973 leaves, numbered consecutively from 1 to 965 with additional leaves interspersed and divided into folders of fifty leaves. There are twenty such folders all with fifty leaves with the exception of the following: number 10 has fifty-two leaves (pp. 460A and 461A); number 14 has fifty-one (468A); number 16 has fifty-four (763A, 781A, 781B, 781C); number 19 has fifty-one (726A); and number 20 has fifteen. In addition, there are nineteen leaves of another draft of chapter XXXVII, numbered 826–7, 827–34, 834, 835–8, 848–51. (There are two each of 827 and 834.) There is the possibility that some leaves, most obviously 826–38 and 848–51, were retained from the earlier manuscript.

THE RELATIONSHIP OF THE MSS TO THE FIRST EDITION

MS A

It is likely that MS A was written before the other MS: how long before is not certain. The MS is heavily corrected in places, but as these corrections are not always carried to the second MS it seems that Meredith was in difficulties with the writing of the first version and was unable to continue it. In the printed version of *One of Our Conquerors* the moral issues are presented more clearly than in the first MS, some of the abstractions have been rendered unnecessary by the redisposition of events, and preoccupation with the relationship between Victor and Nataly has been replaced by a greater emphasis upon Nesta. Whether this is an improvement is open to question. If it could be argued that the urgent attempt to understand and delineate the estrangement between man and woman, rather than to judge it, belonged to an earlier, more mature stage in Meredith's writing life, one could hazard the guess that *One of Our Conquerors* was conceived before 1880. The difference between the style of the two MSS would tend to confirm this.

Meredith's letter to Jessopp dated 30 May 1890 has been preserved with this MS, though it must refer to the final version. 'I am just finishing a novel and am a bit strained – as I have condemned myself both to a broad and a close observation of the modern world in it, – throwing beams both upon its rat-tides and its upper streams' (*Letters* II 999).

MS B

The longer of the two MSS in the Beinecke corresponds closely, but not exactly, to the first edition. There are a number of minor changes that were presumably made in proof. The fact that the MS is made up of bundles of fifty leaves indicates that it was sent part by part to be copied or typed. It does not have the signs of the printing shop as does the MS of *Diana of the Crossways* which was divided in this way.

XIV

LORD ORMONT AND HIS AMINTA

FIRST EDITION

LORD ORMONT AND HIS AMINTA / *A Novel* / BY / GEORGE MEREDITH / IN THREE VOLUMES / VOL. I. / LONDON: CHAPMAN AND HALL, LD. / 1894 / [*All rights reserved*]

VOLUME I

Collation [A]⁴B–P⁸Q⁶ 172 leaves (19.4 × 12.3) [i–viii [1]–235 [236]

Contents [i] halftitle: LORD ORMONT AND HIS AMINTA / VOL. I. [ii] imprint at centre: *This Edition, in 3 Vols., consists of 1500 copies.* [iii] titlepage [iv] printer's imprint at centre: RICHARD CLAY & SONS, LIMITED, / LONDON & BUNGAY. [v] dedication: *Gratefully Inscribed* / TO / GEORGE BUCKSTON BROWNE, / SURGEON. [vi] blank [vii] contents [viii] blank [1]–235 text, on 235: END OF VOL. I. [236 blank

VOLUME II

Collation [A]⁴B–Q⁸ 124 leaves (19.4 × 12.3) [i–viii] [1]–240

Contents [i] blank [ii] blank [iii] halftitle [iv] blank [v] titlepage [vi] printer's imprint [vii] contents [viii] blank [1]–240 text, on 240 at centre: END OF VOL. II.

VOLUME III

Collation [A]⁴B–R⁸S⁵ 137 leaves (19.4 × 12.3) [i–viii] [1]–266 [267–8]

Contents [i] blank [ii] blank [iii] halftitle [iv] blank [v] titlepage [vi] printer's imprint [vii] contents [viii] blank [1]–266 text, on 266 at centre: THE END and on 266 at foot: [short rule] / *Richard Clay & Sons, Limited, London & Bungay.* [267–8] blank

Binding Spine, and boards at front and back, covered in olive-green coarse morocco cloth. Endpapers plain.

Front cover Stamped in black, a three-line horizontal border at top, at bottom a single horizontal line, and immediately above it a stylized floral border between horizontal lines.

Spine Lines and border continue from front cover. Beneath horizontal lines at top, stamped in gilt: LORD / ORMONT / AND HIS / AMINTA / [short rule] / GEORGE / MEREDITH / VOL. I.

Back cover Horizontal lines from front cover continue to back, but not the floral border.

SERIAL PUBLICATION

The serial, published in eight instalments in the *Pall Mall Magazine* between December 1893 and July 1894, is an abbreviated version of the first edition. There were 42 illustrations by J. Gülich.

Chapters 1–3 of the serial appeared in volume II, December, pp. 182–212; chapters 4–7 in volume II, January 1894, pp. 367–97; chapters 8–11 in volume

II, February, pp. 552–73; chapters 12–15 in volume II, March, pp. 817–45; chapters 16–19 in volume II, April, pp. 981–1005; chapters 20–3 in volume III, May, pp. 90–112; chapters 24–7 in volume III, June, pp. 292–318; chapters 28–30 in volume III, July, pp. 465–82.

MANUSCRIPTS

There is one complete and one partial MS of *Lord Ormont and His Aminta*.

MS A

In the Beinecke, 28 leaves, numbered as follows: pp. 1–22, 23–6, 28, 30. These pages are evidently no more than a first attempt at the writing of the first two chapters. There are only five and a half lines on 30. Page 27 of this fragment is in the Library of Sweet Briar College.

MS B

In the Morgan, the fair copy used by the printer. Bound in with this manuscript in the Morgan, is a letter of certification dated 11 September 1909: 'I, Katherine S. West, herewith certify that this original MS / – Lord Ormont & his Aminta / by / George Meredith / is perfect in every respect and tallies paragraph by paragraph, chapter by chapter, with Archibald Constable & Co's revised edition of 1899.'

PUBLICATION

On 7 February 1893, Meredith told Colles: 'I am writing a one volume novel (rather hotter on it at present than on *The Amazing*); and I will send this week the first two chapters to be copied. You shall then have chapters of the other story. But I would rather finish *Lord Ormont and His Aminta* first. That will be about the end of May, and then I could hasten merrily to *The Marriage*' (*Letters* II 1119). A week later he sent Colles 49 MS pages (15 February 1893, to Colles: *Letters* II 1122). At this point he is writing *The Amazing Marriage* and *Lord Ormont and His Aminta* simultaneously, but says he would 'rather finish the Ormont & Aminta first; it is but one volume.' Meredith had been having difficulties with Chapman and Hall because the agreement for the collected edition was about to expire: he had arranged for Scribner's to publish *The Amazing Marriage* and at least considered, encouraged by Clement Shorter, the idea of publishing *Lord Ormont and His Aminta* with Longmans in combination with an American house. The novel was finished by mid-August 1893, for Meredith sent the whole of it except the last chapter to Colles at Deal. On 25 August he sent Colles a complete corrected copy and said: 'Let the Editors now have the whole of the work' (*Letters* II 1140). In Meredith's agreement with W.W. Astor for the publication of *Lord Ormont and His Aminta* in *The Pall Mall Magazine* – an agreement stipulating a payment of £17 per 1000 words – had promised to deliver the novel in two parts by 15 August 1893 and 15 September 1893 (Stark). The agreement with Chapman and Hall was dated 9 April 1894. The publisher agreed to pay a royalty of $22\frac{1}{2}$ per cent on a 1500 copy edition in three volumes and 25 per cent on a one-volume 6s. edition (Beinecke).

XV a

THE AMAZING MARRIAGE

FIRST EDITION

THE AMAZING / MARRIAGE / BY / GEORGE MEREDITH / IN TWO VOLUMES / VOL. I / WESTMINSTER / ARCHIBALD CONSTABLE AND CO. / 1895

VOLUME I

Collation $[\pi]^4$A–R^8 140 leaves (19.5 × 13.3) [i–vii] viii [1]–296 [270-2]

Contents [i] halftitle: THE AMAZING MARRIAGE [ii] blank [iii] titlepage [iv] imprint at foot: Edinburgh: T. and A. CONSTABLE, Printers to Her Majesty [v] dedication: TO MY FRIEND / FREDERICK JAMESON [vi] blank [vii]–viii contents [1]–296 text [270] imprint at foot: Printed by T. and A. CONSTABLE, Printers to Her Majesty / at the Edinburgh University Press [271-2] blank

VOLUME II

Collation $[\pi]^6$A–R^{8}S^6 146 leaves (19.6 × 13.2) [i–viii] [1]–282 [283-4]

Contents [i–ii] blank [iii] halftitle [iv] blank [v] titlepage [vi] imprint [vii–viii (vii misnumbered vi)] contents [1]–282 text, on 282: THE END / [short rule] / imprint [283-4] blank

Binding Spine, and boards at front and back, covered in olive grey cloth with vertical ribbing. Endpapers plain white, with horizontal grain and widely spaced vertical ribbing.

Front cover At upper right, stamped in gilt: The / Amazing / Marriage / [three-lobed stylized leaf hanging from curling vine] At lower right, stamped in gilt: George / Meredith

Spine Stamped in gilt: The / Amazing / Marriage / Volume I / George / Meredith / Constable / Westminster

Back cover Plain.

XV b

FIRST AMERICAN EDITION

THE / AMAZING MARRIAGE / BY / GEORGE MEREDITH / VOLUME I /
NEW YORK / CHARLES SCRIBNER'S SONS / 1895 / [*All rights reserved*]

VOLUME I

Collation [A]⁵B–W⁸X⁶ 159 leaves (19.5 x 13.3) [i–x] 1–318

Contents [i] halftitle: THE AMAZING MARRIAGE [ii] blank [iii] titlepage [iv] imprint: COPYRIGHT, 1895, BY / CHARLES SCRIBNER'S SONS / *Norwood Press* / J.S. Cushing & Co. – Berwick & Smith / Norwood Mass. U.S.A. [v] dedication: *To my Friend / Frederick Jameson* [vi] blank [vii (numbered v)–ix] contents [x] blank 1–316 text 317–18 blank

VOLUME II

Collation [A]⁴B–X⁸Y⁶ 166 leaves (19.6 x 13.2) [i–x] 1–332

Contents [i] halftitle [ii] blank [iii] titlepage [iv] imprint [vii (numbered v)–ix] contents [x] blank 1–330 text, on 330: THE END 331–2 blank

Binding Spine, and boards at front and back, covered in dark blue cloth.

Front cover Margin blind-stamped at each edge and, at centre, Meredith's signature stamped in gilt.

Spine Stamped in gilt: THE / AMAZING / MARRIAGE / I / GEORGE / MEREDITH / SCRIBNERS

Back cover Plain.

SERIAL PUBLICATION

The serial is a severely shortened version of the first edition.

Meredith wrote on 26 October 1894 to E.L. Burlingame, who was acting for Scribner: 'My son has telegraphed that your office is at liberty to reduce for serial purposes the length of my novel. I am sure you have in your staff one to whom I can confide as I would to Mr. Bridges this surgical operation which shall lop excesses without wounding an artery. This without damage to the full publication subsequently, for if I have been criminal in running to this excess, it has come of my conscience in regard to thoroughness' (*Letters* III 1176). Though Meredith wrote to Burlingame directly, the serialization of *The Amazing Marriage* was arranged by The Authors' Syndicate. In the Pforzheimer Library is the Syndicate's bill for a 5 per cent commission on the sale of the world serial rights for £1000.

The Amazing Marriage was published in 12 instalments throughout 1895 in *Scribner's Magazine* (published monthly, with illustrations, by Charles Scribner Sons, New York, and Samson, Low, Marston & Co., Limited, London). January–June constituted volume XVII, and July–December volume XVIII. The 12 issues were numbered 97–108 consecutively, as follows: pp. 33–48, chapters I–IV, January; pp. 229–46, chapters V–VIII, February; pp. 365–82, chapters IX–XII, March; pp. 461–78, chapters XIII–XVI, April; pp. 640–56, chapters XVII–XX, May; pp. 774–88, chapters XXI–XXIV, June; pp. 110–28, chapters XXV–XXVIII, July; pp. 248–61, chapters XXIX–XXXI, August; pp. 328–47, chapters XXXII–XXXVI, September; pp. 444–58, chapters XXXVII–XXXIX, October; pp. 629–50, chapters XL–XLIV, November; pp. 681–92, chapters XLV—XLVI, December.

MANUSCRIPTS

There are four partial MSS of *The Amazing Marriage*. Meredith left these, as other papers, to his nurse, Miss Nicholls, and his gardener, Frank Cole. The division of the papers was not, however, achieved efficiently, probably because Meredith himself had left them in an unsorted state when he finished making his fair copy. Thus, the description of the manuscripts in sale catalogues, as quoted in the Altschul Catalogue, is not reliable.

MS A (Nicholls)

In the Beinecke, 165 leaves, numbered as follows: pp. 118–67, 193–247 (243 and 244 are missing), 248–87, 289–310. The first 103 pages of this MS (i.e. pp. 118–67, 193–247) and 4 other pages (303–[306]) which have now been transferred to the so-called Cole MS in the Beinecke Library (B below), were part of Miss Nicholls' collection, sold at Sotheby's on 1 December 1910. Sotheby's catalogue of this date described Lot 171: '*The Amazing Marriage*, portions of an early unpublished version of the novel, about 110 pp. The manuscript consists of chapters XII–XIV and XVII–XIX, with another version of part of chapter XVIII and the opening page of chapter XLV.'

The remaining 58 pages (i.e. pp. 248–87, 289–310) were transferred to this MS from the Cole MS (see below) when it was realized that they belonged with the papers sold by Miss Nicholls. They are similar in paper and handwriting to the Nicholls MS, and indeed continue it in both pagination and sense without break after 247. This MS is now contained in a box folder of grey boards bound at the spine and corners with dark green tape.

MS B (Cole)

In the Beinecke, 187 leaves, numbered as follows: pp. 118–49 (146 is missing),

150–89, 190–224, 225–51, 252–302 (numbers 255 and 256 given to one page), 303–[306]. These leaves, except for 303–[306] were part of the Cole MS sold at Sotheby's on 19 March 1952. Sotheby's catalogue for 19 March 1952, p. 54, Lot 287, read in part: 'Autograph manuscript of an early draft of *The Amazing Marriage*, with upwards of 240 pp., 4to. In a full brown levant morocco solander case. In a cloth case. The manuscript was afterwards discarded by Meredith for the form in which the book eventually appeared in 1895. [The catalogue lists chapter numbers and titles.] With many autograph corrections by the Author. This manuscript was formerly the property of an English-woman, Mrs. Katherine S. West, who purchased it from Meredith's garderner, Frank Cole. With the W.T.H. Howe bookplate.'

The MS, when first purchased, included pp. 248–60 (chapter XX), 261–87 (chapter XXI), and 289–310 (chapter XXII). As explained above, these have now been added to the so-called Nicholls MS in the Beinecke.

MS C

In the Beinecke Library at Yale, three leaves, described as 'a portion of Chapter 26 and 38 of *The Amazing Marriage*.' The three leaves, of faded white paper yellowed with age, have been torn from a notebook, then held together by string or ribbon threaded through the top left corner. Each has been cut horizontally slightly above centre page, and later taped together again with transparent adhesive tape on the back. The pages are numbered in Meredith's usual fashion at the top right corner as follows:

1 p. 160, headed 'Ch. XXVI' with the title 'State of Parties: Ross Mackrell: Opening of the Grand New Fruitshop.'
2 p. 2 ... (possibly 260 – the corner has been torn); no chapter number or title, but corresponding to pp. 345–6 in the serial.
3 p. 301, headed 'Ch. XXXVIII' but without a title. An upnublished page.

To these three leaves has been added a fourth, taken from the original Nicholls MS (A above). It is marked 'p. 387' at the top right corner, and headed, at centre, 'The Amazing Marriage,' with underneath, 'Chapert XLV.' It is identical in its physical features to the three leaves described above, and clearly belongs with them. On the back of this leaf, p. 387, there is a stanza of an unpublished poem:

> 'The Parting of the Hour'
> He who made age more [as] beautiful to see,
>   more tolerable to bear,
> Than [as] in the flash of morning youth's grim tree,
>   Than youth's light load of care,

The word 'as' in lines 1 and 3 has been left on the page as an undecided alternative.

MS D

In the Morgan, 476 leaves, numbered as follows: pp. 1–8, 9, 11–77, 79–120, 121, 122–44, 145–8 (one page), 149–211, 212a, 212b, 213–14, 214a, 214b, 214c, 214d, 214e, 215–41, 241a, 241b, 242–90, 290a, 291–362, 368–407, 409–68. The leaf numbered 121 was presented to the Morgan in June 1924 by Frank Altschul. The first page of chapter XXV was originally numbered 149, then crossed out and replaced by 145–8.

Bound in at the front of this MS are two letters from Mrs. Katherine S. West of The Gables, Dorking. The first is a handwritten note dated 16 September 1909, to certify that she has compared the MS with the first edition, and has found that the MS lacks the first eight chapters, 'a sentence here and there,' and the last eighteen lines. The second, addressed to Mr. Douglas, c/o Mr. J. Pierpont Morgan, and dated 15 October 1909, is a typewritten letter on the condition of the three MSS she was selling to Mr. Morgan: the MSS of *The Amazing Marriage*, *Diana of the Crossways*, and *Lord Ormont and His Aminta*. She comments on the differences between the MS and the first printed version of *The Amazing Marriage*: 'In The Amazing Marriage I found many more differences, several short passages appearing in the published work and one of considerable length being the last paragraph of the book not be to found in the written MS. These changes must have been made by Mr. Meredith when he was correcting his typewritten MS.' Mrs. West was presumably selling the three MSS on behalf of Frank Cole, Meredith's gardener, to whom Meredith had left them as a legacy. Cole's own letter in which he stipulates a price for the three MSS is bound into the Morgan MS of *Diana of the Crossways*. He asked for £200 for the MS of *The Amazing Marriage*.

THE RELATIONSHIP OF THE MSS TO THE FIRST EDITION

MS A

The Nicholls MS is an early draft, presumably written in 1879 or even before that. Meredith's letter to R.L. Stevenson, 16 April 1879, confirms that Meredith had had the book in mind as early as that. It was the serious book that had to wait while Meredith wrote what he called his pot-boiler, *The Egoist*. 'I am about one quarter through *The Amazing Marriage*, which I promise you, you shall like better' (*Letters* II 569). It is reasonable to conjecture that the 'one quarter' referred to is the first twelve chapters.

That these leaves form part of a rejected draft is clear from the fact that the chapter numbers and titles do not correspond to those of the first edition. The MS consists of chapter XII, 'Lord Fleetwood' (pp. 118–34); chapter XIII,

'Concerning the Jaws of the Dragon and His Group' (pp. 134–53); chapter XIV, 'Showing the Effect of a Natural Condition upon a Natural Philosopher' (pp. 153–67); chapter XVII, 'The Beautiful Cousins' (pp. 193–205); chapter XVIII, 'Of Admiral Fakenham: and of Sir Graham Dobee & Mary Dump & her courier' (pp. 205–22); chapter XIX, no heading (pp. 223–47); chapter XX, 'The First Meeting' (pp. 248–60); chapter XXI, no heading (pp. 261–87); and chapter [XXII], no heading (pp. 289–310).

To deduce from this MS the structure of the novel as it was finally published would be if not impossible, at least extraordinarily difficult, since the later change was a radical one. The MS concerns simply the story of Fleetwood, Woodseer, Chillon Kirby, Carinthia, Livia, and Henrietta, as they meet each other by accident on the Continent, ending with (chapter XXI) Fleetwood's proposal to Henrietta and her rejection of him, and with Chillon Kirby's receiving in England the letter from Henrietta which tells him of his sister's engagement to Fleetwood. There is little to suggest the way in which the novel was to be developed: perhaps at this stage Meredith did not know himself.

This early draft is more theoretical in its description and analysis of character than the first version. (The same is the case with the early MS of *One of Our Conquerors*.) In the final version more is done by the disposition of events, less by psychological narrative. Meredith comments on this (Memorial pp. 132–3) without perhaps realizing the irony of what he says. Other parts of the Nicholls MS, however, are more racily written than the final version, particularly Fleetwood's encounter with Carinthia on the hillside, his improper proposal to Henrietta at the picnic lunch, and Henrietta's letter to Chillon Kirby describing the ball. Meredith must have lost interest in the continental part of the story by the time he came to rewrite it. In any case, in the final version he is more detached. The events are seen in a different perspective, and this difference is reflected in the style, which holds the object at arm's length, in a noun clause or an abstraction.

The Nicholls MS is corrected throughout, but the corrections have no bearing upon the final version. They are incorporated, many of them, into the Cole MS, but are carried no further. This leads one to the view that although Nicholls must have come before Cole, both were early versions. It may be that the parts which are missing from Nicholls are the parts which interested Meredith most.

MS B

It is clear that the Cole MS was written after the Nicholls MS. Changes or corrections that appear in the margin or between the lines in Nicholls are incorporated into Cole. Nevertheless, Cole is nearer to Nicholls than to the final version. Both are concerned with the early meeting and entanglement of the characters on the Continent; neither gets as far as the Welsh episodes, nor gives any hint of the way in which the plot is to be developed and resolved. Meredith eliminates the rather interesting though unfelicitous episode between Sir Graham and Madge, but he retains and rewrites Fleetwood's meetings with Henrietta and Carinthia. A close comparison of episodes that occur both in Nicholls and in Cole, as for example Fleetwood's proposal to Henrietta in Cole XVII and Nicholls XX–XXI, reveals that neither was written with the other at hand. Isolated sentences and short paragraphs correspond exactly, but by and large Cole is not a copy of Nicholls into which changes are introduced, but a rewriting that derives, apparently, from a change of imaginative focus. As was Meredith's custom, the passages of pure analysis of character give way to episodes in which character is seen in action as the novel moves from early drafts to the final version. In this process, there are signs that the Cole MS was never more than a draft. The name Graham Dobee, for example, is changed in Cole to Meeson Corby, but Meredith neglects to make the change throughout the MS, as though it never had more than temporary importance. Although Cole must be linked with Nicholls because of the similarity of the episodes described, stylistically it is less cramped, and to this extent anticipates the final version.

MS C

The four leaves in the Beinecke that are not part of either the Cole or the Nicholls MS were written later than either. The paging goes beyond either early version. P. 387 refers back to episodes in Wales, and p. 160 to Ross Mackrell and the flower shop in Piccadilly, neither of which occurs in Cole or Nicholls. The poem on the back of p. 387 is about old age and is in Meredith's later handwriting. Finally, there are verbal parallels between the MS pages and the same passages in the first edition.

MS D

The MS in the Morgan is an incomplete autograph of the printed version, representing the work that Meredith did on the novel after the publication of *Diana of the Crossways* and probably after *One of Our Conquerors*. Thus this manuscript represents the final stage of Meredith's writing career, whereas the earlier manuscripts are contemporary with *The Egoist* and *The Tragic Comedians*.

The novel was in fact rewritten during the winter of 1893–4. In a letter dated 2 January 1894, Meredith told W. Gordon Clark: 'I am under an engagement with *Scribner's Magazine* to deliver a novel in the Spring, and have to go the round of a well-horse daily' (*Letters* III 1151). On 7 August 1894, he tells his daughter: 'My work will want a chapter or two for finish at the end of the month' (*Letters* III 1168). The process of correction and revision went on until the last moment.

There are, as in most Meredith MSS, heavy deletions and numerous marginal additions. Most but not quite all of these marginal additions were incorporated into the first edition. Leaving out of account these omissions, there are in the body of the MS at least seven passages not printed in the first edition, none of them of great critical significance. The final edition, on the other hand, has one or two passages – the most important being the last eighteen lines of the book – which are not in the MS at all. The Morgan MS is therefore close to the printed version, but not identical with it.

The MS bears the signs of having been sent to someone to be copied or typed: the pages at one time were tied together in bundles of fifty, and on the back of a few pages Meredith has written his name and address. The MS of *The Amazing Marriage* does not have the pencilled marks that appear, for example, on the MS of *Diana of the Crossways*, indicating that it was used by the typesetter. It is possible therefore that there was a typescript between the Morgan MS and the first edition. Whether Meredith made the final changes to the proofs or to the typescript it is impossible to tell. The pagination of this MS has not been done during the writing, but afterwards: the deleted page numbers would relate the Morgan MS to those in the Beinecke.

HANDWRITTEN EMENDATIONS IN PRINTED VOLUMES

There exist several copies of *The Amazing Marriage* with annotations in Meredith's hand.

1 *Corrections to volume I of the copy of the first edition in the Stark*
There are some dozen corrections, about half of them having to do with the wedding night of Fleetwood and Carinthia Jane: slight changes of phrase make Fleetwood's return in the middle of the night less vague. An insertion of two sentences is the largest alteration.

2 *Corrections to volume II of the York University copy of the first edition*
This copy of volume II bears three pencilled corrections of literal errors in the author's hand. On p. 17 the word 'mattins' is altered to 'mass'; at the head of p. 18 two sentences are written out for insertion at the end of the first sentence on the page (' – You will learn the story: it cannot be written. I have to question till I am as broken as she'); and on p. 27 the following sentence is pencilled in the margin for addition to the second paragraph: 'The scene of the night of their marriage, known to him & her only, stood out.' Of these corrections only the substitution of 'mass' for 'mattins' was followed in later editions: the

literal errors remain uncorrected in the one-volume reprint of 1896. The additional sentences supplied by the author in this copy remain unpublished.
3 *Corrections to Meredith's copy of the fourth edition now in the Widener*
This copy of the fourth edition which is interleaved and has pencilled corrections on almost every page was probably used as the basis for the de luxe edition. At any rate, contrary to what is said on the Widener catalogue slip, the corrections were for the most part incorporated into the later edition.

OTHER EDITIONS

The first edition, in two volumes, was published on 15 November 1895. It was reissued almost immediately in two versions. The second 'edition' in two volumes and called 'second edition' on its titlepage appeared on 8 January 1896.

Between the first and the second edition there appeared a further two-volume 'edition' dated 1895, similar in type and setting to the one-volume colonial edition printed for George Bell and Sons, but different from the first edition in signatures and pagination. An example of this edition is in the British Museum (012643.m.11.) and was partially described by Forman (p. 115). The pages are numbered consecutively throughout the two volumes, whereas in the first edition the numbering begins again in volume II. Similarly, whereas in the first edition the two volumes were made separately, in the edition now being described the signatures of volume II are $R^*S-2L^82M^4$. The setting of the first few pages of volume II is different from the equivalent pages in the one-volume edition. The titlepage of volume I is a cancel.

Nowell-Smith has been able to explain this edition, by comparing it with the one-volume edition of 1895 which was for the overseas market only, and by consulting both Meredith's contract with Constable, his new publisher, and the day-book of T. and A. Constable, the printers, to whom the book had been sent by Chapman and Hall, before Meredith changed publishers.

Constable's contract with Meredith was for a two-volume edition of 2000 copies, a colonial edition of 2500, and a one-volume English edition of 4500. The contract is dated 24 September 1895 and is in the Stark. The first two were to be ready by 15 November 1895, but when the two-volume edition had been printed machine changes were necessary before the one-volume edition could be printed. Meanwhile the novel was selling. So that the novel would not become unavailable so soon after publication, a new version was fabricated.

Chapter XXIV was extended, without additional material, to p. 270, and the signatures were altered to suit a one-volume edition. 2500 copies dated 1895 were run off for Bell's on smooth wove paper for the colonial edition at 2s. 6d.

in paper wrappers, and 3s. 6d. in cloth; and 4500 copies dated 1896 were run off for Constable's on a rough imitation-laid paper for a domestic edition at 6s. When the demand for the first edition exceeded the supply, and Constable's presumably wished to meet it before Christmas, 500 copies in two volumes were created by dividing the one-volume edition into two, and adding, as cancels, reprinted versions of signatures R and S. Nowell-Smith shows that these details are confirmed by T. and A. Constable's day-book for December 1895. In addition, perhaps because the printer had dated the titlepages 1896, new singleton titlepages dated 1895 were printed for both volumes and inserted as cancels.

There are, then two versions of the first edition both dated 1895, and a second edition dated 1896, not, as Forman claimed, 'four editions of *The Amazing Marriage* in two volume form' (Forman p. 115).

XVI

CELT AND SAXON

FIRST EDITION

CELT AND SAXON / BY / GEORGE MEREDITH / LONDON / CONSTABLE AND COMPANY LTD / 1910

Collation $[\pi]^4$A–S^{8}T^6 154 leaves (19.0 × 16.6) [i–viii] [1]–297 [298–300]

Contents [i] blank [ii] blank [iii] halftitle: CELT AND SAXON [iv] blank [v] titlepage [vi] blank [vii–viii(misnumbered v–vi)] contents [1]–297 text, on 297 at foot: [short rule] / Printed by T. and A. CONSTABLE, Printers to His Majesty / at the Edinburgh University Press [298–300] blank

Binding Spine, and boards at front and back, covered in deep red cloth with a vertical ribbing, the colour being the same as the first Constable revised edition. Endpapers white.

Front cover Plain.

Spine Stamped in gilt: [three small leaves] / CELT AND / SAXON / [two small leaves] / [one larger leaf] / GEORGE / MEREDITH / CONSTABLE / LONDON

Back cover Plain.

SERIAL PUBLICATION

Celt and Saxon was published simultaneously in 1910 by the *Fortnightly Review* and *The Forum* in New York.

Chapters I–III appeared in the January issue of the *Fortnightly Review*, volume 93, pp. 1–15; chapters 4–6 in February, pp. 207–22; chapters 7–8 in March, pp. 499–516; chapters 9–11 in April, pp. 702–20; chapters 12–13 in May, pp. 874–87; chapters 14–15 in June, pp. 1045–70; chapters 16–17 in volume 94 in July, pp. 109–31; chapters 18–19 in August, pp. 350–66.

Chapters I–IV appeared in volume 43, No. 1 of *The Forum* in January, pp. 21–39; chapters V–VI in No. 2, February, pp. 170–81; chapters VII–VIII in No. 3, March, pp. 238–55; chapter IX in No. 4, April, pp. 409–16; chapter X in No. 5, May, pp. 520–3; chapter XI in No. 6, June, pp. 619–25. The June issue ends with 'To be continued' after the sentence 'Philip signalled – thoughtful of the feelings of his wife.'

MANUSCRIPT

The incomplete manuscript of *Celt and Saxon* was deposited in the British Museum in 1910 by W.M. Meredith where it remained until sold at Christie's on 20 July 1960 as part of the estate of Mrs. M.E. Sturgis. W.M. Meredith's letter about the lending of the MS to the British Museum is bound in with the MS which is now in the Beinecke Library.

The MS is a fair copy to which marginal additions have been made, apparently at a later date, and it is numbered as follows: 1–8, 8–16, 17–34, 35–43, 44–52, 53–74, 75–95, 96–117, 118–36, 136–45, 146–60, 161–71, 172–93, 194–202, 201/2–22, 223–54, 256–81, 282–306, 307–43. The novel appears to have been called *Adianta* at first, and later *The Princess Nikolas*, both titles having been deleted from the headings of various chapters. Though the novel was published from the manuscript in 1910, it is likely for internal reasons that it was written between the completion of *The Tragic Comedians* and the beginning of the writing of *Diana of the Crossways* in 1883.

XVII

THE HOUSE ON THE BEACH

FIRST EDITION

THE HOUSE ON THE BEACH. / *A Realistic Tale.* / BY GEORGE MEREDITH. / [short rule] / NEW YORK: / HARPER & BROTHERS, PUBLISHERS, / FRANKLIN SQUARE. / 1877

Collation 1–9⁸ 72 leaves (12.0 × 7.5) [1]–140 [141–4]

Contents [1]–4 advertisements [5] titlepage [6] blank [7]–140 text, on 140: THE END. [141–4] advertisements

Binding Spine, and boards at front and back, covered in green cloth. Endpapers plain pale brown.

Front cover Stamped in red, a border 1 cm. from spine and top and bottom edges. Within this border, stamped in red and black (the red marked here with an asterisk): HARPER'S* / HALF-HOUR SERIES.* / [double long rule] / THE HOUSE ON THE BEACH. / *A Realistic Tale.* / BY GEORGE MEREDITH. / [double long rule] / [publisher's monogram*] / [rule*] / COPYRIGHT, 1877, BY HARPER & BROTHERS.*

Spine Lengthways from top to bottom: THE HOUSE ON THE BEACH.

Back cover Stamped in black at centre: publisher's monogram.

This edition of *The House on the Beach* was also published on different paper in grey paper wrappers, the front cover being as described above except that at the top is printed: *Price Twenty Cents.* The spine of the paper wrapper gives the number in the series, thus: *22 The House on the Beach.*

SERIAL PUBLICATION

The House on the Beach was first published in the *New Quarterly Magazine* January 1877, pp. 329–410. From Meredith's letter to Janet Ross, dated 17 May 1861, one has to suppose that it was written, at least in part, some sixteen years earlier (*Letters* I 81). Harper's must have asked Meredith for the right to publish it in North America, having seen the serial, since in later correspondence with Chapman and Hall Meredith defends himself for not having offered them the story.

SUBSEQUENT PUBLICATION

The House on the Beach was not published in book form in England until 1894 when it appeared in Ward, Lock and Bowden's *The Tale of Chloe and Other Stories*, a volume which is treated here as part of the first collected edition. The contract for it, now in the Stark Library, was dated 28 July 1894 and specified a one-volume edition to be sold at 3s. 6d., the author to receive a 25 per cent royalty and the agreement to last for three years. When this agreement expired, Constable acquired the copyright. By that time, however, Ward, Lock & Bowden had done rather well from the book, issuing it as least five times and disposing of a large number of copies in the States. The accounts show that there was a first printing on 1 November 1894 of 2241 copies; a second on 13 February 1895 of 1522 copies; a third on 6 May 1895 of 1515 copies; a fourth on 23 July 1895 also of 1515 copies; and a fifth on 1 July 1896 of 2024 copies. Ward, Lock & Bowden's accounts also indicate that 250 copies of a finer edition were prepared in 1894 to be sold at 25s. but no copy has been traced.

XVIII

THE CASE OF GENERAL OPLE AND LADY CAMPER

FIRST EDITION

THE CASE OF / GENERAL OPLE AND / LADY CAMPER. / BY / GEORGE MEREDITH, / AUTHOR OF "CHLOE," "DIANA OF THE CROSSWAYS," "THE / EGOIST," ETC., ETC. / [short rule] / NEW YORK: / JOHN W. LOVELL COMPANY, / 150 WORTH STREET, COR. MISSION PLACE.

Collation 1–4¹⁶ 64 leaves (18.3 x 12.2) [1–5] 6–126 [127–8]

Contents [1] halftitle: THE / Case of General Ople and Lady Camper. [2] blank [3] titlepage [4] imprint: COPYRIGHT, 1890, / BY / JOHN W. LOVELL COMPANY [5]–126 text, on 126: THE END. [127–8] blank

Binding Brown paper wrapper glued onto spine. Advertisements on inside front and back covers.

Front cover Printed in black and with small rectangular picture of buildings at top left: No 3 25 Cts. / LOVELL'S / WESTMINSTER / SERIES / [long rule] / *Entered at the Post Office, New York, as second class matter.* / THE CASE OF / GEN'L OPLE AND / LADY CAMPER / BY / GEORGE MEREDITH / [short rule] / NEW YORK / JOHN W. LOVELL COMPANY / 150 WORTH ST., COR. MISSION PLACE / ISSUED WEEKLY. ANNUAL SUBSCRIPTION, $12.00. JUNE 23, 1890 (EXTRA).

Spine Printed in black from top to bottom: The Case of Gen'l Ople and Lady Camper. By Geo. Meredith. 25 Cts.

Back cover Advertisement for Colgate's soaps and perfumes.

Though at the head of the advertisement for Lovell's Westminster Series there is the statement that the works were published 'by special arrangement with the authors,' there is no record in this instance of communication between Lovell and Meredith. The firm no doubt pirated the serial. The story was published in two other American paperback editions as noted by Forman (p. 93). '*The Case of General Ople and Lady Camper* also appeared as No. 1695 in George Munro's "Seaside Library Pocket Edition," and as No. 145 in "The Surprise Series" published by the International Book Company of New York. Both these issues are from the types of Lovell's edition. Munro's is dated on the front wrapper December 15, 1890 and was sold at ten cents, while the International Book Company's edition is dated June 4, 1891 and was sold at twenty-five cents.'

SERIAL PUBLICATION

The Case of General Ople and Lady Camper was first published in the New *Quarterly Magazine*, July 1877, pp. 428–78. Meredith's only reference to it is quite a casual one. In a letter to William Hardman dated 25 September 1877 he wrote: 'If you have not seen the New Quarterly Magazine for July last, will you commission D'Troia to get it from Mudie's. Run your eyes over *The Case of General Ople and Lady Camper*. I think you will recognize the General and remember the case' (*Letters* I 548). The story was later pirated by the Sunday edition of the New York *Sun* and appeared in three issues: 1 June, chaps. I–III, p. 23; 8 June, chaps. IV–VI, p. 22; 15 June, chaps. VII–VIII, p. 21.

SUBSEQUENT PUBLICATION

The Case of General Ople and Lady Camper was not published in book form in England until 1894 when it appeared in Ward, Lock & Bowden's *The Tale of Chloe and Other Stories*, a volume which is treated here as part of the first collected edition.

XIX

THE TALE OF CHLOE

FIRST EDITION

THE TALE OF CHLOE: / AN EPISODE IN THE HISTORY OF BEAU BEAMISH. / BY / GEORGE MEREDITH, / AUTHOR OF "DIANA OF THE CROSSWAYS," "THE EGOIST," "THE CASE OF GENERAL OPLE AND LADY CAMPER," ETC. / Fair Chloe we toasted of old, / As the queen of our festival meeting; / Now Chloe is lifeless and cold; / You must go to the grave for her greeting. / Her beauty and talents were framed / To enkindle the proudest to win her; / Then let not the mem'ry be blamed / Of the purest that e'er was a sinner! / *Captain Chanter's Collection*. / [short rule] / NEW YORK: / JOHN W. LOVELL COMPANY / 150 WORTH STREET, COR. MISSION PLACE.

Collation 1–4^{16} 72 leaves (16.5 x 10.8) [1–5] 6–144

Contents [1] halftitle: THE TALE OF CHLOE [2] blank [3] titlepage [4] imprint: COPYRIGHT, 1890, / BY JOHN W. LOVELL COMPANY. [5]–144 text

Binding Brown paper wrapper glued onto spine. Advertisements on inside front and back covers.

Front cover Printed in black and with small rectangular picture of buildings at top left: No 6 25 Cts / LOVELL'S / WESTMINSTER / SERIES / *Entered at the Post Office, New York, as second class matter.* / THE TALE OF / CHLOE / BY / GEORGE MEREDITH / [short rule] / NEW YORK / JOHN W. LOVELL COMPANY / 150 WORTH ST., COR. MISSION PLACE / ISSUED WEEKLY. ANNUAL SUBSCRIPTION, $12.00 July 7, 1890

Spine Printed in black from top to bottom: No 6 The Tale of Chloe. By George Meredith. 25 Cts.

Back cover Advertisements.

REISSUE FROM THE SAME PLATES

THE TALE OF CHLOE: / AN EPISODE IN THE HISTORY OF BEAU BEAMISH. / BY / GEORGE MEREDITH, / AUTHOR OF "DIANA OF THE CROSSWAYS," "THE EGOIST," / "THE CASE OF GENERAL OPLE AND LADY CAMPER," ETC. / Fair Chloe was toasted of old, / As the queen of our festival meeting; / Now Chloe is lifeless and cold; / You must go to the grave for her greeting. / Her beauty and talents were framed / To enkindle the proudest to win her; / Then let not the mem'ry be blamed / Of the purest that e'er was a sinner! / CAPTAIN CHANTER'S COLLECTION. / [short rule] / R.F. FENNO & COMPANY, / 112 FIFTH AVENUE, NEW YORK CITY.

Collation 1–4^{16} 72 leaves (16.5 x 10.8) [1–5] 6–144

Contents [1] halftitle: THE TALE OF CHLOE [2] blank [3] titlepage [4] blank [5]–144 text, on 144: THE END.

Binding Apple green textured cloth flecked with darker green on boards. Endpapers white.

Front cover Stamped in black: The Tale of Chloe / GEORGE MEREDITH / [rectangular leafy design at centre with publisher's monogram in shield at bottom left]

Spine The Tale / of / Chloe / [device] / MEREDITH / [device] / R.F. FENNO & CO.

Back cover Plain.

FIRST PUBLICATION IN ENGLAND

THE TALE OF CHLOE – THE / HOUSE ON THE BEACH – / THE CASE OF GENERAL / OPLE AND LADY CAMPER / BY / *George* / *Meredith* / LONDON / WARD, LOCK & BOWDEN, LIMITED / WARWICK HOUSE, SALISBURY SQUARE, E.C. / NEW YORK AND MELBOURNE / 1894 / [*All rights reserved*]

Collation [A]³B–Y⁸Z⁴AA¹ 176 leaves (19.0 x 12.5) [i–vi] 1–345 [346]

Contents [i] halftitle: THE TALE OF CHLOE – THE HOUSE ON THE / BEACH – THE CASE OF GENERAL OPLE / AND LADY CAMPER [ii] blank [iii] titlepage [iv] blank [v(misnumbered vii)] contents [vi] blank 1 flytitle: THE TALE OF CHLOE / AN EPISODE IN THE HISTORY OF BEAU BEAMISH [2] epigraph 3–345 text [346] blank

Binding Spine, and boards at front and back, covered in olive green cloth, virtually identical to that of the first collected edition (see IV). Endpapers plain white.

Front cover A blind-stamped border 3 mm. from all four edges. Otherwise plain.

Spine Stamped in gilt at top and bottom a single horizontal line between which, also in gilt: THE TALE / OF CHLOE / AND OTHER STORIES / GEORGE MEREDITH / WARD, LOCK & BOWDEN. L^D.

Back cover Identical to front cover.

SERIAL PUBLICATION

The Tale of Chloe was first published in *The New Quarterly Magazine*, July 1879, pp. 57–113. The serial was pirated by the Sunday edition of the New York *Sun* and appeared in four issues in 1890: 22 June, chaps. I–III, p. 18; 29 June, chaps. IV–V, p. 15; 6 July, chaps. VI–VIII, p. 16; 13 July, chaps. IX–X, p. 15.

PUBLICATION

The first publication of *The Tale of Chloe* as a book, in Lovell's Westminster Series, was pirated from *The New Quarterly Magazine*. The texts are identical, except for minor typographical differences. From the Lovell plates the story was re-issued in New York during 1891 in the three cheap paperback series published by George Munro, by R. F. Fenno, and by the International Book Company. At least five Meredith titles appeared in the aptly named 'Surprise Series' of the International Book Company. These were *Diana of the Crossways* (No. 350), *Rhoda Fleming* (No. 1146), *The Egoist* (No. 1150), *The Case of General Ople and Lady Camper* (No. 1695), and *The Tale of Chloe* (No. 1807). These novels had earlier appeared as volumes in the Seaside Library of George

Munro, who had purchased the plates from Lovell. These acts of piracy came to an end when the new copyright act was introduced. Meanwhile inexpensive, albeit sometimes mutilated copies of Meredith's work had been available to American readers between 1885 and 1892, a fact which no doubt contributed to American interest in Meredith during the nineties.

In England, too, the *New Quarterly* text was used for the first edition published by Ward, Lock & Bowden in 1894, as described above. This first edition was also issued in a large paper set of 250 numbered copies. The book was reprinted the following year and the titlepage altered by the inclusion of SECOND EDITION. Further re-issues were made during the nineties with no change to the text, apart from the titlepage. Meredith revised the text of *The Tale of Chloe* for the collected editions by Constable and Scribners, just as he had done in the case of *The House on the Beach*, *The Case of General Ople and Lady Camper*, and most novels. The corrected copies are in the Beinecke Library.

MANUSCRIPT

The manuscript of *The Tale of Chloe* was sold at Sotheby's in 1910 and is now in the Widener Collection.

Other Prose

Part II consists of printed volumes of non-fiction prose, collections of letters in book or pamphlet form, and a checklist of prose contributions to journals, magazines, and newspapers. Ephemera have been excluded from Section A, though some items have appeared in other bibliographies. The *George Meredith Calendar*, for example, compiled by Rachel Wheatcroft and published by Cecil Palmer and Hayward is a charming little piece of Meredithiana but cannot be counted as a Meredith publication. The same applies to the *Meredith Birthday Book* printed at the Guild Press, Birmingham, and published in 1898. There has been no attempt in this section to enumerate the occasions when quotations or sets of quotations from Meredith's work have been used for such purposes as gift books and desk calendars. Similarly, separate pulls of articles or addresses privately 'published' for circulation among friends have not been accorded the status of a publication, but have been described in the checklist of contributions to journals, magazines, and newspapers. Thus, the item *George Meredith on John Morley* which, in half a page of print, is Meredith's testimony and support for Morley as a candidate for the Lord Rectorship of Glasgow University in 1902, is not counted as a publication despite Forman's claim that it 'was widely quoted in the press during the last days of October 1902.' Finally, there are two items a person unfamiliar with Meredith might not at first identify. These are *The Idyll of First Love*, a pirated excerpt from *The Ordeal of Richard Feverel* published by Mosher in 1906, and *The Egoist*, a Drama referred to and described briefly in x.

In Professor C.L. Cline's edition of the letters (xxxv) there is clear indication of which letters had been previously published. For this reason, the contents of xxix–xxxiii in this bibliography have not been given in detail; the best guide to the letters which Meredith wrote to Clement Shorter, for example, is Professor Cline's index. An exception is made in xxxiv simply because the 'various correspondents' are more difficult to identify.

A Books

XXI

THE PILGRIM'S SCRIP

FIRST EDITION

THE PILGRIM'S SCRIP: / OR, / *Wit and Wisdom* / OF / GEORGE
MEREDITH. / WITH SELECTIONS FROM HIS POETRY, AND AN /
INTRODUCTION. / Exclusive of the abstract sciences, the largest and worthiest
portion / of our knowledge consists in aphorisms; and the greatest of men
is but / an aphorism. – COLERIDGE, *Aids to Reflection*. / A composer of
aphorisms can pluck blossoms from a razor-crop. / RICHARD FEVEREL. /
BOSTON: / ROBERTS BROTHERS. / 1888.

Collation $[\pi]^4[1-12^{12}13^8]$ 152 leaves (17.6 x 11.6) [1-8] [i-v] vi [vii-ix] x-1
[7]-258 [259-60]

Contents [1-7] blank [8] advertisement: *Popular Edition* / OF / GEORGE
MEREDITH'S WORKS. / Each Novel will be complete in One Volume. / Price,
\$1.50. / [rule] DIANA OF THE CROSSWAYS. / THE ORDEAL OF RICHARD FEVEREL. /
EVAN HARRINGTON. / SANDRA BELLONI. / HARRY RICHMOND. / VITTORIA. /
RHODA FLEMING. / BEAUCHAMPS CAREER. / THE EGOIST. / THE SHAVING OF
SHAGPAT, AND FARINA. / [short rule] / ROBERTS BROTHERS, Publishers. [i] titlepage
[ii] copyright statement and imprint: *Copyright, 1888,* / BY ROBERTS BROTHERS. /
University Press: / JOHN WILSON AND SON, CAMBRIDGE. [iii] epigraph [iv] blank
[v]-vi contents [vii] flytitle: INTRODUCTION. [viii] blank [ix]-1 introduction,
signed at the end: M.R.F. GILMAN / CONCORD, N.H., *September* 1, 1888 [7]-247
text [248] blank [249] halftitle: index [250] blank [251]-8 index on 258 at
foot: [rule] / University Press: John Wilson & Son, Cambridge. [259-60]
blank
Between [8] and [i] is pasted in a reproduction of an etching of Meredith's
profile.

Binding Spine, and boards at front and back, covered in dark green cloth.
Endpapers plain white.

Front cover The front cover is divided slightly to left of centre by a bold
vertical line. To the left of this line, stamped in red, is a design which covers
the whole surface. To the right, stamped in black in pseudo-gothic script:
The Pilgrim's / [device] *Scrip* [device] / [short rule] / Wit and Wisdom / of /
George Meredith / [figure of pilgrim with staff]

Spine The same design is continued from the front cover onto the spine. Towards the top of the spine within a rectangle of three lines stamped in gilt: The / Pilgrim's / Scrip / [short rule] / Wit and Wisdom / of / Geo. Meredith

Back cover Partly plain, partly with design stamped in red carried over from spine.

Contents
Introduction vii; The Ordeal of Richard Feverel 7; Evan Harrington 31; Sandra Belloni 43; Rhoda Fleming 55; Vittoria 63; The Adventures of Harry Richmond 69; The Egoist 83; Beauchamp's Career 95; The Tragic Comedians 133; Diana of the Crossways 141; The House on the Beach 175; Vignettes in Prose 179;

SONNETS
My Theme 199; The World's Advance 200; The Discipline of Wisdom 200; Appreciation 201; Earth's Secret 202; Sense and Spirit 203.

POEMS
Love in the Valley 207; France. – December, 1870 210; Men and Man 223; The Woods of Westermain 224; The Lark Ascending 227; Autumn Even-Song 229; By the Rosanna 230; Ode to the Spirit of Earth in Autumn 231; Spring 236; Modern Love 237; Young Reynard 241; Martin's Puzzle 242.

XXII a

AN ESSAY ON COMEDY

FIRST EDITION

AN ESSAY ON / COMEDY / AND THE USES OF THE / COMIC SPIRIT / BY / GEORGE MEREDITH / WESTMINSTER / ARCHIBALD CONSTABLE AND / COMPANY. 1897

Collation [A]⁸B–G⁸ 56 leaves (19.3 x 12.7) [1–7] 8–105 [106–12]

Contents [1] halftitle: AN ESSAY / ON COMEDY [2] blank [3] titlepage [4] blank [5] note: *This Essay was first published in / 'The New Quarterly Magazine' / for April* 1877 [6] blank [7]–105 text [106] imprint: Printed by T. and A. CONSTABLE, Printers to Her Majesty / at the Edinburgh University Press [107–12] advertisements

Binding Spine, and boards at front and back, covered in light brown glazed calico. Endpapers plain.

Front cover Plain.

Spine Stamped in gilt: AN ESSAY / ON / COMEDY / GEORGE / MEREDITH

Back cover Plain.

XXII b

SECOND EDITION

What is referred to as the second edition, for example by Forman, and is indeed stated to be so on its titlepage, which is dated 1898 and has, after the author's name, 'SECOND EDITION,' is in fact a re-issue of the first edition from the same plates. This re-issue appeared in the red binding of the New Popular Edition 1897–1910 (See LXI, p. 259). In addition to the leaves of advertisements noted above, it has sewn in 16 pages of advertisements, including one for the New Popular Edition of Meredith's work.

XXII c

AMERICAN EDITION

AN ESSAY ON / COMEDY / AND THE USES OF THE / COMIC SPIRIT / BY / GEORGE MEREDITH / NEW YORK / CHARLES SCRIBNER'S SONS / 1897

Collation [1]⁴[2–8]⁸ 56 leaves (19.2 x 12.8) [i–viii] [1]–99 [100–4]

Contents [i–iv] blank [v] titlepage [vi] copyright statement and imprint: *Copyright, 1897,* / BY CHARLES SCRIBNER'S SONS. / *University Press:* / JOHN WILSON AND SON, CAMBRIDGE, U.S.A. [vii] halftitle: AN ESSAY / ON COMEDY [viii] blank [1]–99 text [100–4] blank

Binding Spine, and boards at front and back, covered in dark blue cloth. Endpapers white.

Front cover Meredith's signature stamped in gilt.

Spine Stamped in gilt: AN / ESSAY / ON / COMEDY / GEORGE / MEREDITH / SCRIBNERS.

Back cover Plain.

SERIAL PUBLICATION

The lecture on which publication was based was delivered at the London Institution on 1 February 1877 and a revised version was first printed in the *New*

Quarterly Magazine, April 1877, pp. 1–40. The corrected proof-sheets for this printing are in the British Museum. Meredith's letter to his son dated 12 February 1897 (*Letters* III 1258) about the printing error referred to in an earlier letter confirms that the first edition was set from the serial copy, but in point of fact Meredith did not make extensive changes.

XXIII

ESSAYS

FIRST EDITION

THE WORKS OF / GEORGE MEREDITH / VOLUME XXXII / [device: Meredith's initials entwined in vines and pomegranates] / WESTMINSTER / ARCHIBALD CONSTABLE AND CO. / 2 WHITEHALL GARDENS / 1898

This is a volume in Constable's 'de luxe' edition: see LX pp. 254–5. It contains:
1 'On the Idea of Comedy and of the Uses of the Comic Spirit,' pp. 3–84 (the text of which is the same as that of the first edition: see XXII).
2 'Homer's Iliad: a Review,' pp. 85–91 (reprinted from *The Fortnightly Review*, May 1869: see XXXIV in LX, p. 255.
3 'St. Paul: a Review,' pp. 93–9 (reprinted from *The Fortnightly Review*, January 1868: see XXXIV in LX, p. 255.

XXIV

THE STORY OF BHANAVAR THE BEAUTIFUL

FIRST EDITION

THE STORY OF / BHANAVAR / THE BEAUTIFUL / BY GEORGE MEREDITH / [device of vines and pomegranates within which Meredith's initials are entwined] / WESTMINSTER / ARCHIBALD CONSTABLE / AND COMPANY, LTD. / 1900

Collation [π]²A–H⁸J⁴ 72 leaves [13.9 × 9.5) [i–iv] 1–134 [135–6]

Contents [i] halftitle: THE STORY OF / BHANAVAR THE / BEAUTIFUL [ii] blank [iii] titlepage [iv] imprint: T. and A. CONSTABLE PRINTERS TO HER MAJESTY 1–[135] text, with at foot of [135] the imprint: Edinburgh: T. and A. CONSTABLE / PRINTERS TO HER MAJESTY [136] blank

Binding The spine and 1 cm. of the front and back cover are covered in white vellum. The boards at front and back are covered in stiff brown paper.

Front cover Meredith's signature stamped in gilt at foot.

Spine Stamped in gilt: The Story / of / Bhanavar / The / Beautiful / George Meredith / *West-* / *minster*

Back cover Plain.

XXV

THE MEREDITH POCKET BOOK

THE MEREDITH / POCKET BOOK / LONDON / ARCHIBALD CONSTABLE / AND COMPANY LTD. / 1906

Collation $[\pi]^4$A–K^{8}L^4 89 leaves (12.7 x 8.0) [i–viii] [1]–167 [168–70]

Contents [i–ii] blank [iii] halftitle: THE MEREDITH / POCKET BOOK [iv] blank [v] titlepage [vi] imprint: Edinburgh: T. and A. Constable, Printers to His Majesty [vii] editor's note [viii] blank [1]–167 text, on 167 at foot: [short rule] / Printed by T. and A. CONSTABLE, Printers to His Majesty / At the Edinburgh University Press [168–70] blank

Binding Spine, and boards at front and back, covered in dark blue leather. Endpapers white.

Front cover A blind-stamped border 2 mm. from all edges and stamped in gilt at centre: G.M.

Spine Stamped in gilt: THE / MEREDITH / POCKET / BOOK / [pattern occupying all the space between the words] / CONSTABLE / LONDON

Back cover Plain.

The *Pocket Book* consists of excerpts from Meredith's prose works selected by G.M. Trevelyan.

XXVI

MISCELLANEOUS PROSE

GEORGE MEREDITH / [short rule] / MISCELLANEOUS / PROSE / *Memorial* / *Edition* / LONDON / CONSTABLE AND COMPANY LTD / 1910

This is volume 23 of the Memorial Edition: see LXIV, pp. 264–5. It contains:

1 Essay: On the Idea of Comedy and of the Uses of the Comic Spirit (reprinted from the first edition but not from the same plates). 3–55

2 INTRODUCTIONS TO
Lady Duff Gordon's Letters from Egypt, 1902 59–64
W.M. Thackeray's *The Four Georges* 65–7
The Japanese Spirit by G. Okakura, Constable, 1905 68–70
The Collected Poems of Dora Sigerson Shorter, Hodder and Stoughton, 1907 71–3

3 REVIEWS
Homer's Iliad in English Rhymed Verse by Charles Merivale 77–80 (*Fortnightly Review*, 1 May 1869, pp. 629–30)
La Maison Forestière by MM. Erckmann-Chatrian 81–86 (*Fortnightly Review*, January 1867, New Series, Vol. I, p. 126)
Training in Theory and Practice by Archibald MacLaren 87–91 (*Fortnightly Review*, March 1867, New Series, Vol. I, p. 380)
'St. Paul: a poem' 92–5 (*Fortnightly Review*, January 1868, pp. 115–17)
'Reminiscences of a Septuagenarian from 1802 to 1815' 96 (*Fortnightly Review*, February 1868, p. 229)
'Mr. Robert Lytton's Poems' 103–27 *Chronicles and Characters*, Chapman and Hall, 1867 (*Fortnightly Review*, June 1868, p. 658)
'Mrs. Meynell's Two Books of Essays' 128–39 *The Rhythm of Life* and *The Colour of Life* (*The National Review*, August 1896, pp. 762–70)

4 SHORT ARTICLES
'A Pause in the Strife' (reprinted from the *Pall Mall Gazette*, 9 July 1886, pp. 1–2) 143–5
'Concession to the Celt' (reprinted from the *Fortnightly Review*, October 1886, p. 448) 146–52
'Leslie Stephen' (reprinted from *The Author*, April 1904, p. 187) 153–4

5 CRITICISM
'Fine Passages in Verse and Prose selected by living Men of Letters' (reprinted from the *Fortnightly Review*, August 1887, pp. 297–316) 157–60

6 Correspondence from the Seat of War in Italy: Letters written to the Morning Post from the seat of war in Italy 163–213
The letters are dated: 22 June 1866; 3 July 1866; 7 July 1866; 8 July 1866; 9 July 1866; 12 July 1866; 17 July 1866; 20 July 1866; 22 July 1866; 24 July 1866.

XXVII a

GEORGE MEREDITH AND THE MONTHLY OBSERVER

FIRST EDITION

GEORGE MEREDITH / AND THE / MONTHLY OBSERVER / BY /
MAURICE BUXTON FORMAN / PRIVATELY PRINTED / LONDON / 1911

Collation 12 leaves (19.4 x 13.0) [1–3] 4–22 [23–4]

Contents [1] titlepage [2] publisher's note: *Only twenty-one copies printed* [3]–
22 text [23] imprint: PRINTED BY / WILLIAM CLOWES AND SONS, LIMITED / LONDON
AND BECCLES [24] blank

Binding A grey paper wrapper with the titlepage printed on the front cover.

Meredith contributed to at least five issues of *The Monthly Observer:* no. 11
January 1849; no. 13 March 1849; no. 14 April 1849; no. 16 June 1849; no. 17
July 1849
The manuscripts of these contributions are in the Widener Collection at
Harvard.

XXVII b

GEORGE MEREDITH AND THE MONTHLY OBSERVER

THE CONTRIBUTIONS / OF / GEORGE MEREDITH / TO / THE MONTHLY
OBSERVER / JANUARY–JULY 1849 / EDITED BY / MAURICE BUXTON
FORMAN / EDINBURGH / PRINTED FOR PRIVATE CIRCULATION / 1928

Collation Three gatherings of 8 leaves bound one inside the other: 24 leaves
(20.1 x 13.5) [1–6] 7–45 [46–8]

Contents [1] halftitle: THE CONTRIBUTIONS OF / GEORGE MEREDITH / TO THE
MONTHLY OBSERVER [2] blank [3] titlepage [4] blank [5] publisher's note:
NOTE. / The story of George Meredith's association with / "The Monthly Ob-
server" was told by me in a / pamphlet printed privately at the request of the
late / Luther S. Livingston in 1911. Meredith's contribu-/ tions to the Magazine
are here printed for the first / time with the kind permission of Mr. William
Maxse / Meredith. / M.B.F. [6] blank 7–45 text [46] blank [47] imprint:
EDINBURGH: / PRINTED FOR M. BUXTON FORMAN, PRETORIA. / EDITION LIMITED TO
THIRTY-FIVE COPIES. [48] blank

Binding Grey paper cover sewn on with titlepage printed in black on front cover.

XXVIII

UP TO MIDNIGHT

FIRST EDITION

UP TO MIDNIGHT / BY GEORGE MEREDITH / A SERIES OF DIALOGUES CONTRIBUTED / TO *THE GRAPHIC* / NOW REPRINTED FOR THE FIRST TIME / JOHN W. LUCE AND COMPANY / BOSTON, 1913

Collation [1–6]⁸ 48 leaves (17.75 x 12.0) [i–xii] [1]–84

Contents [i–ii] blank [iii] titlepage [iv] blank [v] flytitle: INTRODUCTION [vi] blank [vii–ix] introduction [x] blank [xi] halftitle: UP TO MIDNIGHT [xii] blank [1]–84 text

Binding Spine, and boards at front and back, covered in black cloth. Except for 1.5 cms. next to spine, both front and back covers are covered with an additional layer of mottle paper. A triangular tip at each corner is not covered with paper. Endpapers plain.

Front cover Pasted onto the front cover is a label with a double red border. From bottom left to top right reads: UP / TO / MIDNIGHT At bottom right: George / Meredith

Spine At the top of an otherwise plain spine a label is pasted, on which is printed in red and black: [rule] / UP TO / MIDNIGHT / BY / GEORGE / MEREDITH / [rule] / LUCE / [rule]

SERIAL PUBLICATION

The dialogues included in this publication were first printed in *The Graphic*.
1 21 December 1872, Vol. VI No. 160, p. 582
2 28 December 1872, Vol. VI No. 161, p. 606
3 4 January 1873, Vol. VII No. 162, pp. 6–7
4 11 January 1873, Vol. VII No. 163, pp. 34–5
5 18 January 1873, Vol. VII No. 164, p. 61
The first two numbers were reprinted in *The Graphic* on 1 and 8 February 1873. A note in the British Museum copy indicates that the editor was restrained from reprinting the others by W.M. Meredith acting for Constable's.

B Collections of Letters in Book Form

By far the best account of the publication of Meredith's letters is the introduction to C.L. Cline's edition: Volume I, pp. xxix–xxxv.

XXIX

THE LETTERS OF GEORGE MEREDITH COLLECTED AND EDITED BY HIS SON

LETTERS OF / GEORGE MEREDITH / COLLECTED AND EDITED BY / HIS SON / IN TWO VOLUMES / [short rule] / VOL. I / 1844–1881 / LONDON / CONSTABLE AND COMPANY LTD / 1912

This edition of letters collected and edited by W.M. Meredith is in two volumes – volumes which are consistent in format with the Memorial Edition (see LXIV, p. 265).

VOLUME I

Collation [π]⁴A–U⁸x⁴ 168 leaves (21.5 x 14.5) [i–iv] v–vi [vii–viii] [1]–328

Contents [i] halftitle: LETTERS OF / GEORGE MEREDITH [ii] blank [iii] titlepage [iv] imprint: T. and A. CONSTABLE, Printers to His Majesty v–vi preface [vii] list of illustrations [viii] blank [1]–328 text, on 328 at foot: END OF VOL. I.

VOLUME II

Collation [π]²A–U⁸x² 164 leaves (21.5 x 14.5) [i–iv] [329]–652

Contents [i] halftitle [ii] blank [iii] titlepage [iv] imprint [329]–652 text, with imprint at foot of 652

Binding Spine, and boards at front and back, covered in green cloth. Endpapers plain white.

Front cover Stamped in gilt Meredith's monogram.

Spine Stamped in gilt at top and bottom one thick and three thin horizontal lines and between the two sets, also stamped in gilt: Letters / of / George Meredith / Vol. I. / CONSTABLE / LONDON

Back cover Plain.

The edition was re-issued in 1912 and called a second edition. 'SECOND EDITION' is on the titlepage.

XXX

LETTERS TO CLODD AND SHORTER

FIRST EDITION

LETTERS / FROM / GEORGE MEREDITH / TO / EDWARD CLODD / AND / CLEMENT K. SHORTER / LONDON: / PRINTED FOR PRIVATE CIRCULATION / 1913

Collation $1^6 2^8 3^6$ 20 leaves (19.0 x 12.5) [1–5] 6–39 [40]

Contents [1] halftitle: LETTERS [2] blank [3] titlepage [4] blank [5]–39 text [40] imprint: LONDON: / Printed for THOMAS J. WISE, Hampstead, N.W. / *Edition limited to Thirty Copies.*

Binding A maroon paper wrapper with the titlepage printed on the front cover.

XXXI

LETTERS TO RICHARD HENRY HORNE

FIRST EDITION

LETTERS / FROM / GEORGE MEREDITH / TO / RICHARD HENRY HORNE / CAPE TOWN / PRINTED FOR PRIVATE CIRCULATION / 1919

Collation 16 leaves (19.8 x 12.8) [1–4] 5–15 [16]

Contents [1] halftitle: LETTERS. [2] blank [3] titlepage [4] blank 5–15 text [16] imprint: CAPE TOWN: / Printed for M. BUXTON FORMAN. / *Edition limited to Thirty Copies.*

Binding A green paper wrapper with the titlepage reproduced on the front cover.

XXXII

LETTERS TO SWINBURNE AND WATTS-DUNTON

FIRST EDITION

LETTERS / FROM / GEORGE MEREDITH / TO / ALGERNON CHARLES SWINBURNE / AND / THEODORE WATTS-DUNTON / PRETORIA / PRINTED FOR PRIVATE CIRCULATION / 1922

Collation 10 leaves (21.5 x 14.0) [1–4] 5–19 [20]

Contents [1] halftitle: LETTERS [2] blank [3] titlepage [4] blank 5–19 text [20] imprint: Printed at Cape Town for M. BUXTON FORMAN, / Pretoria. / *Edition limited to Thirty Copies.*

Binding A grey paper wrapper with the titlepage printed on the front cover.

XXXIII

LETTERS TO ALICE MEYNELL

FIRST EDITION

The Letters of / GEORGE MEREDITH / *to* ALICE MEYNELL / *with annotations thereto* / 1896–1907 / [asterisks] / *The Nonesuch Press* / *London and San Francisco, 1923*

Collation [1⁴2–8⁸] 60 leaves (23.5 x 15.5) [i–vi] [1–7] 8–102 [103] 104 [105–10]

Contents [i–vi] blank [1] halftitle: *The Letters of* / GEORGE MEREDITH / *to* ALICE MEYNELL / 1896–1907 / [asterisk] [2] blank [3] titlepage [4] publisher's statement: PRINTED AND MADE IN ENGLAND [5] contents [6] epigraph: "FOR THE SENTENCES HAD A THROB BENEATH / THEM." / *of Henrietta's letter in "The Amazing Marriage".* [7] editor's note 8–102 text [103] blank 104 publisher's note: *This Edition is limited to 850 copies, / on Ingres paper, for England and / America, of which 780 are for sale. / The type has been distributed. This / is number* [105–10] blank The endpapers are pasted to the first and final leaf.

Binding Spine and one centimetre of front and back covered in straw-coloured buckram. Boards at front and back covered in chocolate-brown stiff paper. Endpapers brown.

Front cover Plain.

Spine Stamped in gilt: LETTERS / G.M. / *to* / A.M.

Contents George Meredith's Letters, with notes 8–83; George Meredith's Article on Alice Meynell's Prose 85–94; "A Remembrance," by Alice Meynell 95–97; Alice Meynell's Column: "The Twenty-First" 99–102

XXXIV

LETTERS TO VARIOUS CORRESPONDENTS

LETTERS / FROM / GEORGE MEREDITH / TO / VARIOUS CORRESPONDENTS
PRETORIA / PRINTED FOR PRIVATE CIRCULATION / 1924

Collation 12 leaves (22.2 x 14.3) [1-4] 5-23 [24]

Contents [1] titlepage [2] blank [3] contents [4] blank 5-23 text [24] imprint:
PRETORIA: / Printed for M. BUXTON FORMAN. / *Edition limited to Thirty Copies.*
The contents are as follows: to James Vizetelly [1851] 5; to W.M. Rossetti, 27
June 1863 6; to Frederick Sandys, [1875] 7; to Dr. W.C. Bennett, 2 November
1883 8; to William Reeves, 24 May 1886 9; to Mrs. Janet Ross, 30 March 1890
10; to William Reeves, 18 December 1891 11; to William Watson, 17 April
1892 12; to David Christie Murray, 12 March 1897 13; to Norman MaColl,
20 December 1897 14; to Norman MacColl, 9 February 1902 15; to Norman
MaColl, 16 April 1902 16; to Miss Nora Senior, 15 May 1904 17; to Mrs.
Janet Ross, 8 July 1904 18; to Chevalier Luigi Ricci, 30 December 1907 19; to
Chevalier Luigi Ricci, 25 July 1908 20; to Ford Madox Hueffer, 28 July 1908
21; to Ford Madox Hueffer, 17 October 1908 22; to an unnamed correspondent, 9 April 1909 23.

XXXV

THE LETTERS

THE LETTERS OF / George Meredith / EDITED BY C.L. CLINE / [double
short rule] / VOLUME I / OXFORD / AT THE CLARENDON PRESS / 1970

VOLUME I

Collation [1]⁶[2]⁸[3]⁶B-z⁸Ac-Mm⁸Nn⁶ 288 leaves (21.5 x 14.0) [i-vi] vii-xlii
1-555 [556]

Contents [i] halftitle: THE LETTERS OF / GEORGE MEREDITH [ii] blank [iii] title-
page [iv] imprint and copyright statement: *Oxford University Press, Ely House,
London W.1.* / GLASGOW NEW YORK TORONTO MELBOURNE WELLINGTON / CAPE
TOWN SALISBURY IBADAN NAIROBI DAR ES SALAAM LUSAKA ADDIS ABABA / BOMBAY
CALCUTTA MADRAS KARACHI LAHORE DACCA / KUALA LUMPUR SINGAPORE HONG
KONG TOKYO / © OXFORD UNIVERSITY PRESS 1970 / PRINTED IN GREAT BRITAIN
[v] contents [vi] blank vii-xxii list of letters xxiii-xxvi acknowledgements
xxviii editorial principles xxix-xxxv introduction xxxvi abbreviations and short

titles xxxvii–xl select bibliography xli–xlii chronology 1–555 text [556] PRINTED IN GREAT BRITAIN / AT THE UNIVERSITY PRESS, OXFORD / BY VIVIAN RIDLER / PRINTER TO THE UNIVERSITY

VOLUME II

Collation [1]⁸[2]⁶B–Z⁸Aa–Oo⁸Pp¹⁰ 312 leaves (21.5 x 14.0) [i–vi] v–xxviii 557–1150 [1151–2]

Contents [i] halftitle [ii] blank [iii] titlepage [iv] imprint and copyright statement v–xxvii list of letters xxviii blank 557–1150 text [1151] imprint [1152] blank

VOLUME III

Collation [1–2]⁸B–Z⁸Aa–Ss⁸ 334 leaves (21.5 x 14.0) [i–iv] v–xxxii 1151–1786 [1787–90]

Contents [i] halftitle [ii] blank [iii] titlepage [iv] imprint and copyright statement v–xxxii list of letters 1151–1786 text [1787] imprint [1788–90] blank

Binding Spine, and boards at front and back, covered in red cloth. Endpapers plain white.

Front cover Plain.

Spine Stamped in gilt: [one ornamental above one plain rule] / Letters of / George Meredith / [rule] / Edited by C.L. Cline / [one plain above one ornamental rule] / VOLUME I / [publisher's emblem] / OXFORD

Back cover Plain.

Slightly more than 2600 letters by Meredith are printed in this edition.

c Contributions to Journals, Magazines, and Newspapers

At various times throughout his life Meredith engaged in rather half-hearted journalism which, once he had made his reputation as a novelist, he preferred to forget. Signed articles were collected either for the Constable collected editions or, after Meredith's death, by Buxton Forman: these collected and signed articles appear in the main entries to Part II, that have already been described.

Unsigned and for the most part unacknowledged articles appeared in the *Ipswich Journal*, to which at the instigation of a friend Meredith contributed for almost a decade (1858–68), the *Westminster Review*, the *Pall Mall Gazette*, the *Fortnightly Review*, the *Morning Post*, the *Monthly Observer*, as well as other journals. Some of these contributions to periodicals can be identified with greater certainty than others. Gordon Haight confirmed Meredith's authorship of the Belles Lettres and Arts' section of the *Westminster Review* for at least four issues, those of April, July, and October 1857, and January 1858, (*MLR*, vol. 53, January 1958, pp. 1–16). With the help of Meredith's notebooks, Gillian Beer identified some of Meredith's contributions to the features' section of the *Pall Mall Gazette*, specifically the following six pieces: 'The Anecdotalist,' 21 March 1868, pp. 10–11; 'The Cynic of Society,' 28 March 1868, pp. 11–12; 'The Consummate Epicure,' 25 April 1868, pp. 10–11; 'A Working Frenchwoman,' 30 April 1868, pp. 10–11; 'The Third-Class Carriage,' 23 May 1868, pp. 10–11; 'English Country Inns,' 27 June 1868, p. 10 ('Meredith's Contributions to the *Pall Mall Gazette*,' *MLR*, July 1966, vol. LXI, pp. 395–400).

But references in the *Letters*, such as Meredith's blunt statement in Letter 411: 'I write almost every week in the *Pall Mall Gazette*' (*Letters* I 375) inclines one to suppose that further work, though necessarily speculative, would be rewarding. Finally, for a short period between November 1867 and January 1868, Meredith took over the editorship of the *Fortnightly Review*, while the editor was in North America. Whether there is unsigned work of Meredith's in the *Fortnightly Review* at that period has not been determined. It seems inappropriate to include unsigned and unacknowledged articles as main entries in this bibliography, though one makes this decision with some regret since Meredith's refusal to identify or remember his early journalism is itself an indication that he probably wrote more than he admitted.

1867
1 The *Fortnightly Review*, 1 January 1867, pp. 126–8. Review of *La Maison Forestière* by MM. Erckmann-Chatrian
2 The *Fortnightly Review*, 1 March 1867, pp. 380–2. Review of *Training in Theory and Practice* by Archibald MacLaren

1868

3   The *Fortnightly Review*, 1 January 1868, pp. 115–17. Review of *Saint Paul. (A Poem.)* by Frederic H. Myers

4   The *Fortnightly Review*, 1 February 1868, pp. 229–32. Review of *Reminiscences of a Septuagenarian from 1802 to 1815* by Emma Sophia, Countess Brownlow

5   The *Fortnightly Review*, 1 June 1868, pp. 658–72. 'Mr. Robert Lytton's Poems,' a review of *Chronicles and Characters* by Robert Lytton

1869

6   The *Fortnightly Review*, 1 May 1869, pp. 629–30. Review of *Homer's Iliad in English Rhymed Verse* by Charles Merivale

1872

7   *The Graphic*, vol. VI, no. 160, 21 December 1872, p. 582. (Reprinted in *Up to Midnight*, see Part II, Section A)

8   *The Graphic*, vol. VI, no. 161, 28 December 1872, p. 606. (Reprinted in *Up to Midnight*, see Part II, Section A)

1873

9   *The Graphic*, vol. VII, no. 162, 4 January 1873. (Reprinted in *Up to Midnight*, see Part II, Section A)

10   *The Graphic*, vol. VII, no. 163, 11 January 1873. (Reprinted in *Up to Midnight*, see Part II, Section A)

1880

11   The *Pall Mall Gazette*, 9 July 1880, pp. 1–2. 'A Pause in the Strife'

1886

12   The *Fortnightly Review*, 1 October 1886, pp. 448–51. 'Concession to the Celt'

1887

13   The *Fortnightly Review*, 1 August 1887, pp. 297–316. 'Fine Passages in Verse and Prose: Selected by Living Men of Letters I'

1890

14   *The Author*, vol. I, no. 2, 16 June 1890, p. 45. 'The Art of Authorship'

1896

15   The *National Review*, vol. 27, August 1896, pp. 762–70. 'Mrs. Meynell's Two Books of Essays,' review of *The Rhythm of Life* and *The Colour of Life*

1902

16   Ross, Janet. *Lady Duff-Gordon's Letters from Egypt*, London, R. Brimley Johnson, 1902. An introduction by Meredith on pp. xi–xvi

1903

17   Thackeray, William Makepeace. *The Four Georges*, London, Blackie and Sons Ltd., 1903. An introduction by Meredith on pp. iii–vi

1904

18 *The Author*, April 1904, p. 187. 'Sir Leslie Stephen, K.C.B.'

1905

19 Okakura Yoshisaburo. *The Japanese Spirit*, London, A. Constable and Co., Ltd., 1905. An introduction by Meredith on pp. ix–xiv

20 *The Queen's Christmas Carol, an Anthology of Poems, Stories, Essays, Drawings and Music by British Authors, Artists and Composers*, London, Manchester and Paris, The Daily Mail. An introduction by Meredith on p. v

1907

21 *The Collected Poems of Dora Sigerson Shorter*, London, Hodder and Stoughton, 1907. An introduction by Meredith on pp. v–viii

22 Stephens, T. (Ed.) *Wales: Today and Tomorrow*, Cardiff, Western Mail Limited, 1907. A 'message' from Meredith, p. xi

1908

23 *The Daily Telegraph*, 26 October 1908, p. 14. 'Food reform. Mr. George Meredith's "vices".'

1912

24 *Maggs Catalogue*, no. 278, January 1912, p. 62. 'Armaments,' unpublished; the MS is described as written in Meredith's early style and consisting of some 24 lines on one full page.

1912

25 *Francis Edward's Catalogue*, no. 326, July 1912, p. 69. Nine aphorisms written by Meredith on the inside of the back cover of *Violin Schule von Hubert Ries*, Leipzig, 1840

1913

26 *Maggs Catalogue*, no. 317, November 1913, pp. 104–6. 'The Art and Science of Cookery.' Two and a half pages of extracts from an unpublished MS described as 'extending to some 50 pages interspersed with pieces of poetry and containing occasional notes by Mrs. M.E. Meredith, the daughter of Thomas Love Peacock. Circa 1849–1850'

1914

27 Maggs Catlogue, no. 320, January–February 1914, pp. 125–6. 'Cookery Recipes.' Extracts from an unpublished manuscript 'extending to some 19 pages and interspersed with occasional notes, etc., by Mrs. M.E. Meredith, the daughter of Thomas Love Peacock. Circa 1849–50'

D Independent Publication of Letters
in Journals, Magazines, and Newspapers

[References in square brackets are to Cline's editions of Meredith's letters.]

1866

1 *The Morning Post*, June and July 1866. 'Correspondence from the Seat of War in Italy'

The Italian Army. Ferrara, 22–6 June, pp. 5–6

The Italian Army. Cremona, 30 June–4 July, p. 6

The Italian Army. Headquarters, 11th Division, Bozzolo, 3 July. Marcaria, 3 July, evening–7 July, p. 6

The Italians in Venetia. General Headquarters of the Italian Army, Torre Malimberti, 7–11 July, p. 6

The Italians in Venetia. Headquarters of the 1st Army Corps, Piadena, 8–12 July, p. 6

The War in Italy. Conzaga, 9–13 July, p. 5

The War in Italy. Conzaga, 12 July and 11–18 July, p. 5

The War in Italy. Noale, near Treviso, 17–23 July, p. 6

The War in Italy. Dolo, near Venice, 20–5 July, p. 6

The Late Events in Italy. Civita Vecchia, 22 July. Marseilles, 24–7 July, p. 6

This correspondence, 'From our own correspondent,' occupies approximately thirteen columns of *The Morning Post*.

1888

2 *The Reflector*, 5 February 1888, pp. 119–20. Undated letter to the editor of *The Reflector*, and poem, 'A Stave of Roving Tim' [II.905]

3 Gilman, M.R.F. *The Pilgrim's Scrip*, Boston, Roberts Brothers, 1888, pp. xvii–xviii. Letter to Mrs. J.B. Gilman dated 16 March 1888 [II.909]

1889

4 Salt, H.S. *The Life of James Thomson ('B.V.') With a Selection from His Letters and a Study of his Writings*. London, Reeves and Turner, and Bertram and Dobel, 1889. Extract of letter to Thomson, p. 137; extract of letter to Thomson [II.575] p. 152; letter to Thomson dated Box Hill, Dorking, 27 April 1880 [II.595] p. 153; extracts from two letters to H.S. Salt [II.917, II.918] p. 179

5 *Sotheby, Wilkinson and Hodge's Sale Catalogue*, 27–8 November 1889, p. 22. Extract from letter to John W. Parker dated 17 December 1850 [I.10]; extract from letter on Edgar Allan Poe's 'Raven' dated 25 June 1869 [I.382].

1890

6 Bainton, George (ed.) *The Art of Authorship*, London, James Clarke and Co., 1890, pp. 129–32. Extracts from two letters to George Bainton [II.906, II.907]

1894

7 *The New York Herald*, 9 October 1894, p. 11. Telegram on the death of

Oliver Wendell Holmes; reprinted in *The Westminster Gazette*, 23 October p. 2 [III.1175]

8 *Sotheby, Wilkinson and Hodge's Sale Catalogue*, 11–12 December 1894, p. 25. Extract from letter to Charles Ollier dated July 1851 [I.15]

1895

9 *The Bookman*, May 1895, p. 37. Letter to T.H. Lewis dated 16 January 1888 [II.901–2]

10 *The Author*, August 1895, p. 67. Letter to the Society of Authors on the occasion of a banquet for Sir Walter Besant on 26 June 1895 [III.1199]

11 *The Academy*, 12 October 1895, p. 296. Letter dated 7 October 1895 to A. Constable and Co. concerning Meredith's change of publishers [III.1211]

12 *The South Wales Daily News*, 23 December 1895, p. 4 [III.1216]

1896

13 *The Daily News*, 4 March 1896, p. 4 [III.1221]

1898

14 *Pen and Pencil*. A Souvenir of the Press Bazaar. Compiled and arranged by the proprietors of *Punch*, *The Daily Graphic*, and *The Daily Chronicle*, for the benefit of the London Hospital. 28–9 June 1898, p. [181); note dated Box Hill, Dorking, 20 May 1898, reproduced in facsimile [II.876]

15 *The Harvard Monthly*, June 1898, pp. 127–8. Letter to G.P. Baker dated 22 July 1887 [II.876]

16 *The Daily News*, 26 July 1898, p. 9. Letter to T.J. Cobden Sanderson dated 18 July 1898 regarding Italian political prisoners [III.1304]. Reprinted with variations in *The Westminster Gazette*, 26 July 1898, p. 9

17 Salt, Henry S. *The Life of James Thomson* ('B.V.') Revised Edition, London, A. and B.B. Bonner, 1898. Letters and extracts as in 1889 edition, pp. 123, 136, 163; extract from letter to H.S. Salt dated 2 February 1891, p. iii [II.1019]

1899

18 *The Daily News*, 13 January 1899, p. 5 [III.1320]

19 *The Morning Post*, 11 February 1899, p. 5 [III.1321]

20 *Free Russia*, April 1899, p. 25. Letter to F. Volkhorsky dated 12 March 1899 [III.1324]

1900

21 *The Evening News*, 27 June 1900, p. 1 [III.1255]

1901

22 *The Sunday Sun*, 16 June 1901, p. 6 [III.1395]

23 *The Author*, 1 July 1901, p. 20 (III.1395]

24 *Humanity*, August 1901, p. 155 [III.1396]

1902

25 *The Daily News*, 25 February 1902, p. 3. 'A plea for Kritzinger' [III.1424]

26 *The Daily Mail*, 4 March 1902, p. 5. 'Mr. Meredith and the Boers. A plea for mercy' [III.1427]

27 Jerrold, Walter. *George Meredith. An Essay towards Appreciation*, London, Greening and Co. Ltd., 1902. Extract from letter to Charles Ollier dated July 1851, p. 7; letter to G.P. Baker dated 22 July 1887, p. 25 [II.876]; letter to the editor of *The Reflector*, p. 30

1903

28 *The Morning Leader*, 23 January 1903, p. 3 [III.1475]

29 *The Daily Chronicle*, 12 February 1903, p. 5 [III.1476]

30 *The Daily Telegraph*, 17 February 1903, p. 6 [III.1479]

31 *The Daily Mail*, 18 November 1903, p. 5 [III.1489]

1904

32 *The Morning Post*, 4 March 1904, p. 8 [III.1491]

33 *The Times*, 4 May 1904, p. 9. 'The late Sir Leslie Stephen' [III.1495]

34 *The Daily News*, 20 May 1904, p. 8. 'Women in Public Life. Message from George Meredith' [III.1497]

35 *The Pall Mall Gazette*, 25 June 1904, p. 4. 'The Hundred Best Books' [III.1503]

36 *The English Historical Review*, July 1904, Vol. 19, p. 492. 'Frederick York Powell' [III.1498]

37 *The Daily Mirror*, 28 October 1904, p. 3 [III.1508]

38 Douglas, James. *Theodore Watts-Dunton: Poet, Novelist, Critic*, London, Hodder and Stoughton, 1904, pp. 417–18. Extracts from letters dated 8 March 1892 [II.1072] and 30 November 1898

39 Burnand, Sir Francis C. *Records and Reminiscences Personal and General*, London, Methuen and Co. Ltd., 1904. Letter to Burnand dated Box Hill, Dorking, 16 June 1886 [II.817]

1905

40 *The Daily Mirror*, 1 February 1905, p. 3 [III.1514]

41 *The Daily News*, 23 March 1905, p. 4. 'Dinner for Mr. F. Greenwood. Mr. Meredith's Appreciation' [III.1516]

42 *The Manchester Guardian*, 28 March 1905, p. 5. 'Meredith's Women' [III.1513]

43 *The Academy*, 13 May 1905, pp. 516–17. 'The Schiller Centenary in Germany' [III.1522]

44 *The Daily Chronicle*, 31 May 1905, p. 5. 'Meredith on the Russo-Japanese War' [III.1527]

45 *The Morning Leader*, 23 June 1905, p. 7. Letter to Miss Nora Senior dated 15 May 1904 printed with facsimile of the autograph original [III.1496]

46 *The South Wales Daily News*, 13 October 1905, p. 5 [III.1542]

47 *The Times*, 24 October 1905, p. 4 [III.1543]

1906

48 *The Westminster Gazette*, 11 January 1906, p. 7. 'The Motorman let loose. Mr. Meredith on Mr. Chamberlain' [III.1549]

49 *The Times*, 20 January 1906. p. 11 [III.1550]

50 *The Tribune*, 22 February 1906, p. 12. 'The Eisteddfod of Wales. Mr. Meredith objects to innovation' [III.1555]

51 *The Times*, 16 April 1906, p. 2. 'The Anglo-Austrian "Entente" ' [III.1556]

52 *The Times*, 3 May 1906, p. 15. 'Rationalist Press Association' [III.1557]

53 *The Speaker*, New Series, 14 July 1906, p. 336. 'England and the Duma' [III.1565]

54 *The Daily Telegraph*, 20 July 1906, p. 7. 'Liberals and the Colonies' [III.1566]

55 Anderson, J.P. (Ed.) *Record of the Celebration of the Quatercentenary of the University of Aberdeen from 25th to 28th September, 1906*, p. 6 [III.1563]

56 *The Times*, 1 November 1906, p. 12. 'Suffrage for Women' [III.1576]

1907

57 Felberman, Louis (Ed.) *British Tribute to Hungary and its King Souvenir Album*, London, Louis Felberman [June 1907], p. 13 [III.1597]

58 *The Times*, 12 July 1907, p. 8. 'Memorial to W.E. Henley' [III.1599]

59 *New York Evening Post*, 13 July 1907, p. 8 [I.14]

60 *The East Anglian Times*, 1 November 1907, p. 4 [III.1611]

61 *The Daily Telegraph*, 5 November 1907, p. 11. 'Censorship of Plays and Public Opinion. Mr. George Meredith's View' [III.1611]

1908

62 *The Times*, 13 February 1908, p. 5. 'Mr. Meredith's Birthday' [III.1623]

63 *The Daily News*, 3 March 1908, p. 8. 'Mr. George Meredith's letter to Welshmen' [III.1636]

64 *The Times*, 27 March 1908, p. 11. 'Mr. Meredith on Research in Wales' [III.1636]

65 *The Standard*, 23 June 1908, p. 8. 'Mr. George Meredith and Dante' [III.1651]

66 *The Times*, 26 November 1908, p. 10. 'The Letters of Queen Victoria' [III.1678]

67 *The Author*, 1 December 1908, p. 59 [III.1679]

68 *A Chorus of Celebrities*. Issued by the Board of Management of the Royal

Hospital for Incurables, Putney Heath, Christmas 1908. Message from Meredith p. 50 [III.1681]

69 Murray, David Christie. *Recollections*, London, John Long, 1908, pp. 287–90 [III.1261]

70 Henderson, M. Sturge. *George Meredith*, 1908, pp. 140–1 and p. 3. Undated letter to the Croydon Electors [III.1549]; extract from undated letter to Mrs. M. Sturge Henderson [III.1582]

1909

71 *The Publishers' Circular*, 23 January 1909, p. 113. 'Thomas B. Mosher, the American book pirate' [III.1684]

72 *The English Review*, January 1909, p. 333. 'A Note on Cheyne Walk' [III.1671]

73 *The Daily Telegraph*, 4 March 1909, p. 15. 'Votes for Women. Mr. George Meredith's advice' [III.1686]

74 *The Western Mail*, 14 April 1909, p. 7. 'Land of the Mountains' [III.1690]

75 *The Times*, 15 April 1909, p. 6. 'Mr. Swinburne' [III.1691]

76 *Messina e Reggio*, April 1909, p. [50]. Milan, Enrico Bonetti. Message dated 9 January 1909 given in facsimile; reprinted in Maggs Brothers' Autograph Catalogue, no. 320, Jan.–Feb. 1914, p. 89 [III.1683]

77 *The Times*, 20 May 1909. 'Mr. Meredith and Vivisection' [III.1571 and III.1572]

78 *The Times*, 20 May 1909, p. 10 [III.1675]

79 *The Athenaeum*, 22 May 1909, p. 619 [III.1583]

80 *The Manchester Despatch*, 22 May 1909, p. 4. 'Meredith and the Jews' [III.1551]

81 *The Observer*, 23 May 1909, p. 8

82 *Vanity Fair*, 26 May 1909, p. 647 [II.1037]

83 *Women's Franchise*, 27 May 1909, p. 598. Reprinted in *The Citizen*, Gloucester, 31 May 1909, p. 3 [II.936]

84 *Justice*, 29 May 1909, p. 6. 'George Meredith' by H.M. Hyndman. Two letters to Hyndman dated 16 February 1908 [III.1629] and 5 January 1909 [III.1683]; reprinted in *The Record of an Adventurous Life* by H.M. Hyndman, 1911, pp. 90–1

85 *The Spectator*, 29 May 1909, p. 856. 'Mr. George Meredith' [II.572]

86 *The Spectator*, 5 June 1909, p. 896. 'Mr. George Meredith' [II.937]

87 *The Bookman*, July 1909, p. 169.

88 *The Observer*, 12 December 1909, p. 9. 'Perils of the new censorship. How *Richard Feverel* was banned'

1910

89 *The Cape Times*, Cape Town, 15 January 1910, p. 6. 'George Meredith

on Himself.' Leading article embodying letter to Dr. H. A[nders] dated 5 April 1906 [III.1556]

90 McKechnie, James. *Meredith's Allegory, The Shaving of Shagpat*, London, Hodder and Stoughton, 1910, pp. 5–8. Letter to the author dated Box Hill, Dorking, 21 May 1906 [III.1559]

91 O'Connor, Mrs. T.P. *I Myself*, London, Methuen and Co., 1910, p. 281. Letter to the author dated Box Hill, Dorking, 29 April 1908 [III.1642]

92 Whiting, Lilian. *Louise Chandler Moulton, Poet and Friend*, London, Hodder and Stoughton, 1910, pp. 179–80 and p. 218. Letters to Louise Chandler Moulton dated 9 March 1890 and 4 January 1889 [II.992 and II.941]

1911

93 *Catalogue of the Library of the Reverend Augustus Jessop*, Messrs. Sotheby, Wilkinson and Hodge, 4 December 1911, pp. 22–3. Extracts from seven letters to Dr. and Mrs. Jessop written on various dates

94 Hyndman, Henry Mayers. *Records of an Adventurous Life*, London, Macmillan and Co., Ltd., 1911, pp. 71–92. Three letters to the author dated 31 October 1899, 16 February 1908, and 5 January 1909 [III.1338, II.1629, and III.1683]

95 *The Life of John Oliver Hobbes, told in her Correspondence with Numerous Friends*, London, John Murray, 1911, p. 236. Two letters to Mrs. Craigie dated 1 April 1902 and 15 May 1903 [III.1434 and III.1483]

96 Hallam, Lord Tennyson (Ed.) *Tennyson and His Friends*, London, Macmillan and Co., Ltd., 1911, p. 257. Letter to Alfred Austin dated Box Hill, Dorking, 5 November 1892 [II.1109]

97 Ellis, S.M. *William Harrison Ainsworth and his Friends*, London, John Lane, 1911, pp. 56–7, 115–16, 117, 119–20, 151, 160, 238, 191, 182, 240, 240–1, 218, 217, 241–2, 256–7, 257, 258, 258–9, 216, 260, 271–2, 260, 261, 280, 318, 225, 369, 135–6, 339. Letters from Meredith to various correspondents appear on these pages [I.15, I.74, I.76, I.84, I.119, I.131, I.135, I.200, I.295, I.296, I.307, I.312, I.340, I.377, I.406, I.416, I.417, I.420, I.425, I.428, I.432, I.438, I.470, I.473, II.598, II.713, II.1381, III. 1691, III.1582]

98 *The Autobiography of Alfred Austin, Poet Laureate 1835–1910*, London, Macmillan and Co., Ltd., 1911, Vol. II, p.257. Letter to Alfred Austin dated Box Hill, Dorking, 5 November 1982 [II.1109]

1912

99 *Der Verlag Bernhard Tauchnitz 1837–1912. Mit einem Anhand enthaltend Auszuge aus den Briefen englischer und amerikanischer Autoren der Tauchnitz Edition*, Leipzig, 1 Februar 1912, pp. 111–12. Letter to Baran Tauchnitz dated Box Hill, Dorking, 29 May 1895 [III.1197]. Published also in *The Harvest: Being the Record of One Hundred Years of Publishing 1837–1937*, Leipzig, 1937, pp. 57–8

100 *Scribner's Magazine*, August 1912, pp. 275–88; October 1912, pp. 385–400. 'Letters of George Meredith.' A selection from the correspondence edited by William Maxse Meredith and published in two volumes in October 1912 by Constable & Co. Ltd.

101 *Sotheby, Wilkinson and Hodge's Sale Catalogue*, 18–19 December 1912, pp. 52–62. Extracts from forty-four letters to the Rev. Augustus and Mrs. Jessop written on various dates, twenty-two reprinted in *Letters*, twenty-two unpublished; extracts from six letters to George Stevenson

102 Livingston, Luther S. *First Editions of George Meredith*, New York, Dodd and Livingston, 1912, p. 22. Letter to Frederick Chapman dated Box Hill, Dorking, 28 February 1893 [II.1124]

103 Harper, J. Henry. *The House of Harper. A Century of Publishing* in Franklin Square, New York and London, Harper and Brothers, 1912, pp. 165–6. Undated letter to Harper and Brothers written at Copsham Cottage, Esher

104 Ross, Janet. *The Fourth Generation*, London, Constable and Co. Ltd., 1912, pp. 51–2, 86, 87, 102–5, 113–18, 120–2, 148–15, 381. Letters to the author written on various dates [1.45, 1.66, 1.68, 1.78, 1.111, 1.132, 1.235, III.1504]

105 Sharp, Elizabeth. *William Sharp (Fiona Macleod) A Memoir*, London, William Heinemann, 1912, pp. 114, 134, 144–5, 150, 156–7, 183–4, 228, 245–6. Eight letters to William Sharp and one to 'Fiona Macleod'

106 *Maggs Catalogue*, 1912, No. 301, p. 112. Letter to W.C. Bonaparte Wyse dated 20 May 1880 [II.598]

1913

107 *The Pall Mall Gazette*, 31 March 1913, p. 9. 'The Muse in Exile. A talk with Mr. William Watson,' by J.P. Collins. Contains a letter to William Watson dated 17 April 1892 [II.1079]

108 *The Pall Mall Gazette*, 9 May 1913, p. 8. 'George Meredith and National Service.' Letter to Seymour Trower dated 2 August 1905 [III.1538]

109 *The Sphere*, 2 August 1913, p. 152. Letter to C.K. Shorter dated 13 November 1908 [III.1676]

110 *Maggs Catalogue*, May–June 1913, No. 309, pp. 94–5. Letter to W.C. Bonaparte Wyse dated Esher, 23 July [1864] [1.276]

111 *Sotheby, Wilkinson and Hodge's Sale Catalogue*, 19 February 1913, p. 32. Three letters to George Stevenson dated 2 October 1890, 25 August 1891, and 12 April 1892 [II.1008, II.1042, II.1077]

112 Wise, Thomas J. *Letters from George Meredith to Edward Clodd and C.K. Shorter*, printed for Private Circulation, 1913. Two letters to C.K. Shorter dated 28 March 1891 and 1 April 1891 and one letter to Edward Clodd dated 27 March 1907 [II.1021, II.1022, III.1590]

1914

113 Carr, J. Comyns. *Coasting Bohemia*, 1914, p. 135, p. 139. Undated letter to Carr and letter dated 9 October 1878 [II.558, II.562]

1915

114 *The Morning Post*, 7 April 1915, p. 8. Letter to Chevalier Luigi Ricci dated 30 December 1907 [III.1621]

115 Harris, Frank. *Contemporary Portraits*, London, Methuen and Co. Ltd., 1915, pp. 181–99. Chapter on George Meredith contains an extract from a letter to the author

1916

116 Hake, Thomas and Compton-Rickett, Arthur. *The Life and Letters of Theodore Watts-Dunton*, London, T.C. and E.C. Jack, Ltd., 1916, Vol. I, pp. 278, 293; Vol. II, pp. 68–9, 138–9 [III.1283, III.1318, III.1393, III.1423]

117 *Anderson Galleries Catalogue*, 27–8 March 1916, p. 54. Letter to George Stevenson dated 2 October 1890 [II.1008]

118 *Anderson Galleries Catalogue*, 24–6 May, 1916, p. 77. Letter to W.C. Bonaparte Wyse dated 4 June 1881 [II.623]

1919

119 Butcher, Lady. *Memories of George Meredith*, London, Constable and Co., Ltd., 1919. Letters to Mrs. Brandreth and Miss Alice Brandreth, afterwards Lady Butcher, pp. 24, 30, 39, 47, 48, 54, 56, 63, 65, 67, 68, 70, 71, 73–5, 85–6, 88, 89, 101, 102, 105, 115, 118–23, 134, 138–41, 143–4, 144–5, 148 [I.511, I.512, I.516, I.518, I.528, I.529, I.531, I.536, II.558, II.683, II.686, II.718, II.764, II.780, II.787, II.794, II.795, II.833, II.915, II.925, II.1063, II.1118, III.1193, III.1201, III.1252, III.1365, III.1397, III.1401, III.1403, III.1404, III.1414, III.1474, III.1541, III.1459, III.1593, III.1602, III.1603, III.1613, III.1620, III.1641, III.1622]

120 *Maggs Catalogue*, 1919, No. 381, p. 125. Letter to Havelock Ellis dated 31 December 1886 [II.846]

1921

121 *The Bookman's Journal and Print Collector*, 11 March, p. 351. 'Notes on Private Collections No. 1: some books and MSS in the library of Dr. A.T. Rake.' Letter to William Michael Rossetti dated 27 June 1863 [I.206]

122 Colvin, Sir Sidney, *Memories and Notes of Persons and Places*, 1852–1912, London, Edward Arnold and Co., 1921, p. 183 [II.986]

123 *The Bookman's Journal*, October 1921, p. 2. 'Chapter from my Reminiscences' by C.K. Shorter. Letter to C.K. Shorter dated 17 May 1891 [II.1028]

1922

124 Forman, Maurice Buxton. *A Bibliography of the Writings of George Meredith*,

Edinburgh, 1922, pp. xxii, 7, 8, 98, 32, 87–8, 140 [I.1, I.3, I.5, I.6, I.9, I.10,
I.14, II.999, II.1074, II.1109, III.1467]

1923

125 *Sotheby, Wilkinson and Hodge's Sale Catalogue*, 26–8 March 1923, p. 21.
Letter to Francis H. Underwood dated 28 August 1893 [II.1141]

1924

126 Forman, Maurice Buxton. *Meredithiana*, Edinburgh, 1924, p. 307. Letter
to A.J. Scott [I.17]

1925

127 *Anderson Galleries Catalogue*, 27 April 1925, p. 22. Letter to Lady Morley
dated 4 October 1908 [III.1670]

128 Le Gallienne, Richard. *The Romantic Nineties*, New York, 1925, pp. 38,
47–50. Letters to Richard Le Gallienne dated 22 December 1891 and 21
December 1894 [II.1054, III.1181]

1926

129 Clodd, Edward. *Memories*, London, Chapman and Hall Ltd., 1926, p. 247.
Letter to the author dated Box Hill, 8 November 1905 [III.1545]

1927

130 Wise, Thomas James. *A Bibliography of the Writings in Prose and Verse of
Algernon Charles Swinburne*, London, William Heinemann Ltd., and New
York, Gabriel Wells, 1927, p. 43. Letter to Thomas Wise dated Box Hill,
Dorking, 23 April 1909, about the writing of Swinburne's *Laus Veneris*.
Same letter appeared in the private edition, London, Richard Clay and
Sons Ltd., 1919, p. 100 [III.1695]

1928

131 *Nineteenth Century*, 1928. 'Unpublished Letters of George Meredith,' by
R.E. Gordon George, pp. 150–2, 153–4, 155–62. Letters written on various
dates to Mlle. Hilda de Longueuil [II.840, II.844, II.851, II.853, II.855, II.861,
II.868, II.872, II.878, II.888]

132 Lucas, E.V. *The Colvins and their Friends*, New York, 1928, pp. 205–6.
Three letters to Sidney Colvin dated 5 July 1886, 22 October 1886, and
4 March 1892 [II.818, II.834, II.1071]

1929

133 Sencourt, Robert E. [R.E. Gordon George] *The Life of George Meredith*,
New York, Scribners and Sons, 1929, pp. 168–70, 235–9, 233–4, 229–30
[I.387, I.389, I.394, II.855, II.681, II.868, II.872, II.840, II.844]

134 HH the Dayang Muda of Sarawak. *Relations and Complications* (c. 1929),
pp. 51–2. Letters to Walter Palmer, Mrs. Palmer, and Gladys Palmer
dated 15 March 1893, 27 June 1894, and 19 May 1901 [II.1125, III.1161,
III.1390]

135 Burr, Ann Robeson. *Weir Mitchell: His Life and Letters*, New York, 1929, pp. 212–15. Letters to S. Weir Mitchell dated 2 April 1885, 27 July 1885, 23 June 1898, and 7 December 1907 [II.765, II.778, III.1301, III.1618]

1930

136 Ellis, S.M. *The Hardman Papers*, 1930, pp. 142, 302–3. Two Letters to William Hardman [I.307, I.383]

137 *Maggs Catalogue*, 1966, No. 902, p. 168. Two letters to Hamilton Aide dated 6 October 1898 and 21 November 1901 [III.1313, III.1407]

1931

138 *Altschul Catalogue*, 1931, pp. 26, 51–2. Two letters to Augustus Jessop and one to Frederic Chapman [I.579, I.663, I.666]

1933

139 Sturge Moore, T. and D.C. *Works and Days from the Journal of Michael Field*, 1933, pp. 66–7, 70–1, 73, 88–91, 109. Several letters to Michael Field and Katherine Bradley [II.962, II.1008, II.1073, II.1144, III.1214, III.1205, III.1341]

1937

140 Horvath, Eugene. *South Eastern Affairs*, 1937, p. 207. Letter to Ferenc Pulszky dated 30 June 1849 [I.4]

1945

141 *More Books: The Bulletin of the Boston Public Library*, October 1945, pp. 357–8. Letter to George Stevenson dated 12 September 1887. [II.886]

1949

142 Doughty, Oswald. *A Victorian Romantic: Dante Gabriel Rossetti*, 1949. Letter to William Michael Rossetti [I.469]

1953

143 Stevenson, Lionel. *The Ordeal of George Meredith*, New York, 1953. Various letters [I.1, I.15, I.71, I.131, I.329, I.353, I.375, I.451, I.453, I.465, I.474, I.477, I.485, I.539, I.546, II.742, II.743, II.837, II.838, II.850, II.872, II.876, II.878, II.999]

1954

144 Ivanyi, B.G. *TLS*, 12 November 1954. Letter to Ferenc Pulszky [I.4]

1958

145 McKay, George L. *A Stevenson Library: Catalogue of a Collection of Writings by and about Robert Louis Stevenson*, formed by Edwin J. Beinecke, New Haven, 1958. Letter to Robert Louis Stevenson dated 25 October 1884 [II.750]

1966

146 *Maggs Catalogue*, 1966, No. 902. Letter to 'Tudie' dated 7 January 1908 [III.1622]

147 Ellis, S.M. *George Meredith, His Life and Friends in Relation to His Work,* London, Grant Richards Ltd., 1920

148 *American Art Association Catalogue,* 8 February [n.y.] Letter to F.G. Aylward dated 21 January 1889 and one to William Tinsley [II.944, I.450]

149 *American Art Association Catalogue,* 2nd December [n.y.] Letter to George Moore dated 13 June 1889 [II.965]

150 Cline, C.L. *19th Century Fiction,* 'The Betrothal of George Meredith to Marie Vulliamy,' pp. 231–43, 235–6. One letter to Maxse and two to Hardman [I.259, I.262, I.274]

151 *Beinecke Catalogue,* pp. 1504–5. One letter to Robert Louis Stevenson dated 26 September 1885 and three to Mrs. Stevenson dated 12 October 1886, 15 October 1886, and 21 October 1886 [II.790, II.831, II.832, II.834]

PART III

The Poems

A Introductory Note to Part III

The description of volumes of poetry is not in format identical to that of the novels in Section I, partly because of the impending publication of Phyllis Bartlett's edition of the poems, partly because it is more important to distinguish between work published in volume form and that which was not, and partly because the structure of Meredith's publishing life as a poet does not correspond, except in broad outline, to his publishing life as a novelist.

Yale University Press is to publish an edition of the poems prepared by the acknowledged authority on the subject, the late Professor Bartlett, an edition which is to include information about the relationship of serial, manuscript and printed book, often with variants in each case. A reader needing information about a volume of poetry might reasonably turn to the bibliography; one seeking information about a single poem would naturally go the definitive edition. For this reason, a detailed discussion of the relationship of the manuscripts of individual poems to the printed version in a magazine or book has not been included.

There remained, however, the problem of identifying single poems. A 'census' of poems has been introduced to facilitate identification, a list which gives, for each poem, its first appearance in a magazine or paper and its first appearance in book form.

Meredith published his first volume of poetry (*Poems* 1851) at the age of twenty-one, his second (*Modern Love* 1862) eleven years later, long before his reputation as a novelist was firmly established. During these years he wrote much more poetry than he was able to publish: many poems had to be omitted from his first volume and later on in his life it becomes clear that he had continued to write poetry during the fifties. Another twenty years were to pass before the relative success of *The Tragic Comedians* and *The Egoist* allowed him to publish a further volume at his own expense. With characteristic determination, Meredith, now aged 55, began an association with Macmillan which allowed him to publish over the next few years, at his own expense, five volumes of poetry: *Poems and Lyrics* 1883, *Ballads and Poems of Tragic Life* 1887, *A Reading of Earth* 1888, *The Empty Purse* 1892, and *Modern Love, a Reprint* 1892. The publication dates give no indication of when the poems were actually written. Often they had been written thirty years or more before publication. Meredith told John Lane, for example, that the work in *Ballads and Poems* had been 'written about 37 years before publication.' Readers of the letters will notice that Meredith had considerable difficulty over the printing of these five volumes. Whatever the cause, whether Meredith who, feeling the luxury of publishing at his own expense, thought he could revise the poems to the last possible opportunity, or the printer who, dissatisfied with manuscript copy that had not been prepared for the Press, treated the work as job work not requiring his full attention, the books were in fact published with innumerable printers' errors, some of which were noted in cancels, errata slips, and re-issues, some of which were not. Since the poems published by Macmillan were included in later collected editions for which Meredith checked the copy, it is unfortunately the case that none of the Macmillan volumes is completely reliable. One of them, however, was relatively successful as a commercial venture: *Modern Love a Reprint* sold well and can be linked with the last novels in the group of works with which he finally made his reputation late in his life.

The North American issues of the volumes of poetry do not have the interest of those of the novels. Roberts Brothers of Boston distributed the books published by Macmillan, providing new prelims to unbound copies that had been printed in England. *Poems* 1851 and *Modern Love* 1862 were not published or issued in the States during this early period. Thus the average American reader, as distinct from those who, by their own initiative, acquainted themselves with the publications of other countries, would have become aware of Meredith as a poet at roughly the same time as the first collected edition became available from Roberts, that is in 1885.

At some point in the early eighteen-nineties, Meredith broke his long-standing arrangement with Chapman and Hall and began to be published by Constable, for whom his son by that time was working. In addition to the important volumes that appeared in three collected editions, Constable published six books of poetry during the last twelve years of Meredith's life: *Selected Poems* 1897, *Odes in Contribution to the Song of French History* 1898, *Poems Written in Early Youth* 1898, *Nature Poems* 1898, *A Reading of Life* 1901, and *Last Poems* 1909. Perhaps regrettably, a large part of this was opportunist publishing deriving from the work that had been done in preparation for Constable's first collected edition, the so-called de luxe edition begun in 1895. W.M. Meredith had in effect taken over from Colles as Meredith's agent and everything that could be published was. The later volumes of poetry were thus carried on the reputation Meredith had made for himself as a novelist.

Everything published by Constable was issued in North America by Scribner with the exception of *Nature Poems* 1898. Though the publications by Scribner were important in that they completed the process by which Meredith came to be known in the States, none of them is of textual significance. A few pirated American publications are of interest, however, notably Mosher's *Modern Love* 1891, and *Modern Love and Other Poems* 1898 – though they both lack the author's authority.

Within the over-all structure, there are only a few volumes that need special notice. There are variant bindings for *Modern Love* 1862, for example, but the different bindings do not signal variations of any other kind. Similarly there are variant re-issues of some of the volumes published by Macmillan but these always derive from mistakes that were made in the original printing. But such variants as exist have been noted in the appropriate place.

The volumes of poetry that were published as part of three collected editions are included in this section, partly because in the section on Collected Editions (Part IV) the contents of each volume are not specified in the detail that is required here, partly because it is the Collected Editions that provide the definitive texts of the poems as they were known in Meredith's lifetime. Further, a reader will as readily come across a single volume of poems in the format of one of the Collected Editions as one of the earlier, rarer volumes. The inclusion of the volumes from the Collected Editions also means that the checklist of titles which follows the Introductory Note can include every volume of poetry that appeared during Meredith's lifetime.

B Checklist of Titles

Table 1: Checklist of titles

BIBLIO-GRAPHY NUMBER	TITLE	ENGLISH PUBLICATION	AMERICAN PUBLICATION
XXXVI	POEMS	J.W. Parker 1851	
XXXVII	MODERN LOVE	Chapman & Hall 1862	Mosher 1891
XXXVIII	POEMS AND LYRICS OF THE JOY OF EARTH	Macmillan (Clay printing) 1883 (Clarke printing) 1883, 1894, 1895	Roberts 1883
XXXIX	BALLADS AND POEMS OF TRAGIC LIFE	Macmillan 1887, 1894, 1897	Roberts 1887
XL	A READING OF EARTH	Macmillan 1888, 1895	Roberts 1888
XLI	JUMP-TO-GLORY JANE	1889, 1892	
XLII	THE EMPTY PURSE	Macmillan 1892, 1895	Roberts 1892
XLIII	MODERN LOVE, A REPRINT	Macmillan 1892, 1894, 1895 Kennerley 1909	Roberts 1892 Mosher 1898, 1904
XLIV	SELECTED POEMS	Constable 1897, 1898, 1903, 1910, 1914	Scribner 1897
XLV	ODES IN CONTRIBUTION TO THE SONG OF FRENCH HISTORY	Constable 1898	Scribner 1898
XLVI	POEMS WRITTEN IN EARLY YOUTH	Constable 1898	Scribner 1898, 1909
XLVII	NATURE POEMS	Constable 1898, 1907	
XLVIII	POEMS: de luxe edition	Constable 1898	
XLIX	A READING OF LIFE	Constable 1901	Scribner 1901
XL	POEMS: pocket edition in two volumes	Constable 1903	
LI	MILTON	British Academy 1908	
LII	LAST POEMS	Constable 1909	Scribner 1909
LIII	CHILLIANWALLAH	Privately printed 1909	
LIV	LOVE IN A VALLEY	Constable 1909	Alderbrinck 1909 Mosher 1910
LV	TWENTY POEMS	Privately printed 1909	
LVI	POEMS: Memorial Edition	Constable 1910	Scribner
LVII	POETICAL WORKS	Constable 1912	

c Descriptions

XXXVI

POEMS

FIRST EDITION

POEMS: / BY / GEORGE MEREDITH. / EOS ! blest Goddess of the Morning, hear / The blind Orion praying on thy hill, / And in thy odorous breath his spirit steep / That he, the soft gold of thy gleaming hand / Passing across his heavy lids, sealed down / With weight of many nights / and night-like days / May feel as keenly as a new-born child, / And, through it, learn as purely to behold / The face of nature ... / His blind eyes wept. / R.H. Horne's "ORION." / [short rule] / LONDON: / JOHN W. PARKER AND SON, / WEST STRAND.

Collation [A]⁴B–K⁸ 84 leaves (13.0 x 8.2) [i–viii] [1] 2–159 [160]

Contents [i] halftitle: POEMS. [ii] blank [iii] titlepage [iv] imprint: LONDON / VIZETELLY AND COMPANY, PRINTERS, / FLEET STREET. [v] dedication: TO / THOMAS LOVE PEACOCK, ESQ. / THIS VOLUME / IS DEDICATED WITH THE PROFOUND ADMIRATION AND AFFECTIONATE / RESPECT OF HIS / SON-IN-LAW. / WEYBRIDGE, / MAY, 1851. [vi] blank [vii–viii] contents [1]–[160] text

Binding Spine, and boards at front and back, covered in dark green cloth with horizontal ribbing. Endpapers plain.

Front cover A blind-blocked design with border and ornamental device at centre on the plain background.

Spine One thick and one thin line stamped in gilt at top and bottom, between which, also stamped in gilt: POEMS / BY / GEORGE / MEREDITH

Back cover Identical to front cover.

Contents The Olive Branch 1; Love within the Lover's Breast 8; The Wild Rose and the Snowdrop 9; The Death of Winter 12; The Moon is Alone in the Sky 14; John Lackland 15; The Sleeping City 16; The Poetry of Chaucer 22; The Poetry of Spenser 22; The Poetry of Shakespeare 22; The Poetry of Milton 23; The Poetry of Southey 23; The Poetry of Coleridge 23; The Poetry of Shelley 24; The Poetry of Wordsworth 24; The Poetry of Keats 24; Violets 25; Angelic Love 26; Twilight Music 28; Requiem 30; The Flower of the Ruins 31; The Rape of Aurora 35; South-West-Wind in the Woodland 38; Will O' the Wisp 44; Fair and False 48; Two Wedded Lovers Watch'd the Rising Moon 49;

I Cannot Lose Thee for a Day 50; Daphne 51; Should Thy Love Die 74; London by Lamplight 75; Under Bows of Breathing May 82; Pastorals 84; Beauty Rohtraut 106; To a Skylark 108; Sorrows and Joys 109; The Flower Unfolds its Dawning Cup 111; Thou to Me Art Such a Spring 112; Antigone 113; Swathed Round in Mist and Crown'd with Cloud 116; No, No, the Falling Blossom is no Sign 118; The Two Blackbirds 119; July 122; I would I were the Drop of Rain 124; Come to Me in any Shape 125; Shipwreck of Idomeneus 127; The Longest Day 144; To Robin Redbreast 146; The Daisy Now is out upon the Green 148; Sunrise 150; Pictures of the Rhine 155; To a Nightingale 160.

PUBLICATION

The first mention of Meredith's first volume appears to be in 1849. On 8 March 1849 he summoned his courage to write to R.H. Horne: 'You are a Poet and a Critic, and from certain of your writings I understand your sympathies in either phase to be with the young Poet – As this is a fact seldom found even among literary men I have taken the liberty to address myself thus abruptly to you – I wish to lay before you certain Poems I have composed ...' (*Letters* I 1–2).

It was not until December of the same year, however, that he sent a collection or a selection of poems to J.W. Parker and a further year was to pass before Parker published some of them. A part of what was no doubt an extensive correspondence about this publication is reproduced in the early pages of Cline's first volume. Of note are those letters, to James Vizetelly, which indicate that Meredith acquired early the habit of making last-minute changes to what he had sent for publication.

> I received this morning from Mr. Horne the proofs of "Daphne" and the "Wild Rose and Snowdrop" and am waiting to correct them when you send me a copy – I enclose you three more poems – "The Olive Branch", "South West Wind in the Woodland" and "Will o' the Wisp". The rest shall shortly follow. Get these out of hand as soon as possible and I think there will be some chance of having the Poems out by the middle of next month – When I re-enclose the revised proofs to you do not make up any of the long slips into *pages* till the *order* in which they fall is settled –
>
> Can you let me know how many pages the poems altogether that I have now sent would make? – and whether you think there would be room for the "Shipwreck of Idomeneus"? [*Letters* I 11]

A copy of *Poems* in the Berg Collection of the New York Public Library, in which manuscript leaves of other poems – the poems that were not or could not be included in the 1851 publication, is described by Phyllis Bartlett in

'George Meredith: Early MS Poems in the Berg Collection' (*Bulletin of the New York Public Library*, LXI, pp. 396–415).

Not surprisingly, Meredith acquired a strong distaste for what he later regarded as juvenilia with direct relationship to his first marriage. In a letter to a Julian Marshall in 1891, for example, he dismissed them as not worth a second glance. A number of poems were reprinted in later volumes but the volume was not included in the Macmillan re-issues of the early nineties. Hardman, indeed, had reported – as early as 1862 in a letter to Holroyd – that Meredith had suppressed the book. 'Well, Sir, I knew that Meredith had published a volume of Poems in 1851, three hundred copies of which he afterwards destroyed' (*A Mid-Victorian Pepys*, p. 87).

XXXVII a

MODERN LOVE

FIRST EDITION

MODERN LOVE / AND / POEMS OF THE ENGLISH ROADSIDE, / WITH / *Poems and Ballads.* / BY / GEORGE MEREDITH, / AUTHOR OF 'THE SHAVING OF SHAGPAT,' / 'THE ORDEAL OF RICHARD / FEVEREL,' ETC. / LONDON: / CHAPMAN & HALL, 193, PICCADILLY. / 1862.

Collation [A]⁴B–O⁸P⁴ 112 leaves (17 × 10.8) [i]–viii [1]–216

Contents [i] halftitle: MODERN LOVE / AND / POEMS OF THE ENGLISH ROADSIDE. [ii] blank [iii] titlepage [iv] imprint: JOHN EDWARD TAYLOR PRINTER, / LITTLE QUEEN STREET, LINCOLN'S INN FIELDS. [v] dedication: *Affectionately Inscribed* / to / CAPTAIN MAXSE, R.N. [vi] blank [vii]–viii contents [1]–216 text, on 216: THE END. and at foot the imprint: JOHN EDWARD TAYLOR, PRINTER, / LITTLE QUEEN STREET, LINCOLN'S INN FIELDS.

Binding Spine, and boards at front and back, covered in dark green cloth with a bold, horizontal wavy grain.

Front cover Blind-stamped double border at all edges, otherwise plain.

Spine Stamped in gilt at top and bottom three horizontal bands, between which, also in gilt: Modern / Love Ec / [rule] / Geo Meredith / CHAPMAN & HALL

Back cover Identical to front cover.

Variant bindings John Carter has noted a number of variants. Arguing that it was not possible to distinguish between the variants in chronological terms, he said:

> Mr. Buxton Forman's description (p. 26) of the blocking and lettering on this book is accurate; but he mentions only one of the four varieties of cloth known to me, all dark green in colour. And since that which he describes, a bold wavy-grain (see Plate IIh and p. 65), has been regarded by some as being prior to any undescribed variants, it may be worth stating that the others I have seen are perfectly appropriate to the date of publication and, having exactly the same blocking and lettering, cannot be held on internal evidence to be any later. One of them is the wide bead-grain shown in Plate IIj; another is of a close-set embossed pattern based on a figure like the letter Y; a third is of similar style, but the pattern based on a rounded and indented lozenge. All these four cloths are of equally good quality and I believe there is nothing to choose between them.

Contents Grandfather Bridgeman 1; The Meeting 29; Modern Love 31; Juggling Jerry 85; The Old Chartist 92; The Beggar's Soliloquy 100; The Patriot Engineer 109; Cassandra 121; The Young Usurper 128; Margaret's Bridal-eve 129; Marian 143; The Head of Bran 145; By Morning Twilight 152; Autumn Even-song 154; Unknown Fair Faces 156; Phantasy 157; Shemselnihar 168; 'A Roar Through the Tall Twin Elm-Trees' 172; 'When I would Image' 174; 'I Chafe at Darkness' 176; By the Rosanna 178; Ode to the Spirit of Earth in Autumn 190; The Doe: A Fragment from 'Wandering Willie' 205.

PUBLICATION

The greater part of the sequence of poems called 'Modern Love,' as distinct from the other poems in this volume, was written during the winter of 1861-2. The first firm mention in the *Letters* is on 19 November 1861 and in January 1862, Meredith sent Frederick Maxse a portion of the proofs. 'I send you a portion of proofs of the "Tragedy of Modern Love." There are wanting to complete it, 13 more sonnets.' Phyllis Bartlett notes that the 36 poems in the Yale manuscript correspond, roughly, to the poems sent to Maxse (*Yale University Library Gazette*, volume 40, April 1966, number 4). Sonnet 10, probably, and the last 13 poems, almost certainly, were those written after Meredith's letter to Maxse in January 1862. The volume was published in May.

XXXVII b

PIRATED AMERICAN EDITION

MODERN LOVE BY / GEORGE MEREDITH / WITH FOREWORD BY /
E. CAVAZZA / PRINTED FOR THOMAS B. MOSHER AND / PUBLISHED
BY HIM AT 37 EXCHANGE / STREET PORTLAND MAINE MDCCCXCI

Collation [8]⁸ 64 leaves (25.0 x 12.5) [i–x] I–XIV [1–104]

Contents [i–ii] blank [iii] halftitle: MODERN LOVE / [short rule] / GEORGE
MEREDITH [iv] editorial note: NOTE. It may be interesting to recall the date of
the / volume of Meredith's verse, which includes *Modern Love.* / It was published in 1862, four years after William Morris' / *Defence of Guenevere,* and one
year later than Dante Gabriel / Rossetti's translations from the *Early Italian
Poets,* and / Algernon C. Swinburne's *Queen Mother and Rosamund –* / three
names which are of morning stars of modern poetry / singing together with
voices harmonious, yet distinct, / raining their influence upon the entire art of
contemporary / verse. [v] publisher's note: *Only Four Hundred copies of this
Small Paper / Edition (Post 8vo.) have been printed. Each / copy numbered, and the
type distributed. / No.* 222 [vi] blank [vii] titlepage [viii] blank [ix] flytitle:
FOREWORD [x] blank I–XIV foreword [1] flytitle: MODERN LOVE [2] epigraph:
This is not meat / For little people or for fools. / BOOK OF THE SAGES. [3–101] text
[102] blank [103] imprint: [rule] / PRESS OF BROWN THURSTON COMPANY
PORTLAND MAINE [104] blank

Binding The boards and spine are enclosed in a removable white paper wrapper
on the front cover of which is: MODERN LOVE BY / GEORGE MEREDITH / E. CAVAZZA
and on the spine: MODERN / LOVE / 1891

XXXVIII a

POEMS AND LYRICS OF THE JOY OF EARTH

FIRST EDITION

POEMS AND LYRICS / OF THE JOY OF EARTH / BY / GEORGE MEREDITH /
London / MACMILLAN AND CO. / 1883

Collation [A]⁴b²B–M⁸N⁴ 98 leaves (17.3 x 12.0) [i–ix] x–xi [xii] [1]–181 [182–
4]

Contents [i] blank [ii] advertisement: WORKS BY THE SAME AUTHOR / THE SHAV-

ING OF SHAGPAT: AN ARABIAN ENTERTAINMENT. / THE ORDEAL OF RICHARD FEVEREL. / EVAN HARRINGTON. / EMILIA IN ENGLAND. / VITTORIA. / BEAUCHAMP'S CAREER. / THE EGOIST. / &c., &c. / *Forthcoming Publications in Verse.* / POEMS. / THE SENTIMENTALISTS: A COMEDY. [iii] halftitle: POEMS AND LYRICS / OF THE JOY OF EARTH [iv] publisher's monogram [v] titlepage [vi] imprint: LONDON: / R. CLAY, SONS, AND TAYLOR, / BREAD STREET HILL, E.C. [vii] dedication: INSCRIBED TO / JAMES COTTER MORISON. / .... / *Antistans mihi milibus trecentis.* [viii] blank [ix]–xi contents [xii] blank [1]–181 text [182] blank [183] note on metres [184] blank

Binding Spine, and boards at front and back, covered in plain dark blue cloth. The endpapers have a design of clusters of five feather shapes on a background of small irregular circles printed in black on a blue-grey ground.

Front cover Plain.

Spine Stamped in gilt on plain cloth: POEMS / AND / LYRICS / GEORGE / MEREDITH / MACMILLAN & Co.

Back cover Plain.

Contents The Woods of Westermain 1; A Ballad of Past Meridian 28; The Day of the Daughter of Hades 30; The Lark Ascending 64; Phoebus with Admetus 71; Melampus 79; Love in the Valley 87; The Three Singers to Young Blood 101; The Orchard and the Heath 105; Martin's Puzzle 109; Earth and Man 115; A Ballad of Fair Ladies in Revolt 130; SONNETS Lucifer in Starlight 157; The Star Sirius 158; Sense and Spirit 159; Earth's Secret 160; The Spirit of Shakespeare 161; The Spirit of Shakespeare – *Continued* 162; Internal Harmony 163; Grace and Love 164; Appreciation 165; The Discipline of Wisdom 166; The State of Age 167; Progress 168; The World's Advance 169; A Certain People 170; The Garden of Epicurus 171; A Later Alexandrian 172; An Orson of the Muse 173; The Point of Taste 174; Camelus Saltat 175; Camelus Saltat – *Continued* 176; To J.M. 177; To a Friend Lost 178; My Theme 179; My Theme – *Continued* 180; Time and Sentiment 181.

XXXVIII b

SECOND EDITION

POEMS AND LYRICS / OF / THE JOY OF EARTH / BY GEORGE MEREDITH / *London* / MACMILLAN AND CO. / 1883

Collation [A]⁵B–M⁸N⁴ 97 leaves (17.3 × 12.0) [i–x] [1]–181

Contents [i] halftitle: POEMS AND LYRICS / OF / THE JOY OF EARTH [ii] publisher's

monogram [iii] titlepage [iv] imprint: *Printed by* R. & R. CLARK, *Edinburgh.*
[v] dedication: INSCRIBED TO / JAMES COTTER MORISON / .... / *Antistans mihi milibus trecentis* [vi] blank [vii]–ix contents [x] blank [1]–181 text [182] blank [183] notes on the metres of 'Phoebus with Admetus,' 'Melampus' and 'Love in the Valley' [184] blank
Between the endpapers and [i] is pasted in a leaf of advertisements. The recto is blank. On the verso: WORKS BY THE SAME AUTHOR / RICHARD FEVEREL. / EVAN HARRINGTON. / EMILIA IN ENGLAND. / VITTORIA. / BEAUCHAMP'S CAREER. / THE EGOIST. / ec. ec. / *Forthcoming publications in verse.* / POEMS. / THE SENTIMEN-TALISTS: A COMEDY.

Binding Spine, and boards at front and back, covered in plain dark blue cloth. The endpapers have a design of clusters of five feather shapes on a background of small irregular circles printed in black on a blue-grey ground.

Front cover Plain.

Spine Stamped in gilt on plain cloth: POEMS / AND LYRICS / GEORGE / MEREDITH / MACMILLAN & Co.

Back cover Plain.

PUBLICATION

It seems probable that many of the poems in *Poems and Lyrics of the Joy of Earth* were written in the spring of 1881, as Cline has noted (*Letters* II 618). Two years passed, however, before Meredith was ready to publish them. A letter (*Letters* II 696) indicates that he corrected proof in April 1883 and the volume was published on 7 June of the same year.
The printing was bungled. There are four versions of the first edition.

VERSION I

As printed, without the corrections that were made to Versions II, III, and IV.

VERSION II

As printed, but with a single correction. The misprint 'Revotl' on p. [ix] has been altered to 'Revolt.' Forman's note reads: 'A copy of this variety was sent by Meredith to G.W. Foote in Holloway Gaol and the foregoing particulars of it were furnished to me by Mr. W.T. Spencer who at one time held it. It is referred to in a letter from Meredith to Admiral Maxse dated July 20, 1883' (Forman p. 69). A copy of this version has not been inspected during the preparation of the present bibliography.

VERSION III

With 'Revotl' corrected and with a new leaf pasted on to the stub of the original pp. 63–4 which is torn or cut out. This second correction must have occurred before publication day, since Meredith's letter to Louisa Lawrence dated 6 June 1883 shows that she had been sent a copy of the book in proof and that Meredith therefore had to arrange for her to be sent the corrected pages. 'By this time you have received the corrected sheet of the poems and perhaps had the curiosity to notice the blunder. Who can fathom the depths of printers! No one can explain how such a hideous *gachis* was brought about. I regret that you will have some trouble in setting your book right' (*Letters* II 700). If the cancel were a last-minute correction, as the date of Meredith's letter to Louisa Lawrence indicates, Meredith's having in hand a copy of Version II to G.W. Foote would be easier to understand.

VERSION IV

With 'Revotl' corrected, the cancel inserted at pp. 63–4, and an errata slip inserted between pp. [xii] and 1. The errata slip reads as follows:

P. ix last line, *for* "Revotl" *read* "Revolt."
P. 19 line 10 from top, *for* "with" *read* "will."
P. 62 line 5 from bottom *for* "the" *read* "he."
P. 77 line 5 from bottom *for* "like" *read* "life."
P. 90 line 8 from bottom *for* "like" *read* "as."
P. 104 line 5 from bottom *for* "Immortal" *read* "Im'mortal," accent on first syllable.
P. 117 line 2 from bottom after "now" insert "———"
P. 162 line 6 from bottom *for* "show" *read* "show us."
P. 165 line 2 from bottom *for* "lead" *read* "read."

Probably this errata slip was not produced until a few weeks after publication, for it was on 26 June that Meredith seems to have protested about the shoddy printing. 'As to the enclosed, from Clay, I left the specially objectionable copy at your [Frederick Macmillan's] house, to be forwarded to him' (*Letters* II 702). One imagines Meredith had deposited a copy in which he had marked the corrections that resulted in the errata slip. Forman states that this version was 'on sale at the publisher's in September 1892 after the second edition printed by Messrs. R. and R. Clark in 1883, described hereafter, had gone out of print' (Forman p. 68).

Since two of these four versions existed before publication day and were replaced by the other two, it is a question of some nicety to decide whether they are all in fact versions of the first edition.

By 20 July 1883 Macmillan had agreed to have the volume re-printed at his own expense, presumably after a wrangle about the responsibility for the error. The result is described here as the second edition, though textually it is the same as a corrected version of the first edition. Macmillan must have forgotten what happened since in 1892 Meredith had to explain why he still had on hand copies of the book as printed by Clay. 'The cause for the rejection of Clay's printing is at pages 49–50, where you find the leaf omitted in the copy you sent and I return. The printers put two lines out of place, destroying the sense in two places. The pages were recast, and the leaf stuck in, but it had a slovenly effect, and it was decided to send the book to Clark. I fear that nothing can be done with the 250, except to sell them in America at 1/– if Americans will buy' (*Letters* II 1062–3).

XXXIX a

BALLADS AND POEMS OF TRAGIC LIFE

FIRST EDITION

BALLADS AND POEMS / OF / TRAGIC LIFE / BY / GEORGE MEREDITH / *London* / MACMILLAN AND CO. / AND NEW YORK / 1887 / *All rights reserved*

Collation [A]⁴B–L⁸ 84 leaves (17.5 × 12.2) [i–viii] [1]–160

Contents [i] blank [ii] publisher's note: *By the same Author.* / POEMS AND LYRICS OF THE JOY OF EARTH. / *Extra Fcap. 8vo. 6s.* / MACMILLAN AND CO. / 1883. / [rule] / *Forthcoming Volume.* / THE READING OF EARTH: / POEMS AND LYRICS. [iii] halftitle: BALLADS AND POEMS / OF / TRAGIC LIFE [iv] publisher's monogram [v] titlepage [vi] blank [vii] contents [viii] blank [1]–160 text, on 160 at centre: THE END and at foot: *Printed by* R. & R. CLARK, *Edinburgh*

Binding Spine, and boards at front and back, covered in dark blue cloth. The endpapers have a design of clusters of five feather shapes on a background of small irregular circles printed in black on a blue-grey ground.

Front cover Plain.

Spine Stamped in gilt: BALLADS / AND / POEMS / GEORGE / MEREDITH / MAC-MILLAN & CO.

Back cover Plain.

Contents The Two Masks 1; Archduchess Anne 3; The Song of Theodolinda 25; A Preaching from a Spanish Ballad 35; The Young Princess 42; King Harald's Trance 58; Whimper of Sympathy 63; Young Reynard 65; Manfred 67; Hernani 69; The Nuptials of Attila 70; Aneurin's Harp 101; France, December 1870 111; Men and Man 127; The Last Contention 129; Periander 133; Solon 143; Bellerophon 148; Phaethon 152; Notes 159.

XXXIX b

AMERICAN ISSUE

Ballads and Poems of Tragic Life was issued simultaneously in the United States by Roberts Brothers. The issue differs from the English first edition only in the following particulars:

Titlepage BALLADS AND POEMS / OF / TRAGIC LIFE / BY / GEORGE MEREDITH / ROBERTS BROTHERS / 3 SOMERSET STREET / BOSTON / 1887 *All rights reserved*

Binding Spine, and boards at front and back, covered in grey cloth with a bevelled edge.

Front cover Plain.

Spine Stamped in gilt: BALLADS / AND / POEMS / [ornament] / GEORGE / MEREDITH / 1887

XXXIX c

SECOND EDITION

The second edition is identical to the first and was printed from the same setting. It differs only in the titlepage, the binding, and its size. The titlepage reads:

BALLADS AND POEMS / OF / TRAGIC LIFE / BY GEORGE MEREDITH / *London* / MACMILLAN AND CO. / AND NEW YORK / 1894 / *All rights reserved*

The lettering on the spine reads:

BALLADS / AND / POEMS / GEORGE / MEREDITH / MACMILLAN

The leaves measure: 18.0 x 12.0
Though termed an edition, this book is in fact a new impression. There was a further re-issue in 1897.

XL a

A READING OF EARTH

FIRST EDITION

A READING OF EARTH / BY / GEORGE MEREDITH / *LONDON* / MACMILLAN AND CO. / AND NEW YORK / 1888 / *All rights reserved*

Collation [A]⁴B–I⁸K⁴ 87 leaves (17.6 × 11.3) [i–viii] [1]–136

Contents [i] blank [ii] blank [iii] halftitle: A READING OF EARTH [iv] publisher's monogram [v] titlepage [vi] blank [vii–viii (viii misnumbered vi)] contents [1]–136 text, at foot of 136 imprint: *Printed by* R & R CLARK, *Edinburgh*. Between [ii] and [iii] is glued in a leaf of publisher's advertisements the verso of which reads: *By the same Author.* / POEMS AND LYRICS OF THE JOY OF EARTH. / *Extra Fcap. 8vo. 6s.* / MACMILLAN AND CO. / 1883. / *Forthcoming Volume.* / THE EMPTY PURSE: / A SERMON TO OUR LATER PRODIGAL SON.

Binding Spine, and boards at front and back, covered in dark blue cloth. The endpapers have a design of clusters of five feather shapes on a background of small irregular circles printed in black on a blue-grey ground.

Front cover Plain.

Spine In gilt on the plain cloth: A / READING / OF / EARTH / GEORGE / MEREDITH / MACMILLAN

Back cover Plain.

Contents Seed-Time 1; Hard Weather 6; The South-Wester 14; The Thrush in February 23; The Appeasement of Demeter 35; Earth and a Wedded Woman 45; Mother to Babe 50; Woodland Peace 52; The Question Whither 55; Outer and Inner 58; Nature and Life 62; Dirge in Woods 64; A Faith on Trial 66; Change in Recurrence 105; Hymn to Colour 108; Meditation under Stars 116; Woodman and Echo 122; The Wisdom of Eld 125; Earth's Preference 127; Society 129; Winter Heavens 131; EPITAPHS M.M. 133; The Lady C.M. 133; J.C.M. 134; Islet the Dachs 134; Gordon of Khartoum 135; The Emperor Frederick of our Time 135; The Year's Sheddings 136.

PUBLICATION

This volume of poems was prepared during the summer and autumn of 1888, though many of the poems had been written earlier. On 22 October 1888, for example, Meredith told Louisa Lawrence: 'I am busy getting out a volume of

verse – *A Reading of Earth!*' (*Letters* II 934). The first edition was published on 20
December 1888 (Forman 84).

XL b

SUBSEQUENT EDITIONS

1 The first edition was published simultaneously in the States and distributed by
Scribner's. The copies inspected did not have the advertisements glued in, as in
the first edition described above.
2 A second edition was published by Macmillan in January 1895 (Forman 87).
W.M. Meredith had written to Frederick Macmillan on 19 November 1894 to
say: 'My father has decided that for the present at least he will not ask you to
reprint the *Reading of Earth* and *The Empty Purse* as he does not think the recent
sales justify him in doing so' (*Letters* III 1177). Meredith in fact agreed to the re-
publication of several volumes, however, as his son's letter of 31 May 1895 to
Frederick Macmillan indicates: 'In reply to yours of May 27, we are quite will-
ing that you should publish an edition of 500 *Modern Love* as you propose on the
same terms as arranged with regard to *The Empty Purse, Joy of Earth* and *Reading
of Earth*' (*Letters* III 1198).

XLI a

JUMP-TO-GLORY JANE

UNAUTHORISED LIMITED EDITION

JUMP-TO-GLORY JANE / A POEM / BY / GEORGE MEREDITH / LONDON /
1889

Collation 8 leaves (18.1 × 12.8) [1–3] 4–15 [16]

Contents [1] titlepage [2] publisher's note: *The following poem appeared in 'The
Universal Review'* / *for the 15th of October* 1889. *The present issue, privately* /
printed for friends, consists of fifty copies only. [3]–15 text [16] blank

Binding A white paper cover, sewn on.

Front cover As titlepage.

Back cover Plain.

XLI b

SECOND EDITION

(Not supervised by author)

JUMP TO GLORY JANE. / BY GEORGE MEREDITH. / EDITED AND
ARRANGED / BY HARRY QUILTER. / [publisher's device: a lion rampant
holding an anchor with dolphin entwined, round which is printed:
WITH FORTY- / FOUR / DE- / SIGNS IN- / VENTED, / DRAWN, AND /
WRITTEN] / BY LAWRENCE HOUSMAN. / SWAN, SONNEN- / SCHEIN &
CO. / PATERNOSTER / SQUARE, LONDON. 1892

Collation [A]⁸B⁸[C–D]⁸ 32 leaves (18.9 x 12.7) [1–7] 8–28 [29] 30–64

Contents [1] titlepage [2] publisher's note: *This edition is limited to an issue of
1,000 copies (250 of / which have been ordered by* MESSRS. MACMILLAN / AND CO. *for
the American market), and a special / issue of 100 copies on Van Gelder paper, bound
in / vellum and gold.* [3] dedication: TO THE RIGHT HON^BLE. JOHN MORLEY, /
SECRETARY OF STATE FOR IRELAND; / in profound admiration of his intellect as a
writer / and his honesty as a politician. Also in memory of / the days when
George Meredith's work found in the / pages of the "Fortnightly Review" that
welcome and / honour which were denied elsewhere: this book is / dedicated
by / HARRY QUILTER. [4] blank [5] contents [6] list of illustrations [7]–21 a
note on George Meredith's writing 22–8 a note on the birth, history, illustrations, and first reception of the poem [29]–64 text

The text of the poem is printed one stanza to each page. The pages are decorated.
The illustrations are not in the positions indicated in the list of illustrations (p.
[6]) but are arranged as follows:

I is the frontispiece and faces p. [1]; II faces p. 1; III faces p. 9; IV faces p. 12;
V faces p. 18; VI faces p. 24; VII faces p. 28; VIII faces p. 36;

Binding Spine, and boards at front and back, covered in stiff white paper.
Endpapers white.

Front cover All printed in brown: a two-lined border around the top, bottom
and five edges; three pictures of Jane jumping arranged diagonally from top left
to bottom right; and at top right: JUMP TO / GLORY / JANE / BY GEORGE /
MEREDITH and at bottom left: EDITED / WITH A NOTE BY / HARRY QUILTER

Spine Printed in brown: JUMP / TO / GLORY / JANE / GEORGE / MEREDITH /
ILLUSTRATED / BY L. HOUSMAN

Back cover Plain.

PUBLICATION

'Jump-to-Glory Jane' was first published in the *Universal Review* on 15 October 1889. Meredith's letter to William Sharp dated 29 July 1889 refers to the editor's bid for the poem.

Interest in the poem was renewed as a result of the unauthorized private printing described above. Probably because Mosher had pirated *Modern Love*, Meredith jumped to the conclusion that the poem had been printed by an American. 'I hear that the printing of my poem "Jump-to-Glory Jane" is an American piratical enterprise. A friend of mine here had the offer of one of the 50 copies (common paper) from his bookseller, for £5' (*Letters* II 1100). There is no clear evidence, however, that the booklet was produced in the States, and though Meredith became somewhat excited about the whole business, it is very likely what it claims to be, a private printing for friends.

A few years later Meredith made an informal copyright arrangement with Quilter, who had been editor of the *Universal Review* at the time the poem was published, whereby Meredith would be able to include the poem in a forthcoming volume, *The Empty Purse*, while Quilter could include it in a selection of poems previously published in the magazine. Quilter seems to have hurried to press, which mildly offended Meredith, since he smelled competition. 'We have no time to lose, and must have the book out,' he wrote in a letter to Frederick Macmillan, 'for in addition to the, as I find it to be, pirated American edition of "J-to-Glory Jane" ... Quilter, who applied to me for the right to include it in selected pieces for his magazine, now writes to say he has printed it singly with Illustrations' (*Letters* II 1100). Meredith wanted his book of poems, *The Empty Purse*, to come out before Christmas and chose this way to apply pressure on Macmillan. Towards Quilter he was being ungenerous: the separate printing of 'Jump-to-Glory Jane' had been proposed by the illustrator, Lawrence Housman.

XLII a

POEMS: THE EMPTY PURSE

FIRST EDITION

POEMS / THE EMPTY PURSE / WITH ODES TO THE COMIC SPIRIT / TO YOUTH IN MEMORY / AND VERSES / BY / GEORGE MEREDITH / *London* / MACMILLAN AND CO. / 1892

Collation [A]⁴B–I⁸K⁴ 72 leaves (17.7 × 11.8) [i–viii] [1]–136

Contents [i] blank [ii] publisher's notice: BY THE SAME AUTHOR / [short rule] / POEMS AND LYRICS OF THE JOY OF EARTH. / POEMS AND BALLADS OF TRAGIC LIFE. / A READING OF EARTH. / MODERN LOVE: A Reprint. Together with / THE SAGE ENAMOURED and THE HONEST LADY / [short rule] / MACMILLAN AND CO., LONDON. [iii] halftitle: POEMS [iv] publisher's mongram [v] titlepage [vi] blank [vii] contents [viii] blank [1]–136 text, on 136 at foot, imprint: *Printed by* R. & R. CLARK, *Edinburgh*

Binding Spine, and boards at front and back, covered in dark blue cloth. End-papers plain.

Front cover Plain.

Spine Stamped in gilt: THE / EMPTY / PURSE / GEORGE / MEREDITH / MACMILLAN & CO.

Back cover Plain.

Contents Wind on the Lyre 1; The Youthful Quest 2; The Empty Purse 4; Jump-to-Glory Jane 48; ODES To the Comic Spirit 69; Youth in Memory 92; VERSES Penetration and Trust 109; Night of Frost in May 111; The Teaching of the Nude 117; Breath of the Briar 120; Empedocles 122; To Colonel Charles 124; England before the Storm 130; Tardy Spring 133.

XLII b

AMERICAN EDITION

Poems: the Empty Purse was issued simultaneously by Roberts Brothers in Boston. The American issue differs from the English first edition in two particulars only:

1 The titlepage reads: POEMS / THE EMPTY PURSE / WITH ODES TO THE COMIC SPIRIT / TO YOUTH IN MEMORY / AND VERSES / BY / GEORGE MEREDITH / *Boston* / ROBERTS BROTHERS / 1892

2 *Binding* The spine, and boards at front and back, covered in grey cloth.

Front cover Plain.

Spine Stamped in gilt: THE / EMPTY / PURSE / [ornament] / GEORGE / MEREDITH

Back cover Plain.

XLIII a

MODERN LOVE, A REPRINT

FIRST EDITION

MODERN LOVE / A REPRINT / TO WHICH IS ADDED / The Sage Enamoured and the Honest Lady / BY / GEORGE MEREDITH / *London* / MACMILLAN AND CO. / AND NEW YORK / 1892 / *All rights reserved*

Collation [π]⁴A–F⁸G⁶ 58 leaves (16.1 x 11.1) [i–viii] [1]–107 [108]

Contents [i–ii] blank [iii] titlepage [iv] blank [v] dedication: TO / ADMIRAL MAXSE / IN CONSTANT FRIENDSHIP [vi] blank [vii] contents [viii] blank [1]–107 text [108] imprint at foot: Printed by T. and A. CONSTABLE, Printers to Her Majesty, / at the Edinburgh University Press.
In some copies there is an errata slip which reads:

Page 8, line 1, *for* what now the man *read* what now of the man.
Page 16, line 8, *for* they *read* thy.
Page 30, line 5 from foot of page, *for* aughed *read* laughed.
Page 61, line 2 from foot, *for* me *read* we.

Binding Spine, and boards at front and back, covered in dark blue cloth. End-papers a maiden hair pattern in black on a light blue background.

Front cover Plain.

Spine Stamped in gilt: MODERN / LOVE / GEORGE / MEREDITH / MACMILLAN & CO.

Variant binding As above but in red cloth with heavy brown endpapers.

Contents The Promise in Disturbance 1; Modern Love 3; The Sage Enamoured and the Honest Lady 69; 'Love is Winged for Two' 103; 'Ask, is Love Divine' 105; 'Joy is Fleet' 106; The Lesson of Grief 107.

AMERICAN ISSUE

The issue of *Modern Love, A Reprint* in the United States differs from the first edition in the following particulars only:

Titlepage MODERN LOVE / A REPRINT / TO WHICH IS ADDED / The Sage Enamoured and the Honest Lady / BY GEORGE MEREDITH / *Boston* / ROBERTS BROTHERS / 1892 / *All rights reserved*

XLIII b

PIRATED AMERICAN EDITION

MODERN LOVE / AND OTHER POEMS BY / GEORGE MEREDITH / [ornament] / Portland, Maine / THOMAS B. MOSHER / Mdcccxcviii

Collation [1–9]⁸[10]⁴ 78 leaves (18.0 x 9.5) [i–xii] 1–141 [143–4]

Contents [i–iv] blank [v] halftitle; *Old World Series* / [ornament] / MODERN LOVE / AND OTHER POEMS / [ornament] [vi] blank [vii] titlepage [viii] publisher's note: *This First Edition on Van Gelder paper consists of 925 copies* [ix (numbered v)–x] contents [xi] flytitle: MODERN LOVE [xii] epigraph: *This is not meat / For little people or for fools.* / BOOK OF THE SAGES. 1–141 text [142] imprint: PRINTED BY / SMITH & SALE / PORTLAND / MAINE [143–4] blank

Binding Spine, and boards at front and back, covered in Japanese vellum on board. Endpapers plain.

Front cover Stamped in brown an ornament within which, also stamped in brown, is: MODERN LOVE

Spine Stamped in brown: MOD- / ERN / LOVE / &c. / 1898

Back cover Plain.

Variant binding Some copies were issued with stiff paper covers, being in all other respects identical.

Contents FROM MODERN LOVE AND POEMS OF THE ENGLISH ROADSIDE WITH POEMS AND BALLADS (1862) I Modern Love 1; II The Meeting 53; FROM POEMS (1851) I South-West Wind in the Woodland 54; II PASTORALS I How Sweet on Sunny Afternoons 58; II Yon Upland Slope which Hides the Sun 60; III Now Standing on this Hedgeside Path 63; IV Lo! As a Tree, whose Wintry Twigs 64; V Now from the Meadow Floods the Wild Duck Clamours 65; VI How Barren would this Valley be 66; VII Summer Glows Warm on the Meadows 67; VIII Song: Spring 71; IX Song: Autumn 72; X Love in the Valley 73; FROM POEMS AND LYRICS OF THE JOY OF EARTH (1883) I The Woods of Westermain 77; II Melampus 93; III Love in the Valley 99; IV Lucifer in Starlight 107; V The Star Sirius 108; VI The Spirit of Shakespeare 109; FROM BALLADS AND POEMS OF TRAGIC LIFE (1887) I The Nuptials of Attila 111; II France, *December, 1870* 131.

Forman notes that this edition was re-issued in 1904 (Forman p. 32). Cline states that 'Mosher printed 400 small-paper copies on Van Gelder handmade paper and 40 large-paper copies on the same kind of paper' (*Letters* II 1056n).

PUBLICATION

Meredith had brooded over the possibility of a new and revised edition of *Modern Love*. Whether Mosher's pirated edition of 1891 precipitated the new edition is hard to determine. At all events he published this one, like the others that he had placed with Macmillan, at his own expense. This fact perhaps explains the peremptory tone of his letters to Frederick Macmillan, including the one dated 16 November 1891:

> Herewith Proofs of *Modern Love* for Press.
> I think you may advise the printers to roll off the remaining sheets *at once*.
> No copy is to be sent out for review.
> The title of the book is
>> *Modern Love: a Reprint*
>>> *To which is added, The Sage Enamoured and the Honest Lady*.
> Advertise to the amount of £15, as with the foregoing volumes, and only in the *Athenaeum*, the *Anti-Jacobin*, the *Pall Mall Gazette*, and your own publications (*Letters* II 1049).

Meredith throughout his life regarded the proofs as sheets produced for his own convenience, which he might give to his friends and on which he might do further work of a kind altogether unanticipated when the poems were first sent to the printers. In no sense did he prepare his early poems for the press and, on one occasion, for example, is perplexed when the printer states he lacks copy for the prelims. The printers for their part do not appear to have served him well, being as perplexed by the poems in manuscript as many readers are by the poems in print. On this occasion, Meredith once again had difficulties. He wrote to Frederick Macmillan on 2 January 1892:

> I do not remember to have seen so laughable a Title-Page. I must have a Revise of it.
> Also Revise of the pages containing the Lyrics. The printers have omitted them in the Contents, and evidently are to be trusted in nothing (*Letters* II 1056).

A month later, still complaining about 'gratuitous ghastly printers' errors,' he asks for an errata slip to be inserted in unbound copies. The book had been published a few days earlier, on 26 January 1892.

It should be mentioned, perhaps, in mitigation of the querulous tone in these and other letters written at the same time, that Meredith was seriously ill while this particular volume was going through the press.

Modern Love, a Reprint sold well and resulted in renewed interest in Meredith as a poet, though he himself referred to his work as 'poetical matter, not poems.'

Subsequent reissues of the book in 1894 and 1895 were called the second and third editions although the only change was to the titlepage.

Buxton Forman noted that this version of the poem 'Modern Love' was printed privately by Mitchell Kennerley for his friends but not sold. It has not proved possible to inspect a copy of his book and Forman's description is therefore produced verbatim.

> In 1909 Mr. Mitchell Kennerley issued the revised version of *Modern Love* in a very small edition as gifts to his friends. No copies were sold. The title-page reads: –

> > Modern / Love / George Meredith / The Introduction / by / Richard Le Gallienne / [*Publisher's monogram*] MK / New York / Mitchell Kennerley / 1909

> > This is a medium octavo book of 74 unnumbered pp. with a frontispiece portrait of Meredith. It is printed on handmade cream laid paper and issued with top edges gilt and others uncut in ornate gold and white paper boards with lilac coloured silk back and a silk label on the front cover on which is stamped *Modern / Love* in bold gold letters. The following note appears on the verso of the title-page: –

> > > The portrait by Joseph Simpson, the introduction by Richard Le Gallienne, and the decorations by Frederic W. Goudy are copyright 1909 by Mitchell Kennerley, and must not be reproduced.

XLIV a

SELECTED POEMS

FIRST EDITION

SELECTED POEMS / BY / GEORGE MEREDITH / WESTMINSTER / ARCHIBALD CONSTABLE AND CO. / 2 WHITEHALL GARDENS / 1897

Collation [π]⁴A–P⁸Q³ 127 leaves (18.0 × 13.0) [i–viii] [1]–245 [246]

Contents [i] halftitle: SELECTED POEMS / BY / GEORGE MEREDITH [ii] blank [iii] titlepage [iv] imprint: Edinburgh: T. and A. CONSTABLE, Printers to Her Majesty [v]–vii contents [viii] publisher's note: *The selection here made has / been under the supervision of / the Author* [1]–245 text [246] imprint: Printed by T. and A. CONSTABLE, Printers to Her Majesty / at the Edinburgh University Press [247–62] publisher's advertisements, including notice of 'The New Popular Edition,' separately paged 1–16

In some copies inspected there were only two pages of advertisements.

Binding Spine, and boards at front and back, covered in light brown calico cloth. Endpapers plain.

Front cover Plain.

Spine Stamped in gilt: Selected / Poems / George / Meredith / *Constable* / *Westminster*

Back cover Plain.

Contents Woodland Peace 1; The Lark Ascending 3; The Orchard and the Heath 9; Seed-time 12; Outer and Inner 15; Wind on the Lyre 18; Dirge in Woods 19; Change in Recurrence 20; Hard Weather 22; The South-Wester 27; The Thrush in February 33; Tardy Spring 42; Breath of the Briar 45; Young Reynard 46; Love in the Valley 47; Marian 61; Hymn to Colour 63; Mother to Babe 69; Night of Frost in May 71; Whimper of Sympathy 75; A Ballad of Past Meridian 76; Phoebus with Admetus 77; Melampus 83; The Appeasement of Demeter 92; The Day of the Daughter of Hades 100; The Young Princess 127; The Song of Theodolinda 139; The Nuptials of Attila 147; Penetration and Trust 173; Lucifer in Starlight 175; The Star Sirius 176; The Spirit of Shakespeare 177; The Spirit of Shakespeare *continued* 178; The World's Advance 179; Earth's Secret 180; Sense and Spirit 181; Grace and Love 182; Winter Heavens 183; Modern Love 184; Juggling Jerry 188; The Old Chartist 194; Martin's Puzzle 201; A Ballad of Fair Ladies in Revolt 207; The Woods of Westermain 225

XLIV b

AMERICAN EDITION

SELECTED POEMS BY / GEORGE MEREDITH / NEW YORK / CHARLES SCRIBNER'S SONS / 1897

Collation [1⁶2–17⁸] 134 leaves (17.5 x 12.0) [1–2] [i–iv] v–vii [viii–x] 1–249 [250–6]

Contents [i–ii] blank [iii] titlepage [iv] copyright statement: Copyright, 1897, by / GEORGE MEREDITH v–vii contents [viii] publisher's note: The selection here made has / been under the supervision / of the Author [ix] halftitle: SELECTED POEMS BY / GEORGE MEREDITH [x] blank 1–249 text [250] imprint: [a device of scroll and tapes] / THE DE VINNE PRESS [251–6] blank

Binding Spine, and boards at front and back, covered in apple green cloth. Endpapers plain white.

Front cover Stamped in gilt a border 6 mm. from all edges with the initials 'MA' in bottom right corner. Towards the top of the rectangle created by the border, also stamped in gilt, a device consisting of leaves, scrolls, branches, and grapes within which is: POEMS / BY / GEORGE / MEREDITH

Spine Stamped in gilt at top and bottom the same border as on the front cover between which: [device of leaves and grapes] / POEMS / BY / GEORGE / MEREDITH / [device] / SCRIBNERS
Though the table of contents is identical to that of Constable's *Selected Poems*, 1897, the poems were in fact reset for Scribner.

Contents Woodland Peace 1; The Lark Ascending 3; The Orchard and the Heath 9; Seed-Time 12; Outer and Inner 15; Wind on the Lyre 18; Dirge in Woods 19; Change in Recurrence 20; Hard Weather 22; The South-Wester 28; The Thrush in February 35; Tardy Spring 44; Breath of the Briar 47; Young Reynard 48; Love in the Valley 49; Marian 61; Hymn to Colour 63; Mother to Babe 69; Night of Frost in May 71; Whimper of Sympathy 75; A Ballad of Past Meridian 76; Phoebus with Admetus 78; Melampus 84; The Appeasement of Demeter 92; The Day of the Daughter of Hades 100; The Young Princess 128; The Song of Theodolinda 140; The Nuptials of Attila 148; Penetration and Trust 175; Lucifer in Starlight 177; The Star Sirius 178; The Spirit of Shakespeare 179; The Spirit of Shakespeare–*continued* 180; The World's Advance 181; Earth's Secret 182; Sense and Spirit 183; Grace and Love 184; Winter Heavens 185; Modern Love 186; Juggling Jerry 190; The Old Chartist 197; Martin's Puzzle 204; A Ballad of Fair Ladies in Revolt 210; The Woods of Westermain 227.

PUBLICATION

The *Selected Poems* was published in September 1897. W.M. Meredith's letter of 28 October 1896 to Frederick Macmillan indicates that the selection did in fact have the blessing of the author.

The edition was re-issued by Constable in April 1898, February 1903, September 1910, and March 1914.

XLV

ODES IN CONTRIBUTION TO THE
SONG OF FRENCH HISTORY

FIRST EDITION

ODES / IN CONTRIBUTION / TO THE SONG / OF FRENCH / HISTORY / BY / GEORGE MEREDITH / WESTMINSTER / ARCHIBALD CONSTABLE AND CO / 2 WHITEHALL GARDENS / 1898

Collation [A]⁴B–F⁸G⁷ 59 leaves (19.4 x 11.5) [i–viii] 3–94 [1]–16

Contents [i] halftitle: ODES / IN CONTRIBUTION TO THE SONG OF / FRENCH HISTORY [ii] blank [iii] titlepage [iv] printer's imprint: BUTLER & TANNER, / THE SELWOOD PRINTING WORKS, / FROME, AND LONDON. [v] dedication: *IN-SCRIBED TO THE / RIGHT HON. JOHN MORLEY, M.P.* [vi] blank [vii] contents [viii] blank [1]–94 text 94 imprint at foot: [short rule] / Butler & Tanner, The Selwood Printing Works, Frome, and London. [95]–[110] publisher's advertisements, separately numbered [1]–16

Binding Spine, and boards at back and front, covered in deep yellowish brown buckram. Endpapers plain white.

Front cover Plain.

Spine Stamped in gilt: Odes / in Contribution / to / the Song of / French / History / George / Meredith / Constable / Westminster

Back cover Plain.

Contents The Revolution 1; Napoleon 19; France, December, 1870 [a Reprint] 53; Alsace-Lorraine 67

PUBLICATION

Meredith seems to have begun to write the three new poems in this volume during the winter of 1896–7, since on 2 December 1896, after a period in which he had been preoccupied with the preparation of Constable's de luxe edition, he wrote: 'I am at work, a Series of Three Odes. The First, "The French Revolution", is done. I am midway in the "Napoleon". The Third is "Alsace-Lorraine". You will catch the idea in the sequence. It is History – my view; and I make History sing! Clio in Calliope' (*Letters* III 1252). A similar letter is addressed to Greenwood on 28 December 1896 (Letters III 1254). Though they were not published in *Cosmopolis* until the spring of 1898, they must have been finished a year earlier, since on 6 March 1897 he told W.S. McCormick: 'Look in *Cosmopolis* in a month or two for an Ode, "The French Revolution", to be followed by "Napolean", and "Alsace-Lorraine". You may like them. I hope to have made History sing, and under sanction of philosophy' (*Letters* III 1261).

It is difficult to know whether or not to attach importance to Meredith's letter of 30 November (1897) to Watts-Dunton, in which he said that he had 'just completed three Odes ...' It may be that the normal, or rather inevitable, process of revision had occupied the intervening months; the very addition of a typescript stage gave Meredith in the latter part of his life a further pretext for emendation. On the other hand, he may simply have been justifying himself to Swinburne when he said in the same sentence that he felt 'for the moment empty' (*Letters* III 1283). Although when Meredith wrote to Morley to ask permission to dedicate the volume to his old friend (*Letters* III 1303) he expected it to be published in September, it was not in fact published until 21 October 1898.

XLVI

POEMS WRITTEN IN EARLY YOUTH

FIRST EDITION

POEMS / WRITTEN IN EARLY YOUTH / (published in 1851) / POEMS FROM 'MODERN LOVE' / (first edition) / AND / SCATTERED POEMS / BY / GEORGE MEREDITH / [ornament] / LONDON / CONSTABLE AND COMPANY LTD. / 1909

Collation [π]⁴A–R⁸ 140 leaves (19.2 x 12.5) [i]–viii [1]–269 [270–2]

Contents [i] halftitle: POEMS WRITTEN IN EARLY YOUTH / POEMS FROM 'MODERN LOVE' / AND SCATTERED POEMS [ii] blank [iii] titlepage [iv] blank v–viii contents [1]–269 text, with imprint on 269: [rule] / Printed by T. and A. CONSTABLE, Printers to His Majesty / at the Edinburgh University Press [270–2] blank

Binding Spine, and boards at front and back, covered in sandy brown buckram. Endpapers plain.

Front cover Plain.

Spine Blindstamped in gilt: Poems / Written / in / Early Youth / George / Meredith / *Constable* / *London*

Back cover Plain.

Contents POEMS WRITTEN IN EARLY YOUTH (POEMS 1851): The Olive Branch 3; Song 9; The Wild Rose and the Snowdrop 10; The Death of Winter 13; Song 15; John Lackland 16; The Sleeping City 17; The Poetry of Chaucer 22;

The Poetry of Spenser 23; The Poetry of Shakespeare 23; The Poetry of Milton 24; The Poetry of Southey 24; The Poetry of Coleridge 25; The Poetry of Shelley 25; The Poetry of Wordsworth 26; The Poetry of Keats 26; Violets 27; Angelic Love 28; Twilight Music 30; Requiem 32; The Flower of the Ruins 34; The Rape of Aurora 38; South-West Wind in the Woodland 40; Will o' the Wisp 45; Song 48; Song 49; Song 50; Daphne 51; Song 70; London by Lamplight 72; Song 78; Pastorals 80; Song – Spring 93; Song – Autumn 94; Love in the Valley 95; Beauty Rohtraut 100; To a Skylark 102; Sorrows and Joys 103; Song 105; Song 106; Antigone 107; Song 111; The Two Blackbirds 112; July 115; Song 117; Song 118; The Shipwreck of Idomeneus 120; The Longest Day 135; To Robin Redbreast 137; Song 139; Sunrise 141; Pictures of the Rhine 145; To a Nightingale 149; POEMS FROM 'MODERN LOVE' (FIRST EDITION) Grandfather Bridgeman 153; The Meeting 172; The Beggar's Soliloquy 173; Cassandra 179; The Young Usurper 184; Margaret's Bridal-eve 185; The Head of Bran the Blest 193; By Morning Twilight 197; Autumn Even-Song 198; Unknown Fair Faces 199; Phantasy 200; Shemselnihar 207; A Roar through the Tall Twin Elm-Trees 210; When I would Image 211; I Chafe at Darkness 212; By the Rosanna: To F.M. 213; Ode to the Spirit of Earth in Autumn 214; The Doe: A Fragment 223; SCATTERED POEMS To Alex Smith, the 'Glasgow Poet' 233; Chillianwallah 234; Invitation to the Country 236; The Sweet o' the Year 238; The Song of Courtesy 240; The Three Maidens 243; The Crown of Love 245; Lines to a Friend Visiting America 247; On the Danger of War 256; To Cardinal Manning 257; To Children: For Tyrants 258; A Stave of Roving Tim 262; On Hearing the News from Venice 267; The Riddle for Men 268

PUBLICATION

As far as can be gathered, *Poems Written in Early Youth* was a piece of opportunist publishing for which no doubt W.M. not G.M. Meredith was largely responsible. Certainly Meredith had written to Frederick Macmillan many years earlier to disclaim any intention of publishing his early work again. 'I hear also of English publishers who are on the look-out for the legal term to elapse (40 years) when they intend to issue my first volume of Poems – written when I was twenty-one. I fairly hoped the book was dead. I suppose there is nothing for me to do but reprint a certain number of them – and it will be exceedingly distasteful to me, a bitter choice of evils' (*Letters* II 1082).

The volume in fact contains the whole of *Poems 1851*, although corrections have been made and some of the poems are simply called 'Song,' the original title having been dropped. It also contains all the poems from *Modern Love and Poems of the English Roadside*, with *Poems and Ballads*, 1862, except 'Modern Love,' 'Juggling Jerry,' 'The Old Chartist,' 'The Patriot Engineer,' and 'Marian'; the poems called 'Scattered Poems' were also published in the edition de luxe; the 'Sonnet to Alex Smith,' and 'Chillianwallah.' In short it is a gathering of minor poems from the period which preceded that in which Meredith's reputation was made.

The book was published simultaneously by Scribner. The contents of the English and American issues are identical. The binding of the American issue is in plain, dark blue cloth on boards.

Front cover Stamped in gilt on plain background, Meredith's signature.

Spine Stamped in gilt: POEMS / WRITTEN / IN EARLY / YOUTH / GEORGE / MEREDITH / SCRIBNERS

Back cover Plain.

XLVII a

THE NATURE POEMS

FIRST EDITION

THE / NATURE POEMS / OF / GEORGE MEREDITH / WITH / 20 FULL-PAGE PICTURES / IN PHOTOGRAVURE / BY / WILLIAM HYDE / [ornament consisting of G.M. intertwined with stylized vines, leaves, and pomegranates] / *Westminster* / ARCHIBALD CONSTABLE AND CO. / 2 WHITEHALL GARDENS / 1898

Collation $[\pi]^4$A–D^{8}E^6 42 leaves (25.4 x 15.5) [i–viii] 1–[76]

Contents [i] blank [ii] certificate of issue: Of this Edition 375 copies have been printed / of which this is / No xv [iii] halftitle: THE NATURE POEMS / OF / GEORGE MEREDITH [iv] blank [v] titlepage [vi] blank [vii] contents [viii] blank 1–[76] text, with at foot of [76] imprint: Edinburgh: T. and A. CONSTABLE, Printers to Her Majesty

Binding Spine, and boards at front and back, covered in ivory buckram. Endpapers plain.

Front cover Stamped in gilt at lower right hand corner, Meredith's signature.

Spine Stamped in gilt: THE / NATURE / POEMS / OF / GEORGE / MEREDITH / *Illustrations* / *by* / *William* / *Hyde* / *Constable* / *Westminster*

Back cover Plain.

Illustrations There are twenty illustrations reproduced in photogravure by the Swan Electric Engraving Co. from drawings by William Hyde. Each is separated from the text by a layer of thin tissue and is pasted onto a stub which has been sewn in. The illustrations are between pp. [viii] and 1, 4 and 5, 8 and 9, 12 and 13, 16 and 17, 20 and 21, 22 and 23, 24 and 25, 26 and 27, 28 and 29, 32 and 33, 34 and 35, 36 and 37, 40 and 41, 44 and 45, 52 and 53, 56 and 57, 58 and 59, 60 and 61, 68 and 69.

Contents Woodland Peace 1; The Lark Ascending 3; The Orchard and the Heath 8; Seed-Time 11; Outer and Inner 14; Dirge in Woods 16; Change in Recurrence 17; Hard Weather 19; The South-Wester 23; The Thrush in February 28; Tardy Spring 35; Breath of the Briar 37; Love in the Valley 38; Hymn to Colour 50; Night of Frost in May 55; Winter Heavens 59; The Woods of Westermain 60

PUBLICATION

The Nature Poems was published in July 1898 at the price of two and a half guineas. According to the Prospectus, 350 copies were printed, 25 of which were presentation copies. Forman notes (*Meredithiana* p. 7) that the first edition was also issued in a larger format. Forman's description reads as follows:

Printed on handmade paper and issued with untrimmed edges. The leaves measure 11 x 7½ inches. Bound in grey paper boards with vellum back and white endpapers. The lettering on the back is the same as that of the ordinary issue, and on the front cover there is a panel measuring 3⅞ x 3, with the wording *The Nature Poems Of / George Meredith / Illustrations by William Hyde* above a conventional tulip design. The panel is in gold and is initialled "L.H."

The Certificate of Issue reads, – *Of this Edition 150 copies have been printed / of which this is / No..... and is signed in pencil "William Hyde".*

XLVII b

SECOND EDITION

THE / NATURE POEMS / OF / GEORGE / MEREDITH / [ornament] / WITH SIXTEEN FULL-PAGE / PICTURES IN PHOTOGRAVURE / BY WILLIAM HYDE / LONDON / ARCHIBALD CONSTABLE & CO. LTD. / 1907

Collation [A]⁴B–F⁸ 44 leaves (25.3 x 16.0) [i–viii] [1–4] 5–75 [76–80]

Contents [i] halftitle: THE NATURE POEMS OF / GEORGE MEREDITH / [ornament] [ii] blank [iii] titlepage [iv] imprint: CHISWICK PRESS: CHARLES WHITTINGHAM AND CO. / TOOKS COURT, CHANCERY LANE, LONDON. [v] contents [vi] blank [vii] list of illustrations [viii] blank [1] printer's device, a lion rampant holding an anchor with a dolphin around the shaft contained within an oval frame of acorns and oak leaves and resting on the monogram of CW, beneath which is the imprint: CHISWICK PRESS: CHARLES WHITTINGHAM AND CO. / TOOKS COURT, CHANCERY LANE, LONDON. [2–4] blank 5–[76] text [77–80]

Binding Spine, and boards at front and back, covered in light blue cloth. Endpapers white.

Front cover Stamped in gilt within a rectangular frame two rows of flowers at the top and six rows of flowers at the bottom, between which, also stamped in gilt: THE NATURE POEMS OF / GEORGE MEREDITH / ILLUSTRATIONS BY WILLIAM HYDE

Spine Stamped in gilt: [rule] / THE / NATURE / POEMS / OF / GEORGE / MEREDITH / ILLUSTRATIONS / BY / WILLIAM / HYDE / [ornament] / CONSTABLE / LONDON

Back cover Plain.

Illustrations The sixteen illustrations are between pp. [ii and iii], [viii and 1], 10 and 11, 12 and 13, 24 and 25, 26 and 27, 28 and 29, 32 and 33, 34 and 35, 36 and 37, 38 and 39, 42 and 43, 50 and 51, 54 and 55, 60 and 61, 64 and 65.

Contents Identical to those of the first edition.

PUBLICATION

Forman notes (*Meredithiana* p. 28): 'Some copies were issued in blue cloth boards gilt and sold at 12s. 6d. net each, and some in vegetable parchment gilt at 15s. net.'

XLVIII

POEMS

DE LUXE COLLECTED EDITION OF 1896-1911

THE WORKS OF / GEORGE MEREDITH / VOLUME XXIX / [floral device with pomegranates within which Meredith's initials are entwined] / WESTMINSTER / ARCHIBALD CONSTABLE AND CO. / 2 WHITEHALL GARDENS / 1898

VOLUME I

Collation [π]⁸A–P⁸Q² 126 leaves (22.0 x 14.5) [i–xviii] 1–233 [234–6]

Contents [i] blank [ii] publisher's note: This Edition is limited to / one thousand and twenty-five copies / all numbered / No ... [iii] halftitle: THE WORKS OF / GEORGE MEREDITH / POEMS / I [iv] blank [v] titlepage [vi] copyright statement: Copyright in the /United States of America by / George Meredith, 1898 [vii] flytitle: POEMS / VOLUME / I [viii] blank [ix–xv] contents [xvi] blank 1–233 text [234] imprint: EDINBURGH: T. and A. CONSTABLE, Printers to Her Majesty [235–6] blank

Binding See main entry.

VOLUMES II, III, and IV

The internal arrangement of the other three volumes is the same as in Volume I. The prelims are identical. Only the contents are different and these are indicated in the tables of contents which follow.

Contents of Volume I
MODERN LOVE
The Promise in Disturbance 5; Modern Love, 7–56; I By this he knew she wept with waking eyes: 7; II It ended, and the morrow brought the task. 8; III This was the woman; what now of the man? 9; IV All other joy of life he strove to warm, 10; V A message from her set his brain aflame. 11; VI It chanced his lips did not meet her forehead cool. 12; VII She issues radiant from her dressing-room, 13; VIII Yet it was plain she struggled, and that salt 14; IX He felt the wild beast in him between whiles 15; X But where began the change; and what's my crime? 16; XI Out in the yellow meadows, where the bee 17; XII Not solely that the Future she destroys, 18; XIII 'I play for Seasons; not Eternities!' 19; XIV What soul would bargain for a cure that brings 20; XV I think she sleeps: it must be sleep, when low 21; XVI In our old shipwrecked days there was an hour, 22; XVII At dinner, she is hostess, I am host. 23; XVIII Here Jack and Tom are paired with Moll and Meg. 24; XIX No state is enviable. To the luck alone 25; XX I am not of those miserable males 26; XXI We three are on the cedar-shadowed lawn; 27; XXII What may the woman labour to confess? 28; XXIII 'Tis Christmas weather, and a country house 29; XXIV The misery is greater, as I live! 30; XXV You like not that French novel? Tell me why. 31; XXVI Love ere he bleeds, an eagle in high skies, 32; XXVII Distraction is the panacea, Sir! 33; XXVIII I must be flattered. The imperious 34; XXIX Am I failing? For no longer can I cast 35; XXX What are we first? First, animals; and next 36; XXXI This golden head has wit in it. I live 37; XXXII Full

Contents of Volume II

Contents of Volume III

Contents of Volume IV

XLIX

A READING OF LIFE

FIRST EDITION

A READING OF LIFE / WITH OTHER POEMS / BY GEORGE MEREDITH / WESTMINSTER / ARCHIBALD CONSTABLE & CO LTD / 2 WHITEHALL GARDENS / 1901

Collation [A]⁴B–I⁸ 68 leaves (19.5 × 12.6) [i]–viii 1–[128]

Contents [i] blank [ii] blank [iii] halftitle: A READING OF LIFE [iv] blank [v] titlepage [vi] imprint: BUTLER & TANNER, / THE SELWOOD PRINTING WORKS, / FROME, AND LONDON. vii–viii contents 1–[128] text 43–4 blank 106 blank 107 flytitle: FRAGMENTS OF THE ILIAD / IN ENGLISH HEXAMETER VERSE 108 blank 128 imprint at foot: [short rule] / Butler & Tanner, The Selwood Printing Works, Frome, and London.

Binding Spine, and boards at front and back, covered in deep yellowish brown buckram. Endpapers plain white.

Front cover Plain.

Spine Stamped in gilt: A Reading / of Life / George / Meredith / *Constable* / *Westminster*

Back cover Plain.

Contents A READING OF LIFE The Vital Choice 1; With the Huntress 3; With the Persuader 8; The Test of Manhood 28; The Cageing of Ares 45; The Night-Walk 55; The Hueless Love 60; Song in the Songless 63; Union in Desseverance 64; The Burden of Strength 65; The Main Regret 66; Alternation 68; Hawarden 69; At the Close 70; Forest History 71; A Garden Idyl 81; Foresight and Patience 88
FRAGMENTS OF THE ILIAD IN ENGLISH HEXAMETER VERSE The Invective of Achilles 109; The Invective of Achilles, *continued* 112; The Marshalling of the Achaians 114; Agememnon in the Fight 117; Paris and Diomedes 119; Hypnos on Ida

121; Clash in Arms of the Achaians and Trojans 122; The Horses of Achilles 123
THE MARES OF THE CAMARGUE From the Mireio 126

PUBLICATION

The poems published in *A Reading of Life* had been written during the previous
decade, though the poems at the beginning of the volume Meredith at one
point seems to have regarded as parts of one poem, 'A Reading of Life,' which
was written in 1900. In October 1900 he told Lady Ulrica Duncombe: 'My
long poem is finished. It is called "A Reading of Life".' About a month later,
he told her: 'My poem "A Reading of Life", will appear one part in Murray's
new Review. He takes "The Vital Choice" and "The Test of Manhood". The
Cornhill takes "With the Huntress". The part concerning Aphrodite is too
much for magazines – and may be for you.' Thus provoked, she evidently
asked him to send what he had withheld, for a week later, on 24 November
1900, he sent it to her in proof: 'Here is the poem, or the part of it.' The
volume was published in May 1901.

There are four versions or issues of the first edition of *A Reading of Life*, all
dated 1901. They can be distinguished by means of a comparison of pp. 66–7
on which the poem 'The Main Regret' is printed. All three versions differ from
the MS at lines 4 and 5. At line 4 'charged on the soul' (MS) is changed to 'they
of the soul', and at line 5 'in the earth' (MS) is changed to 'under soil.'

VERSION I

The first version of the first edition printing of 'The Main Regret' gives at line
2 'strip men' as opposed to 'strip us so' (MS), and 'strike us all' (versions II and
III).

VERSION II

In the second version the leaves which constitute pp. 65–8 (the first two leaves
of signature F), have been cut out, and alternative pages pasted onto the stubs.
The text of the second version of 'The Main Regret' differs from the first
printed version at line 2, line 4, and line 8, as indicated above. There is no
record of the reasons for the changes.

VERSION III

The third version is identical textually to the second. The new leaves are now
sewn, not pasted in.

VERSION IV

For clarity's sake it should be mentioned that Forman had seen versions I and II (Forman 137). The B.M. copy is version II. Luther Livingston knew of the difficulty. 'Almost all copies of "A Reading of Life" have two cancelled leaves pp. 65–68, printed as a separate sheet and pasted on the stub of one of the original leaves, which have been removed. We have never seen a copy containing the originals' (*The Nation*, 28 March 1912, p. 311). He had not, however, seen examples of versions I and III.

The three versions were noted by Simon Nowell-Smith (*TLS*, 25 July 1942 p. 372). He observed that in his copy a coarser thread and the presence of glue, indicated that the cancel was inserted after binding. He also notes the existence of a fourth version in his possession: 'My copy of issue C also contains an erratum slip (unrecorded), tipped in between page viii and page 1 and reading 'Page 1, line 5, *for* "divided" *read* "derided".' 'Divided' is the reading of all issues of this edition, and of the first American edition, Scribner, 1901. '"Derided" had appeared when the poem was first printed in the *Monthly Review*, March 1901, and was restored in Constable's second impression, 1909.' The erratum noted by Nowell-Smith resulted from the instruction Meredith sent his son in a letter dated 4 June 1901:

> 1st page of Poems, 1st verse, last line but one, is printed "Each can torture if divided" which has no meaning.
> It should be
> "Each can torture if derided."
> I am sure the error was not in the New Review.
> – The page must be cancelled in all the unbound copies, and the erratum added to the bound copies.

SECOND IMPRESSION

The second impression referred to above was of version III of the first edition, the changes being kept to the minimum, as Forman noted (Forman 139):

> The last four lines of the title-page of the 1st edition are replaced by three lines reading – *London / Constable & Company Ltd / 1909*, and the words *Second Impression* take the place of the imprint in the centre of p. [vi], while the lettering on the cover reads *Constable / London* in place of *Constable / Westminster*

L

POEMS

VOLUMES FROM THE POCKET EDITION, CONSTABLE 1903–

POEMS / BY GEORGE MEREDITH / VOLUME I / [publisher's monogram entwined in leafy ornament] / WESTMINSTER / ARCHIBALD CONSTABLE & CO LTD / 2 WHITEHALL GARDENS 1903

VOLUME I

Collation [1–13]¹⁶[14]² 109 leaves (16.8 x 10.5) [i–v] vi 1–209 [210–12]

Contents [i] halftitle: POEMS / VOL. I. [ii] blank [iii] titlepage [iv] copyright statement: COPYRIGHT 1897, 1898, BY / GEORGE MEREDITH [v]–vi contents 1–209 text [210] imprint: [short rule] / Butler & Tanner, The Selwood Printing Works, Frome, and London. [211–12] blank

VOLUME II

Collation [1]¹[2–17]¹⁶18³ 134 leaves (16.8 x 10.5) [i–v] vii [viii] 1–257 [258–60]

Contents [i] halftitle: POEMS / VOL. II. [ii] blank [iii] titlepage [iv] copyright statement: COPYRIGHT 1898, BY / GEORGE MEREDITH [v]–vii contents [viii] blank 1–257 text [258] imprint [259–60] blank

Binding Both volumes are uniform with the rest of the edition.

Contents of Volume I
Modern Love 3; The Sage Enamoured and the Honest Lady 53; Love is Winged 69; Ask, is Love Divine 70; Joy is Fleet 71; The Lesson of Grief 72; The Woods of Westermain 73; A Ballad of Past Meridian 89; The Day of the Daughter of Hades 90; The Lark Ascending 111; Phoebus with Admetus 116; Melampus 121; Love in the Valley 127; The Three Singers to Young Blood 136; The Orchard and the Heath 140; Earth and Man 143; A Ballad of Fair Ladies in Revolt 152; Juggling Jerry 168; The Old Chartist 173; Martin's Puzzle 179; Marian 183; SONNETS Lucifer in Starlight 185; The Star Sirius 186; Sense and Spirit 187; Earth's Secret 188; The Spirit of Shakespeare 189, 190; Internal Harmony 191; Grace and Love 192; Appreciation 193; The Discipline of Wisdom 194; The State of Age 195; Progress 196; The World's Advance 197; A Certain People 198; The Garden of Epicurus 199; A Later Alexandrian 200; An Orson of the Muse 201; The Point of Taste 202; Camelus Saltat 203, 204;

LI

THE TERCENTENARY OF MILTON'S BIRTH

FIRST EDITION

THE BRITISH ACADEMY / [double rule] / THE TERCENTENARY / OF / MILTON'S BIRTH / [double rule] / INAUGURAL MEETING / AT THE THEATRE / BURLINGTON GARDENS / TUESDAY, DECEMBER 8, 1908 / (The Eve of the Tercentenary) / [rule] / LINES BY / MR. GEORGE MEREDITH, O.M., / WRITTEN IN HONOUR OF THE OCCASION / [double rule]

This publication is no more than a limited printing, for circulation among friends, of the poem as it was to appear in the proceedings of the Academy.

The proceedings of the one day to which Meredith made a contribution were themselves published separately and the titlepage reads as follows:

THE BRITISH ACADEMY / THE TERCENTENARY OF MILTON'S BIRTH / INAUGURAL MEETING / AT THE THEATRE, BURLINGTON GARDENS, / TUESDAY, DECEMBER 8, 1908 / (*The Eve of the Tercentenary*) / LINES / BY GEORGE MEREDITH, O.M. / ORATION / BY DR. A.W. WARD / MASTER OF PETERHOUSE, CAMBRIDGE; FELLOW OF THE BRITISH ACADEMY / SUMMARY OF ADDRESS ON MILTON / AND MUSIC / BY SIR FREDERICK BRIDGE, M.V.O., M.A., Mus.D. / ORGANIST OF WESTMINSTER ABBEY; KING EDWARD PROFESSOR OF MUSIC IN THE / UNIVERSITY OF LONDON / [*From the Proceedings of the British Academy*, Vol. III] / London / Published for the British Academy / By Henry Frowde, Oxford University Press / Amen Corner, E.C. / Price One Shilling net

LII a

LAST POEMS

FIRST EDITION

LAST POEMS / BY / GEORGE MEREDITH / LONDON / CONSTABLE & COMPANY LTD. / 10 ORANGE STREET, LEICESTER SQUARE / 1909

Collation [A]^{8}B–D^8 32 leaves (19.5 x 12.5) [1–6] 7–62 [63–4]

Contents [1] halftitle: LAST POEMS [2] blank [3] titlepage [4] blank [5] acknowledgement: 'Angela Burdett-Coutts' / 'The Centenary of Garibaldi' and 'The Crisis' / are reprinted by courtesy of / the Proprietor of / *The Times* [6] blank 7–8 contents 9–62 text [63] imprint: Printed by T. and A. CONSTABLE, Printers to His Majesty / at the Edinburgh University Press [64] blank

Binding Spine, and boards at front and back, covered in light brown buckram. Endpapers plain.

Front cover Plain.

Spine Stamped in gilt: Last / Poems / George / Meredith / *Constable* / *London*

Back cover Plain.

Contents On Como 9; The Wild Rose 11; Youth in Age 14; The Labourer 15; 'The Years had Worn their Season's Belt' 17; FRAGMENTS 'Open Horizons Round' 20; 'A Wilding Little Stubble Flower' 21; 'From Labours through the

Night' 22; 'This Love of Nature' 23; Il y a Cent Ans 24; October 21, 1905 28; Trafalgar Day 31; The Voyage of the 'Ophir' 34; Ireland 37; The Call 41; The Crisis 46; The Warning 49; Outside the Crowd 50; 'Atkins' 51; The Centenary of Garibaldi 52; At the Funeral 60; Angela Burdett-Coutts 61; Epitaph 62

PUBLICATION

Published simultaneously in England and America in October 1909.

LII b

AMERICAN EDITION

LAST POEMS / BY / GEORGE MEREDITH / NEW YORK / CHARLES SCRIBNER'S SONS / 1909

Collation [1–4]⁸ 33 leaves (18.8 x 13.6) [1–7] 8 [9–11] 12–64

Contents [1] halftitle: LAST POEMS [2] blank [3] titlepage [4] copyright statement: COPYRIGHT, 1909, BY / CHARLES SCRIBNER'S SONS / [rule] / Published October, 1909 [5] acknowledgement: 'Angela Burdett-Coutts' / 'The Centenary of Garibaldi' and 'The Crisis' / are reprinted by courtesy of / the Proprietor of / *The Times* [6] blank [7]–8 contents [9] flytitle: LAST POEMS [10] blank [11]–64 text

Binding Spine, and boards at front and back, covered in coarse dark blue cloth. Endpapers plain.

Front cover Stamped in gilt, Meredith's signature.

Spine Stamped in gilt: LAST / POEMS / GEORGE / MEREDITH / SCRIBNERS

Back cover Plain.

Contents On Como 11; The Wild Rose 13; Youth in Age 16; The Labourer 17; 'The Years had Worn their Season's Belt' 19; FRAGMENTS 'Open Horizons Round' 22; 'A Wilding Little Stubble Flower' 23; 'From Labours through the Night' 24; 'This Love of Nature' 25; Il y a Cent Ans 26; October 21, 1905 30; Trafalgar Day 33; The Voyage of the 'Ophir' 36; Ireland 39; The Call 43; The Crisis 48; The Warning 51; Outside the Crowd 52; 'Atkins' 53; The Centenary of Garibaldi 54; Milton 58; At the Funeral 62; Angela Burdett-Coutts 63; Epitaph 64

LIII

CHILLIANWALLAH

FIRST EDITION

This book, which is really no more than a pamphlet, is made up of 16 leaves sewn together at the centre. It is unbound and on the first page, which serves also as the cover, is simply: GEORGE MEREDITH'S / CHILLIANWALLAH

The pages are unnumbered and only the recto is used. They measure 22.1 x 18.0. On [p. 29] is the statement: ONE HUNDRED AND TWELVE COPIES / PRINTED AT THE MARION PRESS / JAMAICA QUEENSBOROUGH / NEW YORK / 1909 / *This copy is No. 38.*

The introduction is by William E. Comfort of Des Moines, Iowa, and is dated 3 November 1909.

The first serial printings of 'Chillianwallah' are given in the census of poems.

LIV

LOVE IN THE VALLEY

FIRST AMERICAN EDITION

LOVE IN / THE / VALLEY / AND TWO SONGS / SPRING & AUTUMN / BY / GEORGE / MEREDITH / [square device with, at right, the publisher's monogram] / THE RALPH FLETCHER SEYMOUR CO / MPANY PUBLISHERS CHICAGO

Collation 12 leaves

Contents [1–2] blank [3] halftitle: LOVE IN / THE / VALLEY [4] blank [5] titlepage [6]–19 text [20] blank [21] halftitle: TWO SONGS / SPRING AND AUTUMN [22–3] text [24] publisher's statement: ONE OF THREE HUNDRED COPIES / OF LOVE IN THE VALLEY, AND / TWO SONGS, BY GEORGE MEREDITH. / PRINTED IN NOVEMBER MCMIX / ALDERBRINK PRESS, CHICAGO

Binding Spine, and boards at front and back, covered in heavy pale green paper. Endpapers plain white.

Front cover Stamped in brown, a border in the form of a scroll, and in gilt: LOVE IN / THE / VALLEY / GEORGE / MEREDITH

Spine Plain.

Back cover Plain.

LV

TWENTY POEMS

FIRST EDITION

TWENTY POEMS / BY / GEORGE MEREDITH / LONDON / 1909

Collation [π]⁴A–G⁴F² 26 leaves (19.5 x 12.5) [i]–viii 1–43 [44]

Contents [i] halftitle: TWENTY POEMS [ii] publisher's note: *The issue of this privately / printed book consists of / twenty-five numbered copies. / This is number 4.* [iii] titlepage [iv] blank [v] bibliographical note [vi] blank vii–viii contents 1–[44] text.

Binding Spine and boards bound in glazed ivory calico, with bevelled edges at front and back. Endpapers of the same colour.

Front cover Plain.

Spine Horizontal lines stamped in gilt at top and bottom, and between them, also stamped in gilt: TWENTY / POEMS / [device] / GEORGE / MEREDITH

Back cover Plain.

Bibliographical note, transcribed from p. v.

The authorship of the poems in this volume is disclosed by the entries in the office record of the contributors to *Household Words*. These poems are now collected and reprinted for the first time.

Two poems by Mr Meredith, which are not included in this collection, also made their first appearance in *Household Words*. These are "Sorrows and Joys," which is to be found in the first volume on page 517 in the number dated August 24, 1850, and "The Two Blackbirds," which appeared in the second volume, page 157, in the number for November 9, 1850. Both these poems, with slight alterations, were included in Mr Meredith's first book, "Poems," 1851 ...

Contents

NEW YEAR'S EVE, *Household Words*, volume ii, p. 325, 28 December 1850
THE CONGRESS OF NATIONS, *Household Words*, volume ii, p. 572, 8 March 1851
INFANCY AND AGE, *Household Words*, volume iii, p. 85, 19 April 1851
TIME, *Household Words*, volume iii, p. 204, 24 May 1851
FORCE AND HIS MASTER, *Household Words*, volume iii, p. 588, 13 September 1851
THE GENTLENESS OF DEATH, *Household Words*, volume iv, p. 37, 4 October 1851

A WORD FROM THE CANNON'S MOUTH, *Household Words*, volume iv, p. 109, 23 October 1851

QUEEN JULEIMA, *Household Words*, volume iv, p. 131, 1 November 1851

BRITAIN, *Household Words*, volume iv, p. 204, 22 November 1851

FAMILIAR THINGS, *Household Words*, volume iv, p. 254, 6 December 1851

A CHILD'S PRAYER, *Household Words*, volume iv, p. 277, 13 December 1851

THE GLASTONBURY THORN, *Household Words*, volume iv, p. 307, 20 December 1851

A WASSAIL FOR THE NEW YEAR, *Household Words*, volume iv, p. 348, 3 January 1852

THE LINNET-HAWKER, *Household Words*, volume iv, p. 372, 10 January 1852

WAR, *Household Words*, volume iv, p. 517, 21 February 1852

THE FIRST BORN, *Household Words*, volume v, p. 392, 10 July 1852

HOLIDAYS, *Household Words*, volume viii, p. 397, 24 December 1853

MOTLEY, *Household Words*, volume viii, p. 539, 4 February 1854

RHINE-LAND, *Household Words*, volume xiv, p. 12, 19 July 1856

MONMOUTH, *Household Words*, volume xiv, p. 372, 1 November 1856

The serial publication of these poems is given here rather than in the Census of Poems because it is not certain that all twenty of the poems included in *Twenty Poems* were by Meredith. Only a few of them, identified by means of the office records of the magazine, can be ascribed with certainty.

LVI

POEMS

THE MEMORIAL EDITION

GEORGE MEREDITH / [short rule] / POEMS / VOL. I. / *Memorial* / *Edition* / LONDON / CONSTABLE AND COMPANY LTD / 1910

VOLUME I

Collation [π]⁸A–Q⁸R⁴ 140 leaves (21.5 × 14.5) [i–xvi] [1]–264

Contents [i–ii] blank [iii] title: THE WORKS OF / GEORGE MEREDITH / [short rule] / MEMORIAL EDITION / VOLUME XXIV [iv] blank [v] titlepage [vi] imprint: Edinburgh: T. and A. CONSTABLE, Printers to His Majesty [vii–xv] (misnumbered v–xiii)] contents [xvi] blank [1]–264 text, on 264 at foot: [rule] / Printed by T. and A. CONSTABLE, Printers to Her Majesty / at the Edinburgh University Press

A frontispiece is inserted between [iv] and [v]. The other illustrations are not included in the pagination.

Binding See main entry. On the spine of Volume I of the poems is stamped in gilt: Poems / * / George / Meredith / Memorial / Edition / 24

VOLUMES II and III (volumes 25 and 26 of the Memorial Edition)

The internal arrangement of the other two volumes is the same as in Volume I. The prelims are identical. Only the contents are different and these are indicated in the tables of contents which follow.

Contents of Volume I

Contents of Volume II

Contents of Volume III

LVII

THE POETICAL WORKS

FIRST EDITION

THE POETICAL WORKS / OF / GEORGE MEREDITH / WITH SOME NOTES BY / G.M. TREVELYAN / AUTHOR OF / 'THE PHILOSOPHY AND POETRY OF GEORGE MEREDITH' / LONDON / CONSTABLE AND COMPANY LTD / 1912

Collation [x]²[π]⁸A–2Q⁸ 322 leaves (20.0 x 13.5) [1–2] [1–xvi] [1]–623 [624]

Contents [i] titlepage [ii] blank [iii] preface [iv] blank v–xv contents [xvi] editor's note [1]–623 text, on 623 at foot the imprint: [short rule] / Printed by T. and A. CONSTABLE, Printers to His Majesty / at the Edinburgh University Press [624] blank
Before [i] is pasted on a single leaf with the title: THE POETICAL WORKS OF / GEORGE MEREDITH.
The verso of this leaf is blank.

Binding Spine, and boards at front and back, covered in dark blue cloth. Endpapers plain white.

Front cover Plain.

Spine Two lines at top and bottom stamped in gilt between which, also stamped in gilt: THE / POETICAL / WORKS / OF / GEORGE / MEREDITH / CONSTABLE / LONDON

Back cover Plain.

Contents EARLY POEMS Chillianwallah 1; Beauty Rohtraut 2; The Olive Branch 3; Song 6; The Wild Rose and the Snowdrop 7; The Death of Winter 8; Song 9; John Lackland 10; The Sleeping City 10; The Poetry of Chaucer 14; The Poetry of Spenser 14; The Poetry of Shakespeare 14; The Poetry of Milton 15; The Poetry of Southey 15; The Poetry of Coleridge 15; The Poetry of Shelley 15; The Poetry of Wordsworth 16; The Poetry of Keats 16; Violets 16; Angelic Love 17; Twilight Music 17; Requiem 19; The Flower of the Ruins 19; The Rape of Aurora 22; South-West Wind in the Woodland 23; Will o' the Wisp 26; Song 28; Song 29; Song 29; Daphne 30; Song 42; London by Lamplight 43; Song 46; Pastorals 47; To a Skylark 55; Song – Spring 55; Song – Autumn 56; Sorrows and Joys 56; Song 57; Song 58; Antigone 58; Swathed Round in Mist 60; Song 60; The Two Blackbirds 61; July 62; Song 64; Song 64; The Shipwreck of Idomeneus 65; The Longest Day 75; To Robin Redbreast 76; Song 77; Sunrise 78; Pictures of the Rhine 80; To a Nightingale 82; To Alex. Smith, The 'Glasgow Poet' 83; The Doe: A Fragment 84; Invitation to the Country 89; The Sweet o' the Year 90; ——— Autumn Even-Song 91; The Song of Courtesy 92; The Three Maidens 94; Over the Hills 94; Juggling Jerry 95; The Crown of Love 99; The Head of Bran the Blest 100; The Meeting 102; The Beggar's Soliloquy 103; By the Rosanna 107; Phantasy 112; The Old Chartist 117; Grandfather Bridgeman 121; The Promise in Disturbance 133; Modern Love 133; The Patriot Engineer 155; Cassandra 159; The Young Usurper 163; Margaret's Bridal Eve 163; Marian 169; By Morning Twilight 169; Unknown Fair Faces 170; Shemselnihar 170; A Roar through the Tall Twin Elm-Trees 171; When I would Image 172; Ode to the Spirit of Earth in Autumn 172; Martin's Puzzle 178; I Chafe at Darkness 180; Time and Sentiment 181; Lucifer in Starlight 181; The Star Sirius 182; Sense and Spirit 182; Earth's Secret 183; Internal Harmony 183; Grace and Love 183; The Spirit of Shakespeare 184; The Spirit of Shakespeare (*continued*) 184; Appreciation 185; The Discipline of Widsom 185; The State of Age 186; The World's Advance 186; The Garden of Epicurus 186; A Later Alexandrian 187; An Orson of the Muse 187; The Point of Taste 188; Camelus Saltat 188; Camelus Saltat (*continued*) 189; My Theme 189; My Theme (*continued*) 190; To Children: for Tyrants 190; POEMS AND LYRICS OF THE JOY OF EARTH The Woods of Westermain 193; A Ballad of Past Meridian 205; The Day of the Daughter of Hades 205; The Lark Ascending 221; Phoebus with Admetus 224; Melampus 227; Love in the Valley 230; The Three Singers to Young Blood 236; The Orchard and the Heath 238; Earth and

D Census of poems by first line

1
A Blackbird in a wicker cage,
'The Two Blackbirds,' published in *Household Words*, 9 November 1850, 157;
reprinted in *Poems 1851*, 119–21

2
A breath of the mountains, fresh born in the regions majestic,
'The Poetry of Wordsworth,' published in *Poems 1851*, 4

3
A brook glancing under green leaves, self-delighting, exulting,
'The Poetry of Coleridge,' published in *Poems 1851*, 23

4
A dove flew with an Olive Branch;
'The Olive Branch,' published in *Poems 1851*, 1–7

5
A fountain of our sweetest, quick to spring
'J.C.M.,' published in *A Reading of Earth*, 1888, 134

6
A hundred mares, all white! their manes
'The Mares of the Camargue,' published in *A Reading of Life*, 1901, 126–8

7
A message from her set his brain aflame
Untitled, published in *Modern Love*, 1862, 37

8
A princess in the eastern tale
'The Sleeping City,' published in *Poems 1851*, 16–21

9
A rainless darkness drew o'er the lake
'On Como,' published in *Scribner's Magazine*, December 1908, 682; reprinted
in *Last Poems*, 1909, 9–10

10
A revelation came on Jane,
'Jump-to-Glory Jane,' published in *The Universal Review*, 15 October 1889, 240–52; reprinted in *The Empty Purse*, 1892, 48–66

11
A roar through the tall twin elm-trees
Untitled, published in *Modern Love*, 1862, 172–3

12
A Satyr spied a Goddess in her bath,
'The Teaching of the Nude,' published in *The Athenaeum*, 27 August 1892, 288; reprinted in *The Empty Purse*, 1892, 117–19

13
A wicked man is bad enough on earth;
'John Lackland,' published in *Poems 1851*, 15

14
A wilding little stubble flower
Untitled, published in *The Morning Post*, 20 September 1909, 7; reprinted in *Last Poems*, 1909, 21

15
A wind sways the pines,
'Dirge in Woods,' published in the *Fortnightly Review*, 1 August 1870, 179–83, as section ix of 'In the Woods'; reprinted in *A Reading of Earth*, 1888, 64–5

16
All other joys of life he strove to warm,
Untitled, published in *Modern Love*, 1862, 36

17
Along the garden terrace, under which
Untitled, published in *Modern Love*, 1862, 69

18
Am I failing? For no longer can I cast
Untitled, published in *Modern Love*, 1862, 61

19
An English heart, my commandant,
'To Colonel Charles,' published in the *Pall Mall Gazette*, 16 February 1887, 4;
reprinted in *The Empty Purse*, 1892, 124–9

20
An inspiration caught from dubious hues
'A Later Alexandrian,' published in *Poems and Lyrics of the Joy of Earth*, 172

21
And – 'Yonder look! yoho! yoho!
'The Doe: A Fragment from "Wandering Willie",' published in *Modern Love*,
1862, 205–16

22
Angelic love that stoops with heavenly lips
'Angelic Love,' published in *Poems 1851*, 26–7

23
As Puritans they prominently wax,
'A Certain People,' published in *Poems and Lyrics of the Joy of Earth*, 170

24
Ask, is Love divine,
Untitled, published in *Modern Love, A Reprint*, 105

25
Assured of worthiness we do not dread
'Internal Harmony,' published in *Poems and Lyrics of the Joy of Earth*, 1883, 163

26
At dinner, she is hostess, I am host.
Untitled, published in *Modern Love*, 1862, 49

27
At last we parley; we so strangely dumb
Untitled, published in *Modern Love*, 1862, 78

28
At the coming up of Phoebus the all-luminous charioteer,
'Phaéthôn,' published in the *Fortnightly Review*, 1 September 1867, 293–5;
reprinted in *Ballads and Poems of Tragic Life*, 1887, 152–7

29
Avert, High Wisdom, never vainly wooed.
'On the Danger of War,' published in the *Pall Mall Gazette*, 1 May 1885, 3;
reprinted in Edition de Luxe, vol. xxxi, *Poems iii*, 281

30
Awakes for me and leaps from shroud
'The Night Walk,' published in *The Century Illustrated Monthly Magazine*
August 1899, 566–7; reprinted in *A Reading of Life*, 1901, 55–9

31
Beneath the vans of doom did men pass in.
'Forest History,' published in *Literature*, 9 July 1898, 11–12; reprinted in *A Reading of Life*, 1901, 71–80

32
Between the fountains and the rill
'Alternation,' published in *A Reading of Life*, 1901, 68

33
'*Bibber besotted, with scowl of a cur, having heart of a deer, thou!*
'The Invective of Achilles,' v. 225; Fragments of the Iliad in English Hexameter
Verse, published in *A Reading of Life*, 1901, 112–13.

34
Blue July, bright July,
'July,' published in *Poems 1851*, 122–3

35
Bright Sirius! that when Orion pales
'The Star Sirius,' published in *Poems and Lyrics of the Joy of Earth*, 1883, 158

36
Bursts from a rending East in flaws
'Hard Weather,' published in *A Reading of Earth*, 1888, 6–13

37
Bury thy sorrows, and they shall rise
'Sorrows and Joys,' published in *Household Words*, 24 August 1850, 517–18;
reprinted in *Poems 1851*, 109–10

38
But where began the change; and what's my crime?
Untitled, published in *Modern Love*, 42

39
By this he knew she wept with waking eyes:
'Modern Love,' published in *Modern Love*, 1862, 33

40
Cannon his name,
'Napoléon,' published in *Cosmopolis*, April 1898, 30–51; reprinted in *Odes: French History*, 1898, 21–51

41
Captive on a foreign shore
'Cassandra,' published in *Modern Love*, 1862, 121–7

42
Carols nature, counsel men.
'The Three Singers to Young Blood,' published in *Poems and Lyrics of the Joy of Earth*, 1883, 101–4

43
Chillianwallah, Chillianwallah!
'Chillianwallah,' published in Chambers' *Edinburgh Journal*, 7 July 1849, 16;
reprinted in *Poems Written in Early Youth*, 1909, 234–5; reprinted in *The Novels of George Meredith: A Study*, by Elmer James Bailey, New York 1907, 15–16

44
Cistercians might crack their sides
'Hernani,' published in *Ballads and Poems of Tragic Life*, 1887, 69

45
Close Echo hears the woodman's axe,
'Woodman and Echo,' published in *A Reading of Earth*, 1888, 122–4

46
Come to me in any shape!
'Song,' published in *Poems 1851*, 125–6

47
Day of the cloud in fleets! O day
'The South-Wester,' published in *A Reading of Earth*, 1888, 14–22

48
Days, when the ball of our vision
'Youth in Memory,' published in *The Empty Purse*, 1892, 92–105

49
Demeter devastated our good land
'The Appeasement of Demeter,' published in *Macmillan's Magazine*, September 1887, 374–7; reprinted in *A Reading of Earth*, 1888, 35–44

50
Distraction is the panacea, Sir!
Untitled, published in *Modern Love*, 1862, 59

51
Earth loves her young: a preference manifest
'Earth's Preference,' published in *A Reading of Earth*, 1888, 127–8

52
Earth was not Earth before her sons appeared
'Appreciation,' published in *Poems and Lyrics of the Joy of Earth*, 165

53
Enter these enchanted woods,
'The Woods of Westermain,' published in *Poems and Lyrics of the Joy of Earth*, 1883, 1–27

54
Fair and false! No dawn will greet
'Song,' published in *Poems 1851*, 48

55
Fair Mother Earth lay on her back last night
'Ode to the Spirit of Earth in Autumn,' published in *Modern Love*, 1862, 190–204

56
Fire in her ashes Ireland feels
'Ireland,' published in *Last Poems*, 1909, 37–40

57
Flat as to an eagle's eye,
'The Nuptials of Attila,' published in *The New Quarterly Magazine*, January 1879, 47–62; reprinted in *Ballads and Poems of Tragic Life*, 1887, 70–100

58
Fleck of sky you are,
'Mother to Babe,' published in *The English Illustrated Magazine*, October 1886, [26]; reprinted in *A Reading of Earth*, 1888, 50–1

59
Flowers of the willow-herb are wool:
'Seed-Time,' published in *A Reading of Earth*, 1888, 1–5

60
Follow me, follow me,
'Will o' the Wisp,' published in *Poems 1851*, 44–7

61
For a Heracles in his fighting ire there is never the glory that follows
'The Labourer,' published in *The Westminster Gazette*, 6 February 1893, 3; reprinted in *Last Poems*, 1909, 15–16

62
From labours through the night, outworn
Untitled, published in *The Morning Post*, 20 September 1909, 7; reprinted in *Last Poems*, 1909, 22

63
From twig to twig the spider weaves
'Outer and Inner,' published in *A Reading of Earth*, 1888, 58–61

64
Full faith I have she holds that rarest gift
Untitled, published in *Modern Love*, 1862, 64

65
Give to imagination some pure light
Untitled, published in *Modern Love*, 1862, 70

66
Gracefullest leaper, the dappled fox-cub
'Young Reynard,' published in *Ballads and Poems of Tragic Life*, 1887, 65–6

67
Grey with all honours of age! but fresh-featured and ruddy
'The Poetry of Chaucer,' published in *Poems 1851*, 22

68
Hawk or shrike has done this deed
'Whimper of Sympathy,' published in the *Fortnightly Review*, 1 August 1870, 181; reprinted in *Ballads and Poems of Tragic Life*, 1887, 63; also reprinted as part of 'In the Woods,' *Various Readings and Bibliography*, Memorial Edition

69
He felt the wild beast in him between-whiles
Untitled, published in *Modern Love*, 1862, 41

70
He found her by the ocean's moaning verge,
Untitled, published in *Modern Love*, 1862, 81

71
He leads: we hear our Seaman's call
'Trafalgar Day,' published in *Last Poems*, 1909, 31–3

72
He leaped. With none to hinder,
'Empedocles,' published in *The Empty Purse*, 1892, 122–3

73
He rises and begins to round,
'The Lark Ascending,' published in the *Fortnightly Review*, 1 May 1881, 588–91; reprinted in *Poems and Lyrics of the Joy of Earth*, 1883, 64–70

74
He who has looked upon Earth
'The Day of the Daughter of Hades,' published in *Poems and Lyrics of the Joy of Earth*, 1883, 30–63

75
'Heigh, boys!' cried Grandfather Bridgeman, 'it's time before dinner to-day.'
'Grandfather Bridgeman,' published in *Modern Love*, 1862, 1–28

76
'Heigh me! brazen of front, thou glutton for plunder
'The Invective of Achilles, Iliad, BI, v. 149,' published in *The Illustrated London News*, 11 April 1891, 463; reprinted in *A Reading of Life*, 1901, 109–11

77
Her sacred body bear: the tenement
'At the Funeral,' published in *The Morning Post*, 1 February 1901, 4; reprinted in *Last Poems*, 1909, 60

78
Her son, albeit the Muse's livery
'An Orson of the Muse,' published in *Poems and Lyrics of the Joy of Earth*, 173

79
Here Jack and Tom are paired with Moll and Meg
Untitled, published in *Modern Love*, 1862, 50

80
High climbs June's wild rose,
'The Wild Rose,' published in *Scribner's Magazine*, December 1907, [668]; reprinted in *Last Poems*, 1909, 11–13

81
Hill-sides are dark
'In the Woods,' published in the *Fortnightly Review*, 1 August 1870, 179–83; reprinted in full in Edition de Luxe, *Bibliography and Various Readings*, 273–8. Sections VI, VII, and IX were reprinted, much altered, as 'Whimper of Sympathy,' 'Woodland Peace' and 'Dirge in Woods.' The other six sections reprinted in *The Poetical Works*, 342–5

82
His Lady queen of woods to meet,
'The Youthful Quest,' published in *The Empty Purse*, 1892, 2–3

83
Historic be the survey of our kind,
'Society,' published in *A Reading of Earth*, 1888, 129–30

84
How barren would this valley be
Untitled, published in *Poems 1851*, 93

85
How big of breast our Mother Gaea laughed
'The Cageing of Ares, v. V. 385, (Dedicated to the Council at the Hague),'
published in *A Reading of Life*, 1901, 45–54

86
How died Melissa none dares shape in words.
'Periander,' published in *Ballads and Poems of Tragic Life*, 1887, 133–42

87
How low when angels fall their black descent,
'The Promise in Disturbance,' published in *Modern Love, A Reprint*, 1892, 1–2

88
How many a thing which we cast to the ground
Untitled, published in *Modern Love*, 1862, 73

89
How sweet on sunny afternoons
'Pastorals,' published in *Poems 1851*, 84

90
I am not of those miserable males
Untitled, published in *Modern Love*, 1862, 52

91
I am to follow her. There is much grace
Untitled, published in *Modern Love*, 1862, 74

92
I bade my Lady think what she might mean.
Untitled, published in *Modern Love*, 1862, 72

93
I cannot lose thee for a day
'Song,' published in *Poems 1851*, 50

94
I chafe at darkness in the night;
Untitled, published in *Modern Love*, 1862, 176–7

95
I chanced upon an early walk to spy
'The Orchard and the Heath,' published in *Macmillan's Magazine*, February 1868, 363–6; reprinted in *Poems and Lyrics of the Joy of Earth*, 1883, 105–8

96
I know him, February's thrush,
'The Thrush in February,' published in *Macmillan's Magazine*, August 1885, 265–77; reprinted in *A Reading of Earth*, 1888, 23–4

97
I must be flattered. The imperious
Untitled, published in *Modern Love*, 1862, 60

98
'*I play for Seasons; not Eternities!*'
Untitled, published in *Modern Love*, 1862, 45

99
I see a fair young couple in a wood,
'Time and Sentiment,' published in the *Fortnightly Review*, 1 April 1870, 432, as 'A Mark in Time'; reprinted in *Poems and Lyrics of the Joy of Earth*, 1883, 181

100
I stood at the gate of the cot
'Change in Recurrence,' published in *A Reading of Earth*, 1888, 105–7

101
I think she sleeps: it must be sleep, when low
Untitled, published in *Modern Love*, 1862, 47

102
I, wakeful for the skylark voice in men
'To Cardinal Manning,' published in the *Pall Mall Gazette*, 5 November 1886,
3; reprinted in Edition de Luxe, vol. xxxi, *Poems iii*, 282

103
I would I were the drop of rain
'Song,' published in *Poems 1851*, 124

104
If that that thou hast the gift of strength, then know
'The Burden of Strength,' published in *A Reading of Life*, 1901, 65

105
In middle age an evil thing
'Archduchess Anne,' published in *Ballads and Poems of Tragic Life*, 1887, 3–24

106
In our old shipwrecked days there was an hour,
Untitled, published in *Modern Love*, 1862, 48

107
In Paris, at the Louvre, there have I seen
Untitled, published in *Modern Love*, 1862, 65

108
In Progress you have little faith, say you:
'Progress,' published in *Poems and Lyrics of the Joy of Earth*, 1883, 168

109
It chanced his lips did meet her forehead cool.
Untitled, published in *Modern Love*, 1862, 38

110
It ended, and the morrow brought the task
Untitled, published in *Modern Love*, 1862, 34

111
It is no vulgar nature I have wived.
Untitled, published in *Modern Love*, 1862, 67

112
It is the season of the sweet wild rose,
Untitled, published in *Modern Love*, 1862, 77

113
Joy is Fleet
'Joy is Fleet,' published in *Modern Love, A Reprint*, 1892, 106

114
Judge mildly the tasked world; and disincline
'The World's Advance,' published in *Poems and Lyrics of the Joy of Earth*, 1883, 169

115
Keen as an eagle whose flight towards the dim empyrean
'The Poetry of Southey,' published in *Poems 1851*, 23

116
Know you the low pervading breeze
'Twilight Music,' published in *Poems 1851*, 28–9

117
Ladies who in chains of wedlock
'A Preaching from a Spanish Ballad,' published in *Ballads and Poems of Tragic Life*, 1887, 35–41

118
Lakes where the sunsheen is mystic with splendour and softness
'The Poetry of Spenser,' published in *Poems 1851*, 22

119
Last night returning from my twilight walk
'A Ballad of Past Meridian,' published in *Poems and Lyrics of the Joy of Earth*, 28–9

120
Leave the uproar: at a leap
'Nature and Life,' published in *A Reading of Life*, 1888, 62

121
Let Fate or Insufficiency provide
'To J.M.,' published in the *Fortnightly Review*, 1 June 1867, 696; reprinted in
Poems and Lyrics of the Joy of Earth, 1883, 177

122
Like a flood river whirled at rocky banks,
'The Test of Manhood,' published in *The Monthly Review*, March 1901, 155–64;
reprinted in *A Reading of Life*, 1901, 28–42

123
Like as a terrible fire feeds fast on a forest enormous,
'Marshalling of the Achaians, Iliad, B. II. v. 455,' published in *The Illustrated
London News*, 11 April 1891, 463; reprinted in *A Reading of Life*, 1901, 114–16

124
Like to some deep-chested organ whose grand inspiration,
'The Poetry of Milton,' published in *Poems 1851*, 23

125
Lo! as a tree whose wintry twigs
Untitled, published in *Poems 1851*, 91–3

126
Long with us, now she leaves us; she has rest
'Angela Burdett-Coutts,' published in *Last Poems*, 1909, 61

127
Love ere he bleeds, an eagle in high skies,
Untitled, published in *Modern Love*, 1862, 58

128
Love is winged for two,
Untitled, published in *Modern Love, A Reprint*, 1892, 103–4

129
Love within the lover's breast
'Song' published in *Poems 1851*, 8

130
Madam would speak with me. So, now it comes:
Untitled, published in *Modern Love*, 1862, 66

131
Maimed, beggared, grey; seeking an alms; with nod
'Bellerophon,' published in *Ballads and Poems of Tragic Life*, 1887, 148–51

132
Mark where the pressing wind shoots javelin-like
Untitled, published in *Modern Love*, 1862, 75

133
Melpomene among her livid people,
'The Two Masks,' published in *Ballads and Poems of Tragic Life*, 1887, 1–2

134
Men of our race, we send you one
'The Voyage of the "Ophir",' published in the *Pall Mall Gazette*, May 1901, 1–4; reprinted in *Last Poems*, 1909, 34–6

135
Men and Angels eyed;
'Men and Man,' published in *Ballads and Poems of Tragic Life*, 1887, 127–8

136
Merrily 'mid the faded leaves,
'To Robin Redbreast,' published in *Poems 1851*, 146–7

137
Musing on the fate of Daphne,
'Daphne,' published in *Poems 1851*, 51

138
My Lady unto Madam makes her bow.
Untitled, published in *Modern Love*, 1862, 68

139
Never, O never,
'The Rape of Aurora,' published in *Poems 1851*, 35–7

140
Night like a dying mother,
'By Morning Twilight,' published in *Modern Love*, 1862, 152–3

141
No, no, the falling blossom is no sign
'Song,' published in *Poems 1851*, 118

142
No state is enviable. To the luck alone
Untitled, published in *Modern Love*, 1862, 51

143
Not ere the bitter herb we taste,
'The Lesson of Grief,' published in *Modern Love, A Reprint*, 1892, 107

144
Not less a Queen, because I wear
'Queen Zuleima,' published in *Household Words*, vol. iv, 1 November 1851,
131–2; reprinted in *Twenty Poems*, 1909, 13–15

145
Not solely that the Future she destroys
Untitled, published in *Modern Love*, 1862, 44

146
Not solitarily in fields we find
'Earth's Secret,' published in *Poems and Lyrics of the Joy of Earth*, 1883, 160

147
Not the sea-wave so bellows abroad when it bursts upon shingle,
'Clash in Arms of the Achaians and Trojans, Iliad, B. xiv. v. 394,' published in
The Illustrated London News, 18 April 1891, 507; reprinted in *A Reading of Life*,
1901, 122

148
Not vainly doth the earnest voice of man
'To Alex Smith, "The Glasgow Poet",' published in *The Leader*, 20 December
1851, 1213; reprinted in Edition de Luxe, vol. xxxiii, *Poems iv*, 256

149
Not yet had History's Aetna smoked the skies
'The Revolution,' published in *Cosmopolis*, March 1898, 625–34; reprinted in
Odes in Contribution to the Song of French History, 1898, 3–17

150
Now dumb is he who waked the world to speak
'On Hearing the News from Venice,' published in the *Pall Mall Gazette*,
14 December 1889, 1

151
Now farewell to you! you are
'Lines to a Friend Visiting America,' published in the *Fortnightly Review*, 1
December 1867, 727–31; reprinted in Edition de Luxe, vol. xxxi, *Poems iii*,
274–81

152
Now from the meadow floods the wild duck clamours
Untitled, published in *Poems 1851*, 92

153
Now standing on this hedgeside path,
Untitled, published in *Poems 1851*, 90

154
Now the frog, all lean and weak,
'The Sweet o' the Year,' published in *Fraser's Magazine*, June 1852, 699;
reprinted in Edition de Luxe, vol. xxxi, *Poems iii*, 269–70

155
Now the North wind ceases,
'Tardy Spring,' published in *The Illustrated London News*, 20 June 1891, 803;
reprinted in *The Empty Purse*, 1892, 133–6

156
Now, this, to my notion, is pleasant cheer,
'The Beggar's Soliloquy,' published in *Once a Week*, 30 March 1861, 378–9;
reprinted in *Modern Love*, 1862, 101–8

157
Now 'tis Spring on wood and wold,
'Invitation to the Country,' published in *Fraser's Magazine*, August 1851,
217–18; reprinted in Edition de Luxe, vol. xxxi, *Poems iii*, 267–8

158
O briar-scents, on yon wet wing
'Breath of the Briar,' published in *The Empty Purse*, 1892, 120-1

159
O might I load my arms with thee,
'The Crown of Love,' published in *Once a Week*, 31 December 1859, 10;
reprinted in Edition de Luxe, vol. xxxi, *Poems iii*, 273-4

160
O my lover! the night like a broad smooth
'Shemselnihar,' published in *Modern Love*, 1862, 168-71

161
O Nightingale! how has thou learnt
'To a Nightingale,' published in *Poems 1851*, 160

162
O Skylark! I see thee and call thee joy!
'To a Skylark,' published in *Poems 1851*, 108

163
Of me and of my theme think what thou wilt:
'My Theme (2 Sonnets),' published in *Poems and Lyrics of the Joy of Earth*,
1883, 179-80

164
Of men he would have raised to light he fell:
'Gordon of Khartoum,' published in *A Reading of Earth*, 1888, 135

165
On a starred night Prince Lucifer uprose.
'Lucifer in Starlight,' published in *Poems and Lyrics of the Joy of Earth*, 1883, 157

166
On her great venture, Man,
'Earth and Man,' published in *Poems and Lyrics of the Joy of Earth*, 1883, 115-29

167
On my darling's bosom
'The Young Usurper,' published in *Modern Love*, 1862, 128

168
On the morning of May,
'A Faith on Trial,' published in *A Reading of Earth*, 1888, 66–104

169
On yonder hills soft twilight dwells
'The Longest Day,' published in *Poems 1851*, 144–5

170
Once I was part of the music I heard
'Youth in Age,' published in *Last Poems*, 1909, 14

171
One fairest of the ripe unwedded left
'The Sage Enamoured and the Honest Lady,' published in *Modern Love, A Reprint*, 1892, 69–104

172
Open horizons round,
Untitled, in section 'Fragments,' published in *Last Poems*, 1909, 20

173
Or shall we run with Artemis
'The Vital Choice,' published in *The Monthly Review*, March 1901, 155–64; reprinted in *A Reading of Life*, 1901, 1–2

174
Our Islet out of Helgoland, dismissed
'Islet the Dachs,' published in *A Reading of Earth*, 1888, 134

175
Out in the yellow meadows, where the bee
Untitled, published in *Modern Love*, 1862, 43

176
Picture some Isle smiling green 'mid the white-foaming ocean;
'The Poetry of Shakespeare,' published in *Poems 1851*, 22

177
Pitch here the tent, while the old horse grazes:
'Juggling Jerry,' published in *Once a Week*, 3 September 1859, 189–90; reprinted in *Modern Love*, 1862, 85–91

178
Prince of Bards was old Aneurin
'Aneurin's Harp,' published in *Ballads and Poems of Tragic Life*, 1887, 101–10

179
Projected from the bilious Childe,
'Manfred,' published in *Ballads and Poems of Tragic Life*, 1887, 67–8

180
Queen Theodolind has built
'The Song of Theodolind,' published in *The Cornhill Magazine*, September 1872, 308–12; reprinted in *Ballads and Poems of Tragic Life*, 1887, 25–34

181
Rich labour is the struggle to be wise,
'The Discipline of Wisdom,' published in *Poems and Lyrics of the Joys of Earth*, 1883, 166

182
Rub thou thy battered lamp: nor claim nor beg
'The State of Age,' published in *Poems and Lyrics of the Joy of Earth*, 1883, 167

183
See the sweet women, friend, that lean beneath
'A Ballad of Fair Ladies in Revolt,' published in *Poems and Lyrics of the Joy of Earth*, 130–56

184
Seen, too clear and historic within us, our sins of omission
'The Main Regret,' published in *The May Book*, Macmillan, 1901, 38; reprinted in *A Reading of Life*, 1901, 66–7

185
See'st thou a Skylark whose glistening winglets ascending
'The Poetry of Shelley,' published in *Poems 1851*, 24

186
Sharp is the night, but stars with frost alive
'Winter Heavens,' published in *A Reading of Earth*, 1888, 131-2

187
She can be as wise as we,
'Marian,' published in *Modern Love*, 1862, 143-4

188
She issues radiant from her dressing-room,
Untitled, published in *Modern Love*, 1862, 39

189
She yields: my Lady in her noblest mood
Untitled, published in *Modern Love*, 1862, 71

190
Should thy love die,
'Song,' published in *Poems 1851*, 74

191
Sirs! may I shake your hands?
'The Patriot Engineer,' published in *Once a Week*, 14 December 1861, 685-7;
reprinted in *Modern Love*, 1862, 109-17

192
Sleek as a lizard at round of a stone,
'Penetration and Trust,' published in *The Empty Purse*, 1892, 109-10

193
So he, with a clear shout of laughter,
'Paris and Diomedes, Iliad, B. XI. v. 378,' published in *The Illustrated London
News*, 18 April 1891, 507; reprinted in *A Reading of Life*, 1901, 119-20

194
So now the horses of Aiakides, off wide of the war-ground,
'The Horses of Achilles, Iliad, B. XVII. v. 426,' published in *The Illustrated London
News*, 18 April 1891, 507; reprinted in *A Reading of Life*, 1901, 123-5

195
Spirit of Russia, now has come
'The Crisis,' published in *The Times*, 23 March 1905, 8; reprinted in *Last Poems*, 1909, 46–8

196
Sprung of the father blood, the mother brain
'Foresight and Patience,' published in *The National Review*, April 1894, 164–74; reprinted in *A Reading of Life*, 1901, 88–105

197
Strike not thy dog with a stick!
'To Children: For Tyrants,' published in *The English Illustrated Magazine*, Dec. 1887, 184–6; reprinted in Edition de Luxe, vol. xxxi, *Poems iii*, 282–5

198
Summer glows warm on the meadows, and speedwell, and gold-cups and daisies
Untitled, published in *Poems 1851*, 94–8

199
Sunset worn to its last vermilion hue;
'Union in Disseverance,' published in *A Reading of Life*, 1901, 64

200
Swathed round in mist and crown'd with cloud,
Untitled, published in *Poems 1851*, 116–17

201
Sweet as Eden is the air,
'Woodland Peace,' published in the *Fortnightly Review*, 1 August 1870, 179–83; reprinted in *A Reading of Earth*, 1888, 52–4

202
Sweet is the light of infancy, and sweet
'Infancy and Age,' published in *Household Words*, vol. iii, 19 April 1851, 85; reprinted in *Twenty Poems*, 1909, 5

203
Swept from his fleet upon that fatal night
'The Shipwreck of Idomeneus,' published in *Poems 1851*, 127–43

204
Sword in length a reaping-hook amain
'King Harald's Trance,' published in *Ballads and Poems of Tragic Life*, 1887, 58–62

205
Sword of Common Sense! –
'Ode to the Comic Spirit,' published in *The Empty Purse*, 1892, 69–91

206
Take thy lute and sing
'The Flower of the Ruins,' published in *Poems 1851*, 31–4

207
That Garden of sedate Philosophy
'The Garden of Epicurus,' published in *Poems and Lyrics of the Joy of Earth*, 1883, 171

208
That march of the funeral Past behold;
'Il y a Cent Ans,' published in *Last Poems*, 1909, 24–7

209
That was the chirp of Ariel
'Wind on the Lyre,' published in the *Anti-Jacobin*, no. 45, 5 December 1891, 1112; reprinted in *The Empty Purse*, 1892, 1

210
The buried voice bespake Antigone
'Antigone,' published in *Poems 1851*, 113–15

211
The clouds are withdrawn
'Sunrise,' published in *Poems 1851*, 150–4

212
The daisy now is out upon the green;
'Song,' published in *Poems 1851*, 148–9

213
The day that is the night of days,
'England Before the Storm,' published in *The Athenaeum*, 5 December 1891, 762; reprinted in *The Empty Purse*, 1892, 130–2

214
The Flower unfolds its dawning cup,
'Song,' published in *Poems 1851*, 111

215
The hundred years have passed, and he
'October 21, 1905,' published in *Last Poems*, 1909, 28–30

216
The long cloud edged with streaming gray
'Autumn Even-Song,' published in *Once a Week*, 3 December 1859, 464; reprinted in *Modern Love*, 1862, 154–5

217
The misery is greater, as I live!
Untitled, published in *Modern Love*, 1862, 56

218
The moon is alone in the sky
'Song,' published in *Poems 1851*, 14

219
The old coach-road through a common of furze,
'The Meeting,' published in *Once a Week*, 1 September 1860, 276; reprinted in *Modern Love*, 1862, 29–30

220
The old grey Alp has caught the cloud,
'By the Rosanna. To F.M.,' published in *Once a Week*, 19 October 1861, 460–2; reprinted in *Modern Love*, 1862, 178–89

221
The old grey mother she thrummed on her knee:
'Margaret's Bridal-Eve,' published in *Modern Love*, 1862, 129–42

222
The old hound wags his shaggy tail,
'Over the Hills,' published in *Once a Week*, 20 August 1859, 160; reprinted in *Edition de Luxe*, vol. xxxiv, *Miscellaneous Prose*, 1910, 257

223
The senses loving Earth or well or ill
'Sense and Spirit,' published in *Poems and Lyrics of the Joy of Earth*, 1883, 159

224
The shepherd, with his eye on hazy South,
'Earth and a Wedded Woman,' published in *A Reading of Earth*, 1888, 45–9

225
The silence of preluded song –
'South-West Wind in the Woodland,' published in *Poems 1851*, 38–43

226
The sister Hours in circles linked
'Alsace-Lorraine,' published in *Odes in Contribution to the Song of French History*, 1898, 69–94

227
The Snowdrop is the prophet of the flowers;
'The Wild Rose and the Snowdrop,' published in *Poems 1851*, 9

228
The song of a nightingale sent thro' a slumbrous valley,
'The Poetry of Keats,' published in *Poems 1851*, 24

229
The Spirit of Romance dies not to those
'Pictures of the Rhine,' published in *Poems 1851*, 155–9

230
The Tyrant passed, and friendlier was his eye
'Solon,' published in *Ballads and Poems of Tragic Life*, 1887, 143–7

231
The varied colours are a fitful heap:
'The Year's Sheddings,' published in *A Reading of Earth*, 1888, 136

232
The wind is East, the wind is West
'A Stave of Roving Tim,' published in *The Reflector*, 5 February 1888, 119–20; reprinted in Memorial Edition, vol. xxvi, *Poems iii*, 1910, 1–4

233
The windows flash in Taunton town
'Monmouth,' published in *Household Words*, vol. iv, 1 November 1856, 372–3;
reprinted in *Twenty Poems*, 1909, 39–44

234
The years had worn their seasons' belt,
'The Years had Worn their Seasons' Belt,' published in *Scribner's Magazine*,
October 1909, 407–8; reprinted in *Last Poems*, 1909, 17–19

235
Their sense is with their senses all mixed in,
Untitled, published in *Modern Love*, 1862, 80

236
There she goes up the street with her book in her hand,
'Martin's Puzzle,' published in the *Fortnightly Review*, 1 June 1865, 239–41;
reprinted in *Poems and Lyrics of the Joy of Earth*, 1883, 109–14

237
There stands a singer in the street
'London by Lamplight,' published in *Poems 1851*, 75–81

238
There were three maidens met on the highway;
'The Three Maidens,' published in *Once a Week*, 30 July 1859, 96; reprinted in
Edition de Luxe, vol. xxxi, *Poems iii*, 272

239
These, then, he left, and away where ranks were now clashing the thickest,
'Agamemnon in the Fight, Iliad, B. XI. V. 148,' published in *A Reading of Life*,
1901, 117–18

240
They have no song, the sedges dry,
'Song in the Songless,' published in *A Reading of Life*, 1901, 63

241
They say, that Pity in Love's service dwells,
Untitled, published in *Modern Love*, 1862, 76

242
They then to fountain-abundant Ida, mother of wild beasts,
'Hypnos on Ida, Iliad, B. XIV. V. 283,' published in *The Illustrated London News*,
18 April 1891, 507; reprinted in *A Reading of Life*, 1901, 121

243
This golden head has wit in it. I live
Untitled, published in *Modern Love*, 1862, 63

244
This love of nature, that allures to take
'This Love of Nature,' published in *The Morning Post*, 20 September 1909, 7;
reprinted in *Last Poems*, 1909, 23

245
This Riddle rede or die
'The Riddle for Men,' published in *The Paternoster Review*, November 1890,
101; reprinted in Edition de Luxe, vol. xxxi, *Poems iii*, 289–90

246
This was the woman; what now of the man?
Untitled, published in *Modern Love*, 1862, 35

247
Thou our beloved and light of Earth hast crossed
'Epitaph on the Tombstone of James Christopher Wilson,' published in *Last
Poems*, 1909, 62

248
Thou, run to the dry on this wayside bank,
'The Empty Purse,' published in *The Empty Purse*, 1892, 4–47

249
Thou to me art such a spring
'Song,' published in *Poems 1851*, 112

250
Though I am faithful to my loves lived through,
'Unknown Fair Faces,' published in *Modern Love*, 1862, 156

251
Through the water-eye of night,
'With the Huntress,' published in *The Cornhill Magazine*, January 1901, 1–3;
reprinted in *A Reading of Life*, 1901, 3–7

252
Thus piteously Love closed what he begat:
Untitled, published in *Modern Love*, 1862, 82

253
Thy greatest knew thee, Mother Earth; unsoured
'The Spirit of Shakespeare,' published in *The Athenaeum*, 10 February 1883, 184;
reprinted in *Poems and Lyrics of the Joy of Earth*, 1883, 161–2

254
'Tis Christmas weather, and a country house
Untitled, published in *Modern Love*, 1862, 55

255
To sit on History in an easy chair,
'Outside the Crowd,' published in *The National Review*, September 1896, 26;
reprinted in *Last Poems*, 1909, 50

256
To Thee, dear God of Mercy, both appeal
'At the Close,' published in *A Reading of Life*, 1901, 70

257
To them that knew her, there is a vital flame
'The Lady C.M.,' published in *A Reading of Earth*, 1888, 133

258
Two flower-enfolding crystal vases she
'Grace and Love,' published in *Poems and Lyrics of the Joy of Earth*, 1883, 164

259
Two wedded lovers watched the rising moon,
'Song,' published in *Poems 1851*, 49

260
Under boughs of breathing May,
'Song,' published in *Poems 1851*, 82–3

261
Under what spell are we debased
'The Call,' published in *The Oxford and Cambridge Review*, No. 4, Midsummer Term, 1908, 3–7; reprinted in *Last Poems*, 1909, 41–5

262
Under yonder beech-tree single on the green-sward,
'Love in the Valley,' published in *Macmillan's Magazine*, October 1878, 445–51; reprinted in *Poems and Lyrics of the Joy of Earth*, 1883, 87–100. An early version had previously been published in *Poems 1851*

263
Unhappy poets of a sunken prime!
'The Point of Taste,' published in *Poems and Lyrics of the Joy of Earth*, 1883, 174

264
Unto that love must we through fire attain,
'The Hueless Love,' published in *The New Liberal Review*, April 1901, 297–8; reprinted in *A Reading of Life*, 1901, 60–2

265
Violets, shy violets!
'Violets,' published in *Poems 1851*, 25

266
We have seen mighty men ballooning high,
'The Warning,' published in *Last Poems*, 1909, 49

267
We lean'd beneath the purple vine,
'Rhine-Land,' published in *Household Words*, vol. xiv, 19 July 1856, 12–13; reprinted in *Twenty Poems*, 1909, 36–8

268
We look for her that sunlike stood
'France, December 1870,' published in the *Fortnightly Review*, 1 January 1871, 86–94; reprinted in *Ballads and Poems of Tragic Life*, 1887, 111–26; reprinted in *Odes in Contribution to the Song of French History*, 1898

269
We saw the swallows gathering in the sky,
Untitled, published in *Modern Love*, 1862, 79

270
We spend our lives in learning pilotage,
'The Wisdom of Eld,' published in *A Reading of Earth*, 1888, 125–6

271
We three are on the cedar-shadowed lawn;
Untitled, published in *Modern Love*, 1862, 53

272
We who have seen Italia in the throes,
'The Centenary of Garibaldi,' published in *The Times*, 1 July 1907, 9; reprinted
in *Last Poems*, 1909, 52–5

273
What are we first? First animals; and next
Untitled, published in *Modern Love*, 1862, 62

274
What is the name of King Ringang's daughter?
'Beauty Rohtraut,' published in *The Leader*, 14 September 1850, 597, as 'The
Ballad of Beauty Rohtraut'; reprinted in *Poems 1851*, 106–7

275
What links are ours with orbs that are
'Meditation under Stars,' published in *A Reading of Earth*, 1888, 116–21

276
What may this woman labour to confess?
Untitled, published in *Modern Love*, 1862, 54

277
What say you, critic, now you have become
'Camelus Saltat,' published in *Poems and Lyrics of the Joy of Earth*, 1883, 175–6

278
What soul would bargain for a cure that brings
Untitled, published in *Modern Love*, 1862, 46

279
What splendour of imperial station man,
'Milton,' published in *The Times*, 9 December 1908, 12; reprinted in *Last Poems*, 1909, 56–9

280
Whate'er I be, old England is my dam!
'The Old Chartist,' published in *Once a Week*, 8 February 1862, 182–4; reprinted in *Modern Love*, 1862, 92–100

281
When April with her wild blue eye
'The Death of Winter,' published in *Poems 1851*, 12–13

282
When buds of palm do burst and spread
'Song – Spring,' published in *Poems 1851*, 99

283
When by Zeus relenting the mandate was revoked,
'Phoebus with Admetus," published in *Macmillan's Magazine*, December 1880, 122–4; reprinted in *Poems and Lyrics of the Joy of Earth*, 1883, 71–8

284
When comes the lighted day for men to read
'Hawarden,' published in *A Reading of Life*, 1901, 69

285
When I remember, friend, whom lost I call,
'To a Friend Lost,' published in *The Cornhill Magazine*, October 1880, 497; reprinted in *Poems and Lyrics of the Joy of Earth*, 1883, 178

286
When I would image her features,
'When I would Image,' published in *Modern Love*, 1862, 174–5

287
When nuts behind the hazel-leaf
'Song – Autumn,' published in *Poems 1851*, 100

288
When Sir Gawain was led to his bridal-bed,
'The Song of Courtesy,' published in *Once a Week*, 9 July 1859, 30; reprinted in
Edition de Luxe, vol. xxxi, *Poems iii*, 270–2

289
When the head of Bran
'The Head of Bran,' published in *Once a Week*, 4 February 1860, 131–2; re-
printed in *Modern Love*, 1862, 145–51.

290
When the South sang like a nightingale
'The Young Princess,' published in *The English Illustrated Magazine*, December
1886, 184–90; reprinted in *Ballads and Poems of Tragic Life*, 1887, 42–57

291
When we have thrown off this old suit,
'The Question Whither,' published in *A Reading of Earth*, 1888, 55–7

292
Where faces are hueless, where eyelids are dewless,
'Requiem,' published in *Poems 1851*, 30

293
Who call her Mother and who calls her Wife
'M.M.,' published in *A Reading of Earth*, 1888, 133

294
Who murmurs, hither, hither: who
'With the Persuader,' published in *A Reading of Life*, 1901, 8–27

295
With Alfred and St. Louis he doth win
'The Emperor Frederick of Our Time,' published in *A Reading of Earth*, 1888,
135

296
With Life and Death I walked when Love appeared,
'Hymn to Colour,' published in *A Reading of Earth*, 1888, 108–15

297
With love exceeding a simple love of the things,
'Melampus,' published in *Poems and Lyrics of the Joy of Earth*, 1883, 79–86

298
With sagest craft Arachne worked
'A Garden Idyll,' published in *A Reading of Life*, 1901, 81–7

299
With splendour of a silver day,
'Night of Frost in May,' published in *The Empty Purse*, 1892, 111–16

300
Within a Temple of the Toes,
'Phantasy,' published in *Once a Week*, 23 November, 1861, 601–2; reprinted in *Modern Love*, 1862, 157–67

301
Yet it was plain she struggled, and that salt
Untitled, published in *Modern Love*, 1862, 40

302
Yon upland slope which hides the sun
'Yon Upland Slope which Hides the Sun,' published in *Poems 1851*, 87

303
Yonder's the man with his life in his hand
' "Atkins",' published in The *Westminster Gazette*, 18 February 1901, 2; reprinted in *Last Poems*, 1909, 51

304
You like not that French novel? Tell me why.
Untitled, published in *Modern Love*, 1862, 57

305
Young captain of a crazy bark!
'The Last Contention,' published in *Ballads and Poems of Tragic Life*, 1887, 129–32

Alphabetical list of poems by title

In the following list of Meredith's poems by title, the number which follows the title is that of the same poem in the census of poems by first line (Part III, D).

At the Funeral
77
Her sacred body bear: the tenement

Autumn Even-Song
216
The long cloud edged with streaming grey

Beauty Rohtraut
274
What is the name of King Ringang's daughter?

Bellerophon
131
Maimed, beggared, grey; seeking an alms; with nod

Breath of the Briar
158
O briar-scents, on yon wet wing

By Morning Twilight
140
Night like a dying mother

By the Rosanna. To F.M.
220
The old grey Alp has caught the cloud

Camelus Saltat
277
What say you, critic, now you have become

Cassandra
41
Captive on a foreign shore

Change in Recurrence
100
I stood at the gate of the cot

Epitaph on the Tombstone of James Christopher Wilson
247
Thou our beloved and light of Earth hast crossed

Foresight and Patience
196
Sprung of the father blood, the mother brain

Forest History
31
Beneath the vans of doom did men pass in

France 1870
268
We look for her that sunlike stood

Gordon of Khartoum
164
Of men he would have raised to light he fell:

Grace and Love
258
Two flower-enfolding crystal vases she

Grandfather Bridgeman
75
'Heigh, boys!' cried Grandfather Bridgeman, 'it's time before dinner to-day.'

Hard Weather
36
Bursts from a rending East in flaws

Hawarden
284
When comes the lighted day for men to read

M.M.
293
Who call her Mother and who calls her Wife

Modern Love
39
By this he knew she wept with waking eyes:

Monmouth
233
The windows flash in Taunton town

Mother to Babe
58
Fleck of sky you are,

My Theme [2 Sonnets)
163
Of me and of my theme think what thou wilt:

Napoleon
40
Cannon his name,

Nature and Life
120
Leave the uproar: at a leap

Night of Frost in May
299
With splendour of a silver day,

October 21, 1905
215
The hundred years have passed, and he

Ode to the Comic Spirit
205
Sword of Common Sense! –

Periander
86
How died Melissa none dares shape in words.

Phaéthôn – Attempted in the Galliambic Measure
28
At the coming up of Phoebus the all-luminous charioteer

Phantasy
300
Within a Temple of the Toes,

Phoebus with Admetus
283
When by Zeus relenting the mandate was revoked,

Pictures of the Rhine
229
The spirit of Romance dies not to those

Progress
108
In Progress you have little faith, say you:

Queen Juleima
144
Not less a Queen, because I wear

Requiem
292
Where faces are hueless, where eyelids are dewless,

Rhine-Land
267
We lean'd beneath the purple vine,

Seed-Time
59
Flowers of the willow-herb are wool:

The Death of Winter
281
When April with her wild blue eye

The Discipline of Wisdom
181
Rich labour is the struggle to be wise,

The Doe: A Fragment from "Wandering Willie"
21
And – 'Yonder look! yoho! yoho!

The Emperor Frederick of Our Time
295
With Alfred and St. Louis he doth win

The Empty Purse
248
Thou, run to the dry on this wayside bank,

The Flower of the Ruins
206
Take thy lute and sing

The Garden of Epicurus
207
That Garden of sedate Philosophy

The Head of Bran
289
When the head of Bran

The Horses of Achilles, Iliad, xvii, 426
194
So now the horses of Aiakides, off wide of the war-ground,

The Hueless Love
264
Unto what love must we through fire attain,

The Revolution
149
Not yet had History's Aetna smoked the skies

The Riddle for Men
245
This Riddle rede or die

The Sage Enamoured and the Honest Lady
171
One fairest of the ripe unwedded left

The Shipwreck of Idomeneus
203
Swept from his fleet upon that fatal night

The Sleeping City
8
A princess in the eastern tale

The Song of Courtesy
288
When Sir Gawain was led to his bridal-bed,

The Song of Theodolind
180
Queen Theodolind has built

The South-Wester
47
Day of the cloud in fleets! O day

The Spirit of Shakespeare
253
The greatest knew thee, Mother Earth; unsoured

The Star Sirius
35
Bright Sirius! that when Orion pales

The Voyage of the "Ophir"
134
Men of our race, we send you one

The Warning
266
We have seen mighty men ballooning high

The Wild Rose
80
High climbs June's wild rose,

The Wild Rose and the Snowdrop
227
The Snowdrop is the prophet of the flowers;

The Wisdom of Eld
270
We spend our lives in learning pilotage,

The Woods of Westermain
53
Enter these enchanted woods,

The World's Advance
114
Judge mildly the tasked world: and disincline

The Years had Worn their Seasons' Belt
234
The years had worn their seasons' belt,

The Year's Sheddings
231
The varied colours are a fitful heap:

The Young Princess
290
When the South sang like a nightingale

To Children: For Tyrants
197
Strike not thy dog with a stick!

To Colonel Charles
19
An English heart, my commandant,

To J.M.
121
Let Fate or Insufficiency provide

To Robin Redbreast
136
Merrily 'mid the faded leaves,

Trafalgar Day
71
He leads: we hear our Seaman's call

Twilight Music
116
Know you the low pervading breeze

Two Wedded Lovers watched the Rising Moon
259
Two wedded lovers watched the rising moon,

Under Boughs of Breathing May
260
Under boughs of breathing May,

Union in Disseverance
199
Sunset worn to its last vermilion hue;

Unknown Fair Faces
250
Though I am faithful to my loves lived through,

untitled
7
A message from her set his brain aflame

untitled
11
A roar through the tall twin elm-trees

untitled
14
A wilding little stubble flower

untitled
16
All other joys of life he strove to warm,

untitled
17
Along the garden terrace, under which

untitled
18
Am I failing? For no longer can I cast

untitled
24
Ask, is Love divine,

untitled
26
At dinner, she is hostess, I am host.

untitled
27
At last we parley; we so strangely dumb

untitled
38
But where began the change; and what's my crime?

untitled
50
Distraction is the panacea, Sir!

untitled
62
From labours through the night, outworn

untitled
64
Full faith I have she holds that rarest gift

untitled
65
Give to imagination some pure light

untitled
69
He felt the wild beast in him betweenwhiles

untitled
70
He found her by the ocean's moaning verge,

untitled
79
Here Jack and Tom are paired with Moll and Meg

untitled
84
How barren would this valley be

untitled
88
How many a thing which we cast to the ground

untitled
90
I am not of those miserable males

untitled
91
I am to follow her. There is much grace

untitled
92
I bade my Lady think what she might mean.

untitled
94
I chafe at darkness in the night;

untitled
97
I must be flattered. The imperious

untitled
98
'I play for Seasons; not Eternities!'

untitled
101
I think she sleeps: it must be sleep, when low

untitled
106
In our old shipwrecked days there was an hour,

untitled
107
In Paris, at the Louvre, there have I seen

untitled
109
It chanced his lips did meet her forehead cool.

untitled
110
It ended, and the morrow brought the task

untitled
III
It is no vulgar nature I have wived.

untitled
112
It is the season of the sweet wild rose,

untitled
125
Lo! as a tree whose wintry twigs

untitled
127
Love ere he bleeds, an eagle in high skies,

untitled
128
Love is winged for two,

untitled
130
Madam would speak with me. So, now it comes:

untitled
132
Mark where the pressing wind shoots javelin-like

untitled
138
My Lady unto Madam makes her bow.

untitled
142
No state is enviable. To the luck alone

untitled
145
Not solely that the Future she destroys

untitled
152
Now from the meadow floods the wild duck clamours

untitled
153
Now standing on this hedgeside path,

untitled
172
Open horizons round,

untitled
175
Out in the yellow meadows, where the bee

untitled
188
She issues radiant from her dressing-room

untitled
189
She yields: my Lady in her noblest mood

untitled
198
Summer glows warm on the meadows, and speedwell, and gold-cups and daisies

untitled
200
Swathed round in mist and crown'd with cloud,

untitled
217
The misery is greater, as I live!

untitled
235
Their sense is with their senses all mixed in,

untitled
241
They say, that Pity in Love's service dwells,

untitled
243
This golden head has wit in it. I live

untitled
246
This was the woman; what now of the man?

untitled
252
Thus piteously Love closed what he begat:

untitled
254
'Tis Christmas weather, and a country house

untitled
269
We saw the swallows gathering in the sky,

untitled
271
We three are on the cedar-shadowed lawn;

untitled
273
What are we first? First animals; and next

untitled
276
What may this woman labour to confess?

untitled
278
What soul would bargain for a cure that brings

PART IV

Collected Editions

SUMMARY

The importance of the collected editions of Meredith's works derives not only from the fact that they marked successive steps in the establishment of his reputation towards the end of his life, but also from the fact that he revised the whole of his work at least twice when the two principal collected editions were being prepared. No prose work escaped the second revision and no prose work, except *Celt and Saxon*, appeared after it had occurred. Consequently what for the moment has to be regarded as the definitive text of Meredith's work is the 'de luxe' edition published by Constable in 1896 and subsequent years. The relation of one edition to another can be seen in broad outline in the summary which follows.

LVIII CHAPMAN AND HALL, 1885–95

The publication of this edition is undoubtedly the most important event in Meredith's writing career. For it he corrected copies of all his previously published novels and later corrected the proofs. Although, in a strict sense, it became obsolete when Constable published the 'de luxe' edition, it remains significant for anyone interested in the process of emendation and change from first edition to definitive text, since in some novels the differences between the Chapman and Hall 'collected' text and both the first edition and the later Constable text are substantial. Complete sets are relatively rare. Colonial editions were prepared from the plates of this edition.

LIX ROBERTS BROTHERS, 1886–95

Roberts Brothers at first sold copies of LVIII with a titlepage and binding of their own and then re-set the novels for an 'edition' of their own. Neither Meredith nor Chapman and Hall seem to have known about the reprinting until after it had occurred. The edition has no textual importance. The plates were later sold to Scribner but not used.

LX CONSTABLE, 1896–8

This edition established the standard text of the greater part of Meredith's work. Meredith corrected work sheets, the originals of which are now in the Beinecke Library at Yale, made up for him specially from dismembered copies of LVIII and the corrections were in fact incorporated into the new edition.

LXI CONSTABLE, 1897–1910

Textually almost identical to LX, though printed from different plates.

LXII SCRIBNER, 1898–1910
This edition was prepared in the same way as LX; that is, work sheets were made for Meredith from dismembered copies of LVIII for the majority of the volumes. Both the books of corrected leaves and the copies of volumes from which this edition was set are now in the Lilly Library in the University of Indiana at Bloomington. Though they are not identical there are no significant differences between LX and LXII.

LXIII CONSTABLE, 1902 – The Pocket Edition.

LXIV CONSTABLE, 1909–11
The Memorial Edition printed from new plates set up from LX.

LXV THE TIMES BOOK CLUB, 1912
A limited reprinting from the plates of LXIV, described here as a separate entry only because it has assumed the role of one of the standard editions of Meredith's work.

LVIII

CHAPMAN AND HALL, 1885–95
(with Ward, Lock & Bowden)

EXAMPLE

DIANA OF THE CROSSWAYS / *A Novel* / BY / GEORGE MEREDITH / [short rule] / LONDON: CHAPMAN AND HALL / LIMITED / [short rule] / 1885.

Collation [A]³B–2C⁸ 153 leaves (19.0 x 13.0) [i–v] vi [1]–398 [299–300]

Contents [i] halftitle: DIANA OF THE CROSSWAYS [ii] advertisement for other volumes in this edition [iii] titlepage [iv] imprint: WESTMINSTER: / PRINTED BY NICHOLS AND SONS, / 25, PARLIAMENT STREET. [v]–vi contents [1]–398 text, on 398 at centre: THE END. and at foot: [rule] / WESTMINSTER: / PRINTED BY NICHOLS AND SONS, 25, PARLIAMENT STREET. [299–300]

Binding Spine, and boards at front and back, covered in olive-grey cloth. Dark green endpapers.

Front cover Plain, with a blind stamped border .25 cms. from all edges.

Spine Single line stamped in gilt at top and bottom between which, also stamped in gilt: DIANA / OF THE / CROSSWAYS / GEORGE MEREDITH / CHAPMAN & HALL

Back cover Identical to front cover.

PUBLICATION

Chapman and Hall's part of this first collected edition, to which Ward, Lock and Bowden contributed two volumes, was printed twice. In advertisements it was referred to as the 'New' edition, though not on the titlepage.

The first version is on relatively heavy paper and is bound in olive-green cloth; from these plates was later produced the 'colonial' edition for sale in Australia.

The second version is on lighter paper and is bound in royal blue cloth. The first was sold at 6s. a copy; the second at 3s. 6d. Meredith corrected the proof of the first, but not for the second, though he did grumble about the mistakes.

The edition consists of the following novels:

The novels, all published by Chapman and Hall except *The Tragic Comedians* and *The Tale of Chloe*	First version printing by Virtue sold at 6s.	'Colonial' Issue of first impression by George Bell	Second version printing by Clowes sold at 3s. 6d.
1 Diana of the Crossways	1885	1894	1890
2 Evan Harrington	1885	1895	1890
3 The Ordeal of Richard Feverel	1885	1895	1890
4 The Adventures of Harry Richmond	1885	1894	1890
5 Sandra Belloni	1886		1890
6 Vittoria	1886		1889
7 Rhoda Fleming	1886	1895	1890
8 Beauchamp's Career	1886		1889
9 The Egoist	1886	1895	1889
10 The Shaving of Shagpat and Farina	1887		1889
11 One of our Conquerors	1891		1892
12 The Tragic Comedians	1892		1892
13 The Tale of Chloe	1894		
14 Lord Ormont and His Aminta	1895	1895	1897

THE FIRST PRINTING BY VIRTUE

The first collected edition of Meredith's novels was a turning point in his literary career, since the long awaited recognition it represented released him, as it were, for the writing of the last group of novels.

Forman (p. 279) noted some of the contemporary announcements of the first collected edition of Meredith's work. In the 'Literary Gossip' of the *Athenaeum* for 30 May 1890, it was announced that: 'Messrs. Chapman and Hall talk of publishing a uniform edition of Mr. George Meredith's novels, the great majority of which are quite out of print.' On 4 June 1885 there was a notice in the *St. James's Gazette* (p. 4): 'Last week's *Athenaeum* contained a welcome piece of news. Messrs. Chapman and Hall, it is intimated, intend to publish a uniform edition of Mr. George Meredith's novels. Such a re-issue would be most welcome. Some of the best of Mr. Meredith's novels have long been out of print; and if you want to read them you must pay for the privilege of having a first edition, which is not easily to be obtained. *Diana of the Crossways* has brought Mr. Meredith's name before the world again very prominently, and it is in the nature of things that many people would be glad of the opportunity of reading some of his earlier novels – *The Ordeal of Richard Feverel, Rhoda Fleming, Emilia in England* – originally produced when they were at school.'

As noted above, Meredith corrected and in a few instances amended earlier editions for this first collected edition by Chapman and Hall. He had reconsidered, corrected, and partly rewritten *The Ordeal of Richard Feverel* for the Tauchnitz edition of which text was then used by Kegan Paul for the second edition published in 1878. But *The Ordeal of Richard Feverel* is the exception. Meredith for the most part had no cause to revise his other early novels until 1885, when the collected edition being described here gave him the occasion for the first serious review of his work to that date. The collected edition by Chapman and Hall is therefore a major landmark in Meredith's writing life.

The edition is in three parts.

A Ten novels published by Chapman and Hall, 1885–7.

B Two further volumes, *The Tragic Comedians*, 1892, and *The Tale of Chloe*, 1894, published by Ward, Lock and Bowden in a format identical to the Chapman and Hall 'New Edition.'

C Two later novels, *One of Our Conquerors*, 1891, and *Lord Ormont and His Aminta*, 1895, published by Chapman and Hall in the 'New Edition' format.

Individual volumes of this edition are relatively scarce and not too easy to identify, since Chapman and Hall re-issued them from time to time during the course of the next eight years, changing only the titlepage and therefore the date with the new issue.

The three parts will be referred to in turn.

A *The edition as at first conceived*

In the agreement between Meredith and Chapman and Hall dated 2 June 1885 (Beinecke), Chapman and Hall purchased the right to publish *The Ordeal of Richard Feverel, Emilia in England* (*Sandra Belloni*), *Vittoria, Rhoda Fleming*, and *Beauchamp's Career* for a period of 7 years and for this right agreed to pay Meredith £500: £250 on the signing of the agreement and £250 six months later. In the same agreement, Chapman and Hall offered to purchase the copyright of *Evan Harrington, The Adventures of Harry Richmond*, and *The Egoist* for the same period (by implication), if Meredith could negotiate their release, Meredith to be paid £100 for each novel. *The Shaving of Shagpat* and *Farina* are not mentioned. There had never been a formal agreement for the publication of *The Shaving of Shagpat*. Several years later, in a letter dated 15 April 1893, Meredith told Colles: 'I sold to Edward Chapman, then head of the Firm, the original first *edition* of it, only the edition, for £80. No agreement of any kind was written' (*Letters* II 1129). *Diana of the Crossways* was covered by the agreement for the three-volume first edition which was published in 1885.

Within the next two years, Chapman and Hall published these ten novels according to the following schedule:

Diana of the Crossways	20 July 1885
Evan Harrington	14 September 1885
The Ordeal of Richard Feverel	1 November 1885
The Adventures of Harry Richmond	24 December 1885
Sandra Belloni	3 February 1886
Vittoria	18 March 1886
Rhoda Fleming	13 May 1886
Beauchamp's Career	4 August 1886
The Egoist	25 October 1886
The Shaving of Shagpat and *Farina*	30 March 1886

Publication dates of this first issue are given in a letter from Chapman and Hall to Lane (Beinecke). The 'work' that Meredith referred to in his letter to Mrs. Grant Allen dated 29 December 1885 was presumably the correction of the proofs: 'I have to go to Effingham Hill this week, when I have finished work that claims me here. Thence to Eastbourne to bring back my girl' (Stark).

B *The addition of two volumes by Ward, Lock and Bowden*

Ward, Lock and Bowden published *The Tragic Comedians*, 1892, and *The Tale of Chloe*, 1894, in a format identical to the Chapman and Hall 'New

Edition.' In the agreement dated 28 July 1894, Ward, Lock and Bowden agreed to publish a one-volume edition of 'The House on the Beach,' 'The Case of General Ople and Lady Camper,' and 'The Tale of Chloe,' at not less than 3s. 6d. a copy. Meredith was to have a royalty of 25 per cent and the agreement was to last for three years (Stark).

Ward, Lock and Bowden's accounts show that 2241 copies of *The Tale of Chloe* were printed on 1 November 1894; 1522 copies on 13 February 1895; 1515 copies on 6 May 1895; and 1515 copies on 23 July 1895 (Stark). Of these at least 900 copies were 'supplied to American house,' 300 copies being shipped on each of the following dates: 8 February 1895, 15 March 1895, and 22 March 1895 (Stark). Thus the firm did rather well from the arrangement it made with Chapman and Hall.

c *Later additions by Chapman and Hall*

Chapman and Hall published *One of Our Conquerors*, 1891, and *Lord Ormont and His Aminta*, 1895 (but not *The Amazing Marriage*) in the 'New Edition' format.

Meredith corrected the proofs for the three-volume and the one-volume 6s. edition of *One of Our Conquerors* simultaneously, or at least was at work on the proofs of the one-volume edition before the novel was first published, as is made clear in a letter he wrote to Chapman on 17 December 1890: 'I did well in determining to see these Proofs of the Cheap Edition. They have been put in the hands of careless compositors – who now and then take it upon them to amend my corrected proofs of the three volumes and produce a totally different phrase. Pray, speak emphatically to Clowes – otherwise we shall have these present corrections disregarded, and once more an edition to make an author groan. Oblige me by causing duplicate proofs to be sent. I wish you to tell Clowes, that the ante-penultimate chapter of the 3rd Volume, now headed '*Penance*,' should have for heading '*An Expiation*' (*Letters* II 1014). He continued to work at both sets of proofs during January 1891. 'I posted Virtue's proofs to you very soon after they were received,' he told Chapman on 27 January 1891, 'together with some of the cheap edition for Clowes' (*Letters* II 1017).

THE SECOND IMPRESSION

In the agreement between Meredith and Chapman and Hall dated 9 April 1894 (Beinecke), an agreement for the three-volume edition of *Lord Ormont and His Aminta*, Chapman and Hall obtained the right to publish a one-volume edition to be sold at not less than 6s., Meredith to be paid on the one-volume edition a royalty of 25 per cent. *Lord Ormont and His Aminta* was nonetheless also published in the 3s. 6d. version of the 'New Edition.'

The first ten novels in the Chapman and Hall 'New Edition' (the first collected edition) were reissued at 3s. 6d. on cheaper paper from the same plates. Chapman and Hall's letter to Lane (Beinecke) states that this second, cheaper impression was issued in two batches: *Diana of the Crossways, The Ordeal of Richard Feverel, Rhoda Fleming*, and *The Egoist* on 22 January 1890; and *Evan Harrington, The Adventures of Harry Richmond, Sandra Belloni, Vittoria, Beauchamp's Career*, and *The Shaving of Shagpat* and *Farina* on 15 February 1890. He again had problems with the compositors, if it can be assumed that his letter of 2 November 1888 refers to the 3s. 6d. rather than to the 6s. edition. 'As to the New Edition – the errors of print in this one are horrible. Let me know the order of the issues, and I will endeavour to make some corrections, though I can't offer to go through the volumes again' (*Letters* II 935).

THE REISSUE OF THE 'NEW EDITION'

Chapman and Hall continued not only to sell, but also to print, copies of the 'New Edition' after the seven years stipulated in the agreement of 2 July 1885 had elapsed. Perhaps it was when Meredith put his affairs into the hands of an agent that he realized that his relationship with Chapman and Hall had been too casual. The Society of Authors was, in any case, making novelists more aware of the need for sensible business arrangements. Meredith, who had for the most part sold the copyright of his novels for a fixed sum and a fixed term, without royalties, had previously adopted the position that serious writers should not write for money. Whether this was a deep-rooted conviction or an affectation that made his early lack of popularity palatable, he now adopted a more business-like attitude. On 7 February 1893 he wrote to his agent, W.M. Colles: 'Four or five of my novels have fallen in. Chapman writes that he will make a proposal – after saying no word of copyright fallen due to me. I feel bound to give the Firm the chance of the proposal, but expect niggardliness. You shall hear when I have heard, and I will send dates of the books' (*Letters* II 1119).

A little later Meredith authorized Colles to negotiate with Chapman and Hall. On 25 March 1893 he wrote: ' ... we may engage with them for 2 years. It is to be advised, because they have two novels running on to next year, and I in '97. Put it to them that I require a good Royalty and name it. I have told Chapman that I cannot have haggling. Only he must not juggle to withhold what is rightly mine of the sale' (*Letters* II 1127). Presumably 'the two novels running on to next year' were *The Shaving of Shagpat* and *One of Our Conquerors*, and the 'I in 97' was *Lord Ormont and His Aminta*. In a new agreement dated 19 July 1893 (Beinecke), Chapman and Hall purchased the right to publish the 'New Edition' for a further three years, and agreed to pay Meredith a royalty of 25 per cent on all copies in stock on the day that the seven-year agreement came to an end.

This contract includes a list of the novels with, in each case, the number of copies unsold, a list which indicates, though none too accurately, the relative popularity of the novels. The contract refers to earlier agreements of 21 July 1884 and 2 June 1885 covering the novels listed in Schedule I, and of 12 April 1887 for the novels listed in Schedule II, stipulating that 'The Company shall have the exclusive right to print publish and sell the Books specified in the First and Second Schedules hereto in the United Kingdom for a period of three years from the date of the Agreement' (Beinecke).

	Expiration of Licence		No. of Copies in stock at expiration date		No. of Copies printed since	
SCHEDULE I			3s. 6d.	6s.	3s. 6d.	6s.
Diana of the Crossways	16 Feb	90	2006	47	250	4000
Evan Harrington	14 Sept	92	936	176	—	—
The Ordeal of Richard Feverel	1 Nov	92	297	244	2000	—
The Adventures of Harry Richmond	24 Dec	92	1659	222		
Sandra Belloni	3 Feb	93	1733	263		
Vittoria	18 March	93	1782	227		
Rhoda Fleming	13 May	93	599	104		
SCHEDULE II						
Beauchamp's Career	5 Aug	93	201	143		
The Egoist	25 Oct	93	516	123		
The Shaving of Shagpat	30 March	93	338	92		

Chapman and Hall evidently honoured this agreement, for on 29 November 1893 E. Hayward, on the firm's behalf, wrote to Colles: 'We have today given an order to print 2000 copies of "Diana of the Crossways" 3/6 edition, and in accordance with the agreement we send cheque for the royalty thereon, viz. 2000 − 13 as 12 = 1846 at 10% = £80.15.3. Will you please forward cheque to Mr. Meredith & let us have his receipt' (Beinecke).

THE COLONIAL ISSUE FROM CHAPMAN AND HALL PLATES

In the agreement between Chapman and Hall and Messrs. Bell and Sons dated 15 November 1894, Chapman and Hall agreed to sell to Messrs. Bell and Sons unbound copies of the 'New Edition,' according to the following schedule:

Diana of the Crossways	1000 copies	December 1894
The Adventures of Harry Richmond	750 copies	December 1894
The Ordeal of Richard Feverel	1000 copies	January 1894 [sic]
Lord Ormont and His Aminta	1000 copies	February 1895
Evan Harrington	1000 copies	March 1895
The Egoist	750 copies	April 1895
Rhoda Fleming	750 copies	May 1895

Meredith was to have 4d. per copy sold, half on the date of sale, half three months later. Each copy was to marked 'Printed for Colonial Circulation only' (Beinecke).

It may be assumed that Chapman and Hall were anxious to dispose of copies they had in stock when Meredith changed publishers.

The volumes of this first collected edition had previously been issued in Australia with the imprint: George Robertson & Co. Melbourne & Sydney; London & Bungay.

LIX

ROBERTS BROTHERS, BOSTON

Chapman and Hall's 'New Edition' was first distributed, then published in the United States by Roberts Brothers of Boston. The publisher advertised an English edition in ten volumes at $2.00 a volume, or bound in half-calf at $25.00 the set. Roberts bought unbound copies from Chapman and Hall, and apart from the binding changed only the titlepage, on which 'Author's Edition' replaces 'New Edition' and 'ROBERTS BROTHERS. / 3, SOMERSET STREET, / BOSTON.' replaces 'LONDON: CHAPMAN AND HALL / LIMITED'. When it became necessary, however, Roberts Brothers printed their own copies.

Roberts Brothers published Meredith for about ten years. The firm's accounts are not available but when, in 1895, Scribner bought the American rights as well as the plates from Roberts Brothers, a report was drawn up on printing and sales during the previous eight or nine years. These accounts are dated 1 January 1895 and are in the Stark Library at Texas. The chart of sales, reproduced below, reveals that the earlier bookkeeping had been something less than exact.

Roberts Brothers published what in England had been called the 'New Edition' and what they subsequently called the 'Author's Edition' in two bindings, selling the one at $1.50 and the other at $1.00. Esdaile stated (p. 39) that both Chapman and Hall editions were 'issued sumultaneously by Roberts Bros., Boston.' This statement conceals the fact that, when they had sold the copies purchased from Chapman and Hall, or in some cases before they had sold them all, they printed their own. Scribner accounts for 6 October 1898 (Stark) indicate that Scribner paid Roberts Brothers $6000 for the plates, and at various points make clear that both the $1.50 edition and the $1.00 reissue consisted of twelve novels, the eleven novels listed in the agreement with Scribner and *The Tragic Comedians*.

The publication of *One of Our Conquerors* by Roberts Brothers is part of the evidence which confirms the independent printing: it was published in one volume in Boston in 1891. Indeed, Meredith or his agent must have negotiated directly with Roberts Brothers rather than through Chapman and Hall, since there is a letter in which he reassures Niles, of Roberts Brothers, that he has the right to dispose of the book rights. 'In the agreement with the *Sun* for Serial issue of *One of Our Conquerors*, I distinctly reserve the right of publication in book form. And Mr. Balestier, who was agent in the matter, undertook to apprise you of the estimated period of the close of the work in Serial issue, so that you may be ready with the book a little before the last chapters' (20 August 1890: *Letters* II 1002). Presumably because of the rapidly increasing interest in Meredith, they printed additional copies before they had sold the ones bought from Chapman and Hall. Indeed, the advertisements on the verso preceding the titlepage of *One of Our Conquerors* distinguish between '10 volumes, English Edition, half calf. Extra, $25.00 the set' and '11 volumes, Popular American Edition, 16 mo. cloth Price $1.50'.

In summary, three 'editions' of the collected edition by Roberts Brothers were published between 1885 and 1895. They were:

A *The English 'New Edition' by Chapman and Hall with the Roberts Brothers titlepage and binding*

One example is all that is necessary:

ONE OF OUR CONQUERORS / BY / GEORGE MEREDITH / *Author's Edition* / ROBERTS BROTHERS, / 3, SOMERSET STREET, / BOSTON. / 1891.

Binding Olive-green cloth on boards.

Front cover Plain.

Spine Stamped in gilt: [long rule] / ONE OF OUR / CONQUERORS / [short rule] / GEORGE MEREDITH / [long rule] / R.B. / [long rule]

Back cover Plain.

There is no printer's imprint. On the verso of the flytitle, there is an advertisement for George Meredith's works: 'Each novel will be complete in One Volume, price 6s.'

Roberts Brothers' copies dated 1886 are necessarily Chapman and Hall printings.

B(i) *The 'Author's Edition' with the imprint of the American Printer, but with the advertisement unchanged, for example:*

EVAN HARRINGTON / A NOVEL / BY / GEORGE MEREDITH / AUTHOR'S EDITION / BOSTON / ROBERTS BROTHERS / 1896

Binding Brown cloth on boards.

Front cover Stamped in gilt: G.M.'s head and shoulders
Stamped in black: very truly yours / George Meredith.

Spine Stamped in black: five pairs of horizontal lines with a device at top and beneath the lower three sets of lines.
Stamped in gilt: GEORGE / MEREDITH'S / NOVELS / EVAN HARRINGTON

Back cover Plain.

On verso of titlepage: PRESSWORK BY JOHN WILSON AND SON, / UNIVERSITY PRESS. on verso of flytitle, an advertisement for George Meredith's works: 'Each novel will be complete in One Volume, price 6s.'

B(ii) *An alternative version has an identical titlepage but two distinguishing marks:*

a The advertisement on verso of flytitle reads:
Popular Edition / OF GEORGE MEREDITH'S WORKS. / Each novel will be complete in One Volume. Price, $1.50.
b On the verso of the titlepage:
Presswork by / JOHN WILSON AND SON, CAMBRIDGE

Roberts Brothers' records and accounts did not survive. The most illuminating statement of the firm's practice is thus the stock report to Scribner already referred to.

Table 2: Stocklists of copies held by Roberts Brothers when the plates were purchased by Scribners

TITLE	TOTAL	'Impressions' obtained from Chapman and Hall			
		Credited		On Hand	I TOTAL
		To Date	Now		
Rhoda Fleming	500 (Dec 86)				500 (Nov 91)
The Egoist					514 (Mar 93)
The Ordeal of Richard Feverel	500 (Dec 87)	380	84	36	527 (Nov 93)
Evan Harrington	250 (Dec 87)	170	37	43	519 (Dec 88)
The Adventures of Harry Richmond	240 (Dec 87)	125	31	94	500 (Mar 93)
Diana of the Crossways	497 (Dec 87)	470	27		539 (Sept 93)
Sandra Belloni	250 (Dec 87)	60	110	80	500 (Sept 94)
Vittoria	250 (Dec 87)			250	517 (Sept 89)
Beauchamp's Career	250 (Dec 87)	130	26	94	500 (Nov 92)
The Shaving of Shagpat	250 (Dec 87)	175	40	35	500 (Oct 92)
LISTED SEPARATELY					
One of Our Conquerors	270 (May 91)	125	25	120	500 (Oct 91)

Not listed here is *The Tragic Comedians*, for which Roberts had a separate agreement with Ward, Lock & Bowden. Roberts took unbound copies of *The Tragic Comedians* and published them in the same format as the edition being described here, the only textual change being the new titlepage.

| TITLE | Subsequent Printings by Roberts Brothers | | | | | | |
| | Credited | | | | Credited | | |
	To Date	Now	On Hand	II TOTAL	To Date	Now	On Hand
Rhoda Fleming	215	170		280 (Apr 93)	15	20	
The Egoist	164	354		500 (Sept 94)		30	470
The Ordeal of Richard Feverel	30	497					
Evan Harrington	480	39		280 (Mar 93)	73		207
The Adventures of Harry Richmond	55	103	340				
Diana of the Crossways	80	459		500 (Sept 94)		50	450
Sandra Belloni		500					
Vittoria	410	77	30				
Beauchamp's Career	100	135	265				
The Shaving of Shagpat	45	100	355				
LISTED SEPARATELY							
One of Our Conquerors	240	110	150				

LX

A. CONSTABLE AND CO., 1896–8, 1910–11 (The 'De Luxe' Edition)

EXAMPLE

THE WORKS OF / GEORGE MEREDITH / VOLUME I / [device: Meredith's initials entwined in vines and pomegranates] / WESTMINSTER / ARCHIBALD CONSTABLE AND CO. / 2 WHITEHALL GARDENS / 1896

Collation [1]⁴[2]²A–T⁸U² 160 leaves (22.0 x 14.5) [i–viii] ix–xi [xii] 1–[308]

Contents [i] blank [ii] publisher's note: This Edition is limited to / one thousand and twenty-five copies / all numbered / No ... [iii] halftitle: THE

WORKS OF / GEORGE MEREDITH / RICHARD FEVEREL / I [iv] blank [v] titlepage [vi] blank [vii] halftitle: THE ORDEAL OF / RICHARD FEVEREL / A HISTORY OF A / FATHER AND SON / VOLUME / I [viii] note: Originally published / 3 vols.: London 1859 ix–xi contents [xii] blank 1–[308] text, on [308] at foot the imprint: [short rule] / EDINBURGH: T. and A. CONSTABLE, Printers to Her Majesty
The frontispiece is pasted in between [iv] and [v]

Binding Spine and about 1 cm. of each cover in white buckram: the front and back boards in mauve cloth.

Front cover Plain.

Spine Stamped in blue: THE ORDEAL / OF RICHARD / FEVEREL / *by* / GEORGE MEREDITH / VOL. I / A. CONSTABLE / & CO. / WESTMINSTER

Back cover Plain.

The edition consists of 36 volumes, as follows:

I and II	*The Ordeal of Richard Feverel*, 1896
III and IV	*Evan Harrington*, 1896
V and VI	*Sandra Belloni*, 1897
VII and VIII	*Vittoria*, 1897
IX and X	*Rhoda Fleming*, 1897
XI and XII	*The Adventures of Harry Richmond*, 1897
XIII and XIV	*Beauchamp's Career*, 1897
XV and XVI	*The Egoist*, 1897
XVII and XVIII	*Diana of the Crossways*, 1897
XIX and XX	*One of Our Conquerors*, 1897
XXI and XXII	*Lord Ormont and His Aminta*, 1897
XXIII and XXIV	*The Amazing Marriage*, 1897
XXV	*The Shaving of Shagpat*, 1898
XXVI	*The Tragic Comedians*, 1898
XXVII	*The Tale of Chloe* and *The House on the Beach*, 1898
XXVIII	*Farina* and *The Case of General Ople and Lady Camper*, 1898
XXIX–XXXI	*Poems*, 1898 [see PART III, pp. 154–9]
XXXII	*Essays*, 1898 [see PART II, p. 91]
XXXIII	*Poems*, 1910
XXXIV	*Miscellaneous Prose*, 1910 [see PART III, pp. 168–71]
XXXV	*Celt and Saxon*, 1911
XXXVI	*Bibliography and Various Readings*, 1911

Forman notes that both the sets of illustrations for the Memorial Edition which were gathered together in one volume in 1911, and the two-volume edition of letters that was prepared by W.M. Meredith and published in 1912, were bound to match the earlier de luxe edition, which thus in a sense consists of 39 volumes.

PUBLICATION

Meredith changed publisher in 1895 and at the same time put his affairs into the hands of his son. A natural first step for the new publisher, Constable, was the production of a collected edition, since as soon as Chapman and Hall's stock was disposed of the novels were out of print except for those published by Ward, Lock & Bowden. Since Meredith was still enjoying the popularity that had begun with the publication of *Diana of the Crossways* – a popularity that had been greatly enhanced by heavy sales in North America – it was not surprising that Constable should have hurried to launch a collected edition of their own. Time had to pass, however, before Constable could acquire the rights.

Meredith's son had joined the staff of Constable. A year or two earlier, Meredith had put his literary affairs into the hands of the agent, Colles. Though for both of these reasons it was natural for him to think of looking for a better arrangement than he had enjoyed with Chapman and Hall, it was probably not Colles but Scribner's agent, Burlingame, who indirectly brought about the change. Scribner bought the American rights of *The Amazing Marriage* and in doing so brought Meredith's relationship with Roberts Brothers to an end, despite a certain amount of disagreement and unpleasantness. Perhaps in part because of this, Colles was able to persuade Meredith, as he had persuaded other authors, that a change would be beneficial, Chapman and Hall having continued to sell their first collected edition after the contract had expired. The rearrangement, managed for the most part by Colles and W.M. Meredith, took about two years (1893–5), because with at least some of the novels neither Chapman and Hall nor Meredith were very clear about the ownership of the rights.

Chapman and Hall's attitude had indeed been somewhat casual. They had sold the rights for publication in Germany without telling Meredith. They had sold the 'New Edition' to Roberts Brothers without in the first instance making any provision for paying him. Almost four years had passed before Meredith had complained about this to Frederic Chapman: 'You have not sent word concerning the American Royalty. I hold to the sum as being mine. More hangs on the question than you seem to think' (30 March 1889: *Letters* II 951). The matter was eventually settled, for on 4 February 1890 Meredith wrote to Chapman and Hall again: 'I have received the Order of Roberts, Brothers upon Baring which you were good enough to send, with the cession of your claim on the royalty' (*Letters* II 990). Nevertheless, it seems to have been this episode which gave Meredith the notion that his affairs could be more business-like, for whereas he had always affected a disdain for mere writing for profit, the sentiment was largely an English one that apparently did not apply when he began to have dealings with Americans. At all events, his mood had changed by the time that the seven-year agreements for the individual volumes of the Chapman and Hall edition started to terminate one by one, and Colles was therefore permitted to begin his enquiries about rights.

As mentioned already, Meredith wrote to Colles on 7 February 1893: 'Four or five of my novels have fallen in. Chapman writes that he will make a proposal – after saying no word of copyright fallen due to me. I feel bound to give the Firm the chance of the proposal, but expect niggardliness. You shall hear when I have heard, & I will send dates of the books' (*Letters* II 1119). There are a number of other letters that testify to the extent of the confusion, Meredith not helping much by being querulous and critical of Chapman and Hall, who had been no more unbusiness-like than Meredith himself. Whatever his sense of propriety, he clearly wished to obtain a release from Chapman and Hall. On 15 April 1893, for example, he wrote a tetchy letter to Colles: 'As to *Shagpat*, this is the case. I sold to Edward Chapman, then head of the Firm, the original first *Edition* of it, only the Edition, for £80. No agreement of any kind was written. Later on, F. Chapman ... came into the Firm. He pretended a claim, based on nothing, then paid me £5 (for corrections he tells you!) for the right to issue a cheap edition. He is luckless; he reminds me of another...

'Now, as you tell me, he pretends that the payment of £65 for the issue of *Shagpat* was written down by him in purchase of copyright of *Shagpat*. How of *Farina*, included in the volume? But there was no agreement or under-standing of any kind beyond the purchase of rights for the term of years. I confess that this fellow moves my wrath. Please apply to the Firm for a formal *written* renouncement of his knavish claim. If it is not sent to you before the 20th of the month, I break off all connection with the Firm and I make my reasons publicly known. I have borne with the man much too long. very truly yours, George Meredith.' Meredith's postscript indicated the direction of the mind: he had been flattered by Scribner's agent. 'I take warmly to Mr. Burlingame' (*Letters* II 1129–30). It is likely that Meredith was simply muddled, more than forty years having passed since he published his first book. At this stage in his life he was incapable of remembering his earlier occasional writings, and his blustering with Colles probably derived as much from his own un-certainty as from any real dissatisfaction with Chapman and Hall.

A short time later, in his letter to Colles dated 22 May, he backed down a little: 'I do not think that £100 was paid for *Shagpat* and *Farina*: but that the sums were £50 & £15. But let it pass: as there was no signed agreement, the inference is, that I allowed the date from publication 7 years to be implied as the term' (*Letters* II 1132). Chapman and Hall's inability to confute this did not make them any more anxious to lose an author at the very moment he was achieving popularity. Similar difficulties were encountered with Ward and Lock. 'The behaviour of Ward & Lock is bad,' Meredith exclaimed in a letter to Colles dated 21 October 1893. 'Considering the profit they had out of *The Tragic Comedians*, they should be civil and obliging. As I have a letter from them offering me "a Royalty" for the publication of the stories, they acknowledge my right in a way to quash any claim they may have in their minds' (*Letters* II 1146).

Colles was apparently energetic in his attempts to collect the rights in anticipation of the Constable collected edition, for Meredith soon wrote to him again: 'Please let Messrs Ward & Lock have the notification for you. Their success with *The Tragic Comedians* should render them civil. Enclosed is your "authority" ' (Beinecke). Whatever the legal difficulties, at least it can be supposed that the existence of the Chapman and Hall edition made it easier for Meredith to get his affairs into some semblance of order, since for the collected edition there had been a contract. Indeed, the further agreement of 19 July 1893 between Meredith and Chapman and Hall, also in the Beinecke Library, shows that the firm had accepted some of the responsibility. Chapman and Hall were to pay Meredith a royalty of 25 per cent on all books in stock at the termination of the original contract, were to have the right to sell for a further three years, and were to render their accounts on 1 March and 1 September each year. The Constable collected edition could not be published, of course, until these three years had elapsed. Much greater disagreement would have been likely if Colles had had to recall the undocumented arrangements of the publication of Meredith's earlier work.

It is possible that Meredith worked at the correction of the novels for two years, 1893 to 1895, since as early as October 1893 he told Colles ominously: 'I propose to add bits to the novels as well as excise' (*Letters* II 1145-6). The contract for the so-called 'Edition de Luxe' was signed on 1 February 1896, 1025 complete sets to be printed, and Meredith to be paid £2600 between August 1896 and February 1897 (Stark). Meredith used volumes from the Chapman and Hall edition to make corrections for the press; these corrected pages are in the Beinecke Library.

Forman noted (pp. 282–3) the prospectus with which Constable announced what was called 'the first uniform and complete edition.' There is a copy of this prospectus in the Beinecke Library.

LXI

A. CONSTABLE AND CO., 1897–1910
(The 'Library' Edition, sometimes called the 'New Popular Edition' or the 'Revised Edition')

EXAMPLE

THE ORDEAL / OF / RICHARD FEVEREL / *A history of a Father and Son* / BY / GEORGE MEREDITH / REVISED EDITION / WESTMINSTER / ARCHIBALD CONSTABLE & CO. / 1897

Collation $[\pi]^4 1-28^8 29^4 [30]^8$ 240 leaves (19.0 x 12.5) [i–v] vi–vii [viii] [1]–455 [456]

Contents [i] halftitle: THE ORDEAL OF RICHARD FEVEREL [ii] blank [iii] titlepage [iv] copyright statement: COPYRIGHT, 1896, BY / GEORGE MEREDITH [v]–vii contents [viii] blank [1]–455 text, on 455: THE END [456] blank 1–16 publisher's advertisements bound in
Frontispiece bound in between [ii] and [iii]

Binding Spine, and boards at front and back, covered in deep red cloth with a faint vertical ribbing. Endpapers plain white.

Front cover At the top left hand corner a large, stylized design of stems and flowers is blind-stamped, within which and still to left of centre is a square containing a monogram stamped in gilt.

Spine Stamped in gilt: THE / ORDEAL OF / RICHARD / FEVEREL / [device] / GEORGE / MEREDITH / WESTMINSTER / CONSTABLE & CO.

Back cover A blind-stamped device at centre.

PUBLICATION

In the prospectus issued in September 1897, a copy of which is in the Beinecke Library, Constable announced the first collected illustrated edition of Meredith's works. 'This edition will be printed from new type on fine laid paper, and the volumes will be attractively bound in a handsome cover specially designed by Mr. A.A. Turbayne.' As mentioned on p.419 Meredith had revised the novels for Constable during the years preceding the publication of the de luxe edition. It is that revision which permits the statement in the prospectus: 'For some time Mr. George Meredith has been carefully revising his works, and the text of Constable's Edition is the one which Mr. George Meredith wishes to be considered as final.' Though in subsequent advertisements it was referred to as the 'New Popular Uniform Edition,' with the result that over the years librarians and readers have called it, variously, the 'New,' the 'New Popular,' the 'Popular,' or the 'Uniform' edition, it is in fact called 'Revised Edition' on the titlepage. The safeguard for the person who has seen individual copies but not the complete set is the uniformity of format: this edition was bound only in red and is not to be confused with Constable's latter blue bound reprint of the Memorial Edition.

The agreement for the edition, now in the Stark Library, is dated 30 November 1896. The agreement was for three years and specified a sale price of 6/-, a limit of 2000 copies, and a payment to Meredith of £2737 10s. The plates were to be the property of the author.

Despite the agreement, the edition was kept in print by silent re-issue of individual volumes when necessary. The edition was sold both in sets and single volumes. Paper and type vary from volume to volume.

The edition consists of the following volumes:

The Ordeal of Richard Feverel, 1897

Rhoda Fleming, 1897

Sandra Belloni, 1897

Vittoria, 1897

Diana of the Crossways, 1897

The Adventures of Harry Richmond, 1897

Beauchamp's Career, 1897

The Egoist, 1897

Evan Harrington, 1898

The Tale of Chloe and Other Stories, 1898 (The other stories are *The House on the Beach*, *Farina*, and *The Case of General Ople and Lady Camper*.)

The Shaving of Shagpat, 1898

One of Our Conquerors, 1898

Poems, 1898

The Amazing Marriage, 1898 (Printed from the plates of the second edition. See Part I, pp. 68–76.)

The Tragic Comedians, 1898. (Printed by Butler and Tanner from the plates of the earlier editions published by Ward, Lock & Bowden.)

An Essay on Comedy, 1898. (See Part II, p. 89.)

Lord Ormont and His Aminta, 1899. (This volume has the imprint: The Guild Press, 45 Great Charles Street, Birmingham. It was in fact printed from the plates of Chapman and Hall's one-volume edition of 1895 which had been printed by Clowes.)

Celt and Saxon, 1910. (The first edition of *Celt and Saxon* was published by

Constable in a size and binding almost consistent with this collected edition.
See Part I, p. 77.)

LXII

CHARLES SCRIBNER'S SONS
(Boxhill Edition)

EXAMPLE

THE EGOIST / *A Comedy in Narrative* / BY / GEORGE MEREDITH /
REVISED EDITION / NEW YORK / CHARLES SCRIBNER'S SONS / 1913

Collation [1–32]⁸[33]¹⁰ 266 leaves (18.5 x 12.5) [i–v] vi–vii [viii] [1]–523
[524]

Contents [i] halftitle: THE EGOIST [ii] advertisement [iii] titlepage [iv] copy-
right statement and imprint: COPYRIGHT, 1897, BY / GEORGE MEREDITH / THE
SCRIBNER PRESS [v]–vii contents [viii] blank [1]–523 text [524] blank
The frontispiece is pasted in between [ii] and [iii]

Binding Spine and boards at front and back covered in light green cloth.
Endpapers plain.

Front cover Stamped in darker green a border with a simple leaf design 2 mm.
from all edges. Stamped in gilt at centre, a tree.

Spine Stamped in dark green at top and bottom the same border as on front
cover. Between the borders, stamped in gilt: THE EGOIST / [device stamped in
green] / GEORGE / MEREDITH / SCRIBNERS

Back cover Identical to front cover but without central device.

The advertisement on [ii] gives the details both of this issue and of the pocket
edition. It reads as follows:

THE WORKS OF / GEORGE MEREDITH / [rule] / *THE BOXHILL EDITION IN*
17 *VOLS.* / *With Photogravure Frontispieces* / *Each, Crown 8vo, $1.50* / CELT
AND SAXON / THE ORDEAL OF RICHARD FEVEREL / DIANA OF THE CROSSWAYS /
SANDRA BELLONI / VITTORIA / RHODA FLEMING / THE EGOIST / THE ADVENTURES
OF HARRY RICHMOND / BEAUCHAMP'S CAREER / EVAN HARRINGTON / ONE OF
OUR CONQUERORS / THE SHAVING OF SHAGPAT / THE TRAGIC COMEDIANS / LORD
ORMONT AND HIS AMINTA / THE AMAZING MARRIAGE / SHORT STORIES / POEMS /
THE POCKET EDITION IN 18 VOLS. / (*Including THE POETRY AND*
PHILOSOPHY OF / *GEORGE MEREDITH by George Macaulay Trevelyan*) /
Each volume sold separately / *Limp Leather, $1.25 net Cloth, $1.00* / [rule] AN

ESSAY ON COMEDY AND THE USES / OF THE COMIC SPIRIT .... $1.25 / POEMS WRITTEN IN EARLY YOUTH / net, $1.50 / LAST POEMS ...... net, $1.25 / THE MEREDITH POCKET BOOK / Leather, net, $0.75 / [rule] / CHARLES SCRIBNER'S SONS, NEW YORK

This edition or issue was kept in print for at least fifteen years and it should be noted that some copies have on [iv] the imprint: TYPOGRAPHY BY J.S. CUSHING & CO. / [short rule] / PRESSWORK BY UNIVERSITY PRESS, CAMBRIDGE, U.S.A. and that others have the imprint: University Press / JOHN WILSON AND SON, CAMBRIDGE, U.S.A.

PUBLICATION

Meredith signed an agreement with Scribner in September 1895, but negotiations for an American collected edition had been in progress for some time. As early as 21 October 1893 he told Colles: 'Roberts have sent me an indignant letter because of the engagement with Scribners' (*Letters* II 1146). No doubt the discussions for collected editions to be published by Scribner's and Constable were simultaneous. Lionel Stevenson's account (pp. 329–30) makes it seem as though the initiative came from Constable. He claims that the project of a new collected edition in England 'led to the final round in the combat between the American houses of Roberts and Scribner.' Stevenson's account continues: 'On a visit to New York, Otto Kyllman of Constable & Company discussed with Charles Scribner the desirability of issuing the collected edition concurrently in the United States. The obstacle was Roberts' possession of the rights for the earlier novels. After returning to London, Kyllman proposed that Scribner's could take out a fresh copyright on all the books, in view of the changes that had been made in the text. Meredith wished "some friendly arrangement" with Roberts Brothers by which they would consent to discontinue their edition; but if they rejected "a reasonable proposal" Scribner's would be legally justified in bringing out the revised volumes.

'Scribner's replied cautiously that they would like to issue the revised edition, but that it would be difficult for them to purchase the rights from Roberts and that Meredith had better make the arrangement himself. "So far as my father and myself are aware," Will Meredith protested, "they have no claim whatever upon those works of his which they have published ... I do not feel that we need consider them further in the matter." He proceeded to send Scribner's the proofs of the revised *Richard Feverel* so that their edition could be set up immediately.

'Charles Scribner refused to run the risk of infringing the rights of the rival firm. Roberts Brothers reasserted their claim through advertisements warning purchasers against the "mutilated" new edition, and they notified Scribner's that they were prepared to embark upon a price-cutting war if necessary. Will Meredith began to realize with dismay that the whole American copyright of his father's works might be lost in the struggle, for the revised edition was on the eve of appearing in England, with no agreement for its protection in the United States. He suggested desperately that Scribner's and Roberts should enter into a joint agreement for the issuing of uniform complete sets. When this fantastic scheme was rejected, Kyllman managed to persuade Roberts Brothers to surrender their plates and stock of the Meredith novels for the comfortable sum of $6000.'

LXIII

A. CONSTABLE AND CO., 1902–
(The 'Pocket' Edition)

EXAMPLE

THE ORDEAL / OF RICHARD / FEVEREL / A HISTORY OF A FATHER / AND SON / BY GEORGE MEREDITH / [publisher's monogram entwined in a rectangular design of vines] / WESTMINSTER / ARCHIBALD CONSTABLE & CO LTD / 2 WHITEHALL GARDENS 1902

Collation $[\pi]^4$1–28^{8}29^4 232 leaves (16.5 x 10.5) [i–v] vi–vii [viii] [1]–455 [456]

Contents [i] halftitle: THE ORDEAL OF RICHARD FEVEREL [ii] blank [iii] titlepage [iv] copyright statement: COPYRIGHT, 1896, BY / GEORGE MEREDITH [v]–vii contents [viii] blank [1]–455 text, on 455: THE END and at foot: [rule] / Butler & Tanner, The Selwood Printing Works, Frome, and London. [456] blank

Binding Spine, and boards at front and back, covered in crimson red cloth with a distinct vertical ribbing. Endpapers plain white.

Front cover Stamped in gilt, a border .25 cms. from all edges and within this rectangle at top left and also in gilt Meredith's signature.

Spine Stamped in gilt: GEORGE / MEREDITH / THE / ORDEAL / OF / RICHARD / FEVEREL / CONSTABLE / WESTMINSTER

Back cover Plain.

This edition was advertised as the 'New Uniform Pocket Edition' and consisted in the first instance of 15 volumes, the first seven of which appeared towards the end of 1901 but all of which are dated 1902.

The Ordeal of Richard Feverel
Beauchamp's Career
The Egoist
Evan Harrington
Diana of the Crossways
Sandra Belloni
Vittoria
Rhoda Fleming
The Adventures of Harry Richmond
One of Our Conquerors
Lord Ormont and His Aminta
The Amazing Marriage
The Shaving of Shagpat
The Tragic Comedians
Short Stories

To this list were later added:

The Poems Volumes I and II 1903, Volume III 1904. (See Part III, pp. 162–3.)
An Essay on Comedy 1906. (See Part II, pp. 89–90.)

G.M. Trevelyan's *The Poetry and Philosophy of George Meredith*, 1912, was also published in the same format.

In this edition, *An Essay on Comedy* was printed from the plates of the first edition (see Part II, pp. 89–90) and *Lord Ormont and His Aminta* and *The Tragic Comedians* were reset. The other volumes were printed from the plates of LXIII. Though the format remained more or less constant, the volumes were re-issued year by year, sometimes with a cloth, sometimes with a leather binding.

At one stage the edition was issued in a dark green leather binding: of this issue the copies inspected were dated 1902.

The American re-issue of the pocket edition by Scribner is different only in binding and prelims. The binding is in green cloth and has Meredith's monogram stamped in gilt on the front cover. The titlepage reads, for example: THE ADVENTURES / OF / HARRY RICHMOND / BY / GEORGE MEREDITH / REVISED EDITION / NEW YORK / CHARLES SCRIBNER'S SONS / 1906. Facing the titlepage is the advertisement for the edition which in leather cost $1.25 and in cloth $1.00.

LXIV

A. CONSTABLE AND CO.
(The 'Memorial' Edition)

EXAMPLE

GEORGE MEREDITH / [short rule] / THE / SHAVING OF SHAGPAT / AN
ARABIAN ENTERTAINMENT / *Memorial* / *Edition* / LONDON / CONSTABLE
AND COMPANY LTD / 1909

Collation [π]⁴A–T⁸U² 158 leaves (21.4 × 14.5) [i–iv] v–vi [vii–viii] [1]–307
[308]

Contents [i] halftitle: THE WORKS OF / GEORGE MEREDITH / [short rule] / MEMORIAL
EDITION / VOLUME / I [ii] blank [iii] titlepage [iv] imprint: Edinburgh: T. and
A. CONSTABLE, Printers to His Majesty v–vi contents [vii] list of illustrations
[viii] blank [1]–307 text, on 307 at foot the imprint: [rule] / Printed by T. and
A. CONSTABLE, Printers to His Majesty / at the Edinburgh University Press
[308] blank
The frontispiece is bound in between [ii] and [iii]

Binding Spine, and boards at front and back, covered in green cloth. Endpapers
plain white.

Front cover Plain.

Spine Stamped in gilt: The / Shaving of / Shagpat / George / Meredith /
Memorial / Edition / 1

Back cover Plain.

The edition consists of 27 volumes, volumes I–IV dated 1909, volumes V–XXVI
dated 1910, and volume XXVII dated 1911.

I	*The Shaving of Shagpat*
II	*The Ordeal of Richard Feverel*
III & IV	*Sandra Belloni*
V	*Rhoda Fleming*
VI	*Evan Harrington*
VII & VIII	*Vittoria*
IX & X	*The Adventures of Harry Richmond*
XI & XII	*Beauchamp's Career*
XIII & XIV	*The Egoist*
XV	*The Tragic Comedians*
XVI	*Diana of the Crossways*
XVII	*One of Our Conquerors*
XVIII	*Lord Ormont and His Aminta*
XIX	*The Amazing Marriage*

XX *Celt and Saxon*

XXI *Short Stories (Farina, General Ople, & Tale of Chloe)*

XXII *Short Stories (The House on the Beach, The Gentleman of Fifty, & The Sentimentalists*

XXIII *Miscellaneous Prose (An Essay on Comedy, Introductions, Reviews, Short Articles, Criticism, Correspondence from the Seat of War in Italy)*

XXIV–XXVI *Poems*

XXVII *Bibliography and Various Readings*

Though the Memorial Edition was printed from new plates, the text is virtually the same: there are only typographical differences of a minor kind.

REPRINT OF THE MEMORIAL EDITION: 1914-19

Constable's 'Standard Edition' which was published between 1914 and 1919 and which can be identified by its blue binding was a reprint from the plates of the Memorial Edition of the fifteen novels, *An Essay on Comedy*, and a single volume of short stories.

LXIV

CHARLES SCRIBNER'S SONS
(Memorial Edition)

A version of the Constable Memorial Edition was reset and printed by Scribner. It consisted of the following volumes:

I *The Shaving of Shagpat* 1909

II *The Ordeal of Richard Feverel* 1909

III & IV *Sandra Belloni* 1909

V *Rhoda Fleming* 1910

VI *Evan Harrington* 1910

VII & VIII *Vittoria* 1910

IX & X *The Adventures of Harry Richmond* 1910

XI & XII *Beauchamp's Career* 1910

XIII & XIV *The Egoist* 1910

XV *The Tragic Comedians* 1910

XVI *Diana of the Crossways* 1910

XVII *One of Our Conquerors* 1910

XVIII *Lord Ormont and His Aminta* 1910

XIX *The Amazing Marriage* 1910

XX *Celt and Saxon* 1910

LXVII

THE TIMES BOOK CLUB
(The 'Surrey' Edition)

EXAMPLE

THE / AMAZING MARRIAGE / BY / GEORGE MEREDITH / SURREY EDITION / LONDON / THE TIMES BOOK CLUB / 376–84 OXFORD STREET, W. / 1912

Collation $[\pi]^5$A–21^8 261 leaves (21.5 x 14.5) [i–vi] vii–x [1]–511 [512]

Contents [i] halftitle: THE AMAZING MARRIAGE [ii] blank [iii] titlepage [iv] imprint: Edinburgh: T. and A. CONSTABLE, Printers to His Majesty [v] dedication: TO MY FRIEND / FREDERICK JAMESON [vi] blank vii–x contents [1]–511 text, on 511 at centre: THE END and at foot: [rule] / Printed by T. and A. CONSTABLE, Printers to His Majesty / at the Edinburgh University Press [512] blank
The frontispiece, entitled 'Carinthia,' is pasted in between [ii] and [iii].

Binding Spine, and boards at front and back, covered in blue-green cloth. Endpapers plain white.

Front cover A double three-lined border is blind-stamped on the front cover, one border precisely at the edge and the other 2.5 cms. from all four edges. Within this framework is a stamped rectangle at the centre of which an oval piece of green fabric has been pasted on. Around and containing this oval fabric are three gilt lines within which is a design consisting of a small circle, an ear of corn, and the letter M.

Spine A three-lined border stamped in gilt at top and bottom, between which, also stamped in gilt, is a rectangle, containing at the top: THE / AMAZING / MARRIAGE / [device] / GEORGE / MEREDITH

Back cover Plain.

PUBLICATION

The Times Book Club printing from the plates of the Memorial Edition was for 650 sets in 24 volumes, for sale at £8 a set, or £5 10s. in cash. Three volumes were not included: volumes XXII, XXIII, and XXVII. Apart from the omission of these three volumes, the Times Book Club edition corresponds precisely to the Memorial Edition.

PART V

Translations

I
THE SHAVING OF SHAGPAT
FRENCH

Boussinesq, Hélène and René Galland, *Shagpat rasé* Editions de la Nouvelle Revue française. Paris 1921

II
FARINA
GERMAN

Wollmann, Paul (ed.) Velhagen and Klasing, Series of Modern Language Texts, no. 194. Bielefeld 1931

III
THE ORDEAL OF RICHARD FEVEREL
GERMAN

Tauchnitz. Copyright edition in Collection of British Authors, vols. 1508-9. Leipzig 1875

Sotteck, Julie *Richard Feverel. Eine Geschichte von Vater und Sohn* Fischer, Collected Novels, vol. 1, 1904. Berlin 1904 etc.

Greve, F.P. *Richard Feverels Prüfung* J.C.C. Bruns. Minden 1904

Richard Feverels Prüfung 'Meisterromane der modernen Weltliteratur,' 6 vols. J.C.C. Bruns. Minden, vol. 5, 1912

Wollmann, Paul (ed.) Sample excerpts from *The Ordeal of Richard Feverel* Velhagen and Klasing. Bielefeld 1930

Kraushaar, Richard *Richard Feverel* Manesse. Zürich 1961

FRENCH

Forgues, E.D. 'Revue des Deux Mondes,' 14 April 1865, pp. 911-60; 1 May, pp. 137-76; 15 May, pp. 315-56

Weill-Raphaël *Richard Feverel* Editions de la Nouvelle Revue française, 2 vols., 1938

ITALIAN

Padoa, L. *Riccardo Feverel* Emilio Croci, 2 vols. Milan 1873

Riccardo Feverel 'Nuova raccolta di amene letture,' no. 26. Milan 1873

YUGOSLAVIAN

Savic, Vladislav *Iskusenja Ricarda Feverela* Nolit. Beograd 1957

Brusar, Branko *Iskusenja Richarda Feverela* Zora. Zagreb 1965

Moder, Janko *Richard Feverel na preizkusnji* Cankarjeva zalo zba. Ljubljana 1967

CZECH

Prusik, Boryvoj *Zkouska Richarda Feverela* Nakladem J. Otty, 'English Library,' 2 vols., 1902. Prague 1899 etc.

Bartos, J. (ed.) *Zkouska Richarda Feverela*. Prague, 1904

HUNGARIAN

Sandor, Biro. *Tökeletes férfi; regény*. Dante Kiadas, 2 vols. Budapest 193(?)

FINNISH

Kivivuori, Kristina. *Nuoren Feverelin Tulikoe*. Werner Söderström. Helsinki 1953

MALAYAM, INDIA

Variyar, Venmani S. Sankara. *Richard Feverel*. Sahittya Pravarthaka C.S. Kottayam 1961

IV

EVAN HARRINGTON

FRENCH

Mme. le Corbeiller and René Galland. Editions de la Nouvelle Revue française. Paris 1934

V

EMILIA IN ENGLAND

FRENCH

Forgues, E.D. *Sandra Belloni* 'Revue des Deux Mondes,' 15 November 1864, pp. 444–82; 1 December, pp. 550–98; 15 December, pp. 908–47

With 'L'Anneau d'Amasis' (E.R. Bulwer-Lytton), 'La Famille du docteur,' 'Imitations de l'anglais' par E.-D. Forgues. Librairie de L. Hachette and Cie. Paris 1866

Forgues, E.D. *Sandra Belloni* Pätz, 2 vols. Naumburg 1865

VI
RHODA FLEMING
GERMAN
von Harbou, S. J.C.C. Bruns. Minden 1905

Beyer, Werner and Ruprecht Willnow. Dieterich. Leipzig 1964

SLOVAKIAN
Novotneho, Miloslava. Druzstevni Praci Series. Prague 1927

VIII
THE ADVENTURES OF HARRY RICHMOND
GERMAN
Copyright Edition, Heinemann and Balestier, 'English Library,' vols. 86–7. Leipzig 1892

Greve, Felix Paul *Harry Richmonds Abenteuer*. J.C.C. Bruns, Minden 1904

FRENCH
Canque, Yvonne *Les aventures de Harry Richmond* Gallimard, Les Classiques Anglais. Paris 1948

IX
BEAUCHAMP'S CAREER
FRENCH
Monod, Auguste *La Carrière de Beauchamp* Gallimard, Editions de la Nouvelle Revue française, 2 vols. Paris 1928

GERMAN
Copyright Edition. Tauchnitz, Collection of British Authors, vols. 1565–6. Leipzig 1876

Brodt, Peter (ed.) *Beauchamp's Career. A Selection* Westermann, Westermann texts 73. Braunschweig 1931

X
THE EGOIST
GERMAN
Sotteck, Julie *Der Egoist* Fischer, Collected Novels, vol. 2, 1905. Berlin 1904 etc.

Reisiger, H. *Der Egoist* P. List. Leipzig 1925, 1958, and 1966

German Book Company, 2 vols. Berlin, 1932 and Berlin, Darmstadt 1955

P. List. Munich 1955, 1966, and 1969

FRENCH
Strauss, Maurice *L'Egoiste* C. Carrington, 2 vols. Paris 1904

Canque, Yvonne *L'Egoiste* Editions de la Nouvelle Revue française, 2 vols. Paris 1924

Gallimard, 2 vols. Paris 1949

Editions Rencontre. Lausanne 1962

ITALIAN
Torreta, Laura *L'Egoista* Milan 1922

Ottolino, Pino *L'Egoista* Casa edit. Maja. Milan 1929

PORTUGUESE
da Costa Pires, Mario *O grande egoista* Romano Torres. Lisboa 1959

YUGOSLAV
Ujevic, Tin *Egoist* Zora. Zagreb 1953

Markovic, Bozidar *Egoist* Prosveta. Beograd 1962

HUNGARIAN
Babits, Mihaly and Arpad Toth *Az önzö* Szinhaztudomanyi Intézet. Intézet, Budapest 1964

ROMANIAN
Alexandrescu, Sorin *Egoistul* Editura pentru literatura universala. Bucoresti 1966

RUSSIAN
Vengerovoj, Zenaida A. *Egoist* Lederle and Co., 'Moia Biblioteka,' no. 108–12. St. Petersburg 1894

XI
THE TRAGIC COMEDIANS
GERMAN
Copyright Edition. Tauchnitz, Collection of British Authors, vol. 1956. Leipzig 1881; 2nd edition 1891

Sotteck, Julie *Die tragischen Komödianten* Fischer, Collected Novels, vol. 4, 1908. Berlin 1904 etc.

Benecke, J.L. *Die tragischen Komödianten* Siegle Hill and Co. London and Altenburg 1909

FRENCH

Ritt, Claude and Joël *Tragi-comédie d'amour* F. Juven. Paris 1909

Néel, Philippe *Les Comédiens tragiques* Gallimard, Editions de la Nouvelle Revue française. Paris 1927

ITALIAN

Castellini, Itala B. Lossetti *I tragici Commedianti* Rizzoli. Milan 1951

XII
DIANA OF THE CROSSWAYS

GERMAN

Greve, Felix Paul *Diana vom Kreuzweg* J.C.C. Bruns. Minden 1905

Ehm, Emi *Diana vom Kreuzweg* Fischer. Frankfurt and Hamburg 1962

FRENCH

Wolff, Lucien *Diane de la croisée des chemins* Gallimard, 2 vols. Paris 1931

ITALIAN

Pàntini, Romualdo *Diana de' Crossways* 'Nuova Antologia,' 1 September–16 December 1906

Pàntini, Romualdo *Diana de' Crossways*. Reprinted in book form, Fratelli Treves. Milan 1909

Messina, Nora e Anna *Diana di Crossways* Garzanti. Milano 1953

PORTUGUESE

Pires, Mario da Costa *Os três amores de Diana* Romano Torres. Lisbon 1967

BOHEMIAN

Hrusa, Prelozil Joril *Diana z Rozcesti* 1928

XIII
ONE OF OUR CONQUERORS

FRENCH

Lalou, Christine and René *Un de nos conquérants* Editions de la Nouvelle Revue française. Paris 1935

GERMAN
Copyright Edition in Heinemann and Balestier, 'The English Library,' vols.
28–9. Leipzig 1891

XIV
LORD ORMONT AND HIS AMINTA
GERMAN
Copyright Edition. Tauchnitz, Collection of British Authors, vols. 3077–8.
Leipzig 1895

Sotteck, Julie. Fischer, Collected Novels, vol. 3, 1907. Berlin 1904 etc.

YUGOSLAV
Semenovic, Luka *Lord Ormont i njegova Aminta* Subotika. Beograd 1968

XV
THE AMAZING MARRIAGE
FRENCH
Weill-Raphaël *L'Etonnant mariage* Gallimard, Editions de la Nouvelle Revue
française. Paris 1939

GERMAN
Copyright Edition. Tauchnitz, Collection of British Authors, vols. 3195–6.
Leipzig 1897

DUTCH
In condensed form, *Het Geruchtmakend Huwelijk*, *De Gids* Amsterdam, August
1896, pp. 283–317; September, pp. 456–502

XXII
ESSAY ON COMEDY
FRENCH
Davray, Henry-D. 'Essai sur la comédie,' Société du 'Mercure de France.' Paris
1898

GERMAN
Dick, Ernst 'Ein Essay über die Komödie' in *George Meredith. Drei Versuche*
Wiegandt and Grieben. Berlin 1910

JAPANESE
Sagara, Tokuzô. Kigeki-ron. Iwanami Shoten. Tokyo 1953

XIX
THE TALE OF CHLOE
FRENCH

Yersin, Marguerite 'Mercure de France' Paris, 16 February 1908, pp. 635–75; 1 March, pp. 89–113; 16 March, pp. 264–89

Dourgnon, D. *Le Conte de Chloé* Editions de la Nouvelle Revue française, 3rd edition. Paris 1931

GERMAN

Blei, F. *Chloes Geschichte. Eine Novelle* Müller and Company, Sanssouci-Bücher, vol. 7. Potsdam 1923

Blei, F. *Chloes Geschichte. Eine Novelle* Propyläen. Berlin 1925

von Bomhard, Bettina *Die Geschichte von Chloe* Sherpe. Krefeld 1949

XIX
THE HOUSE ON THE BEACH
FRENCH

Connes, Mme. Georges *La Maison de la grève* Gallimard. Paris 1929

XXXVII
MODERN LOVE
FRENCH

Fontainas, André *L'Amour moderne* Editions de 'La Phalange' Paris 1910

L'Amour moderne 'Commerce,' cahier xxv, pp. 163–220. Paris 1930

ITALIAN (with English text)
Serpieri, Alessandro *Modern Love* De Donato. Bari 1968

JAPANESE
Hamayotsu, Ichizô *Tanima ni Shitau. Ukiyo no aiyoku* (and *Love in the Valley*) Hokuseieidô Shoten. Tokyo 1958

XLV
ODE TO FRANCE
FRENCH

Pierrotet, Maurice *L'Ode à la France* Editions de la Nouvelle Revue française. Paris 1916

SELECTED WORKS

FRENCH

Garnier, C.M. *Florilège de George Meredith. Pensées cueillies aux romans et aux poèmes* Paris 1925

Cazamian, M. and L. *Poèmes choisis* Collection bilingue. Editions Montaigne 1969

GERMAN

Stoy, F. (ed.) *The Meredith Textbook* English Library Series for Schools, G. Kühtmann, vol. 39. Dresden 1911

Chronological listing of all Meredith's
publications

1851 *Poems*, first edition, J.W. Parker (1 volume)

1856 *The Shaving of Shagpat*, first edition, Chapman and Hall (1 volume)

1857 *Farina*, first edition, Smith, Elder and Co. (1 volume)

1859 *The Ordeal of Richard Feverel*, first edition, Chapman and Hall (3 volumes)

1860 *Evan Harrington*, serial publication in *Once a Week*, Volume II, February–October 1860

Evan Harrington, first edition, Harper and Bros. (1 volume)

1861 *Evan Harrington*, first English edition, Bradbury and Evans (3 volumes)

1862 *Modern Love*, first edition, Chapman and Hall (1 volume)

1864 *Emilia in England*, serial publication in *Revue des deux Mondes*, 15 November, 1 December, and 15 December 1864

Emilia in England, first edition, Chapman and Hall (3 volumes)

1865 *Rhoda Fleming*, first edition, Tinsley Bros. (3 volumes)

The Shaving of Shagpat, second edition, Chapman and Hall (1 volume)

Farina, second edition, Smith, Elder and Co. (1 volume); variant of second edition also published by Smith, Elder and Co.

The Ordeal of Richard Feverel, serial publication under the title 'L'Epreuve de Richard Feverel, Roman de la vie anglaise,' in *Revue des deux Mondes*, 15 April, 1 May, and 15 May 1865

1866 *Vittoria*, serial publication in the *Fortnightly Review*, January–December 1866

Vittoria, first edition, Chapman and Hall (3 volumes)

Evan Harrington, second edition, Bradbury, Evans and Co. (1 volume)

1868 *Farina*, third edition, Chapman and Hall (1 volume)

1871 *The Adventures of Harry Richmond*, first edition, Smith, Elder and Co. (3 volumes); re-issued by Smith, Elder and Co.

1874 *Beauchamp's Career*, serial publication in the *Fortnightly Review*, August 1874–December 1875

1875 *The Ordeal of Richard Feverel*, 'Collection of British Authors,' Tauchnitz (volumes 1508–9)

1876 *Beauchamp's Career*, first edition, Chapman and Hall (3 volumes)

1877 *The House on the Beach*, serial publication in the *New Quarterly Magazine* January 1877

The House on the Beach, first edition, Harper and Bros. (1 volume)

The Case of General Ople and Lady Camper, serial publication in the *New Quarterly Magazine*, July 1877

Essay on Comedy, serial publication in the *New Quarterly Magazine*, April 1877

1878 *The Ordeal of Richard Feverel*, second edition, C. Kegan Paul and Co. (1 volume)

1879 *The Egoist*, serial publication under the title 'Sir Willoughby Patterne the Egoist' in the *Glasgow Weekly Herald*, June 1879–January 1880
The Egoist, first edition, C. Kegan Paul and Co. (3 volumes)

1880 *The Egoist*, second edition, C. Kegan Paul and Co. (1 volume)
The Tragic Comedians, serial publication in the *Fortnightly Review*, October 1880–February 1881
The Tragic Comedians, first edition, Chapman and Hall (2 volumes)

1881 *The Tragic Comedians*, second version of first edition, Chapman and Hall (1 volume)

1881 *The Tragic Comedians*, paperback edition, Ward, Lock & Bowden (1 volume); 1-volume American edition by George Munro

1883 *Poems and Lyrics of the Joy of Earth*, first edition printed by Clay, Macmillan and Co. (1 volume); second edition printed by Clark, also published by Macmillan and Co.; American edition by Roberts Brothers

1884 *Diana of the Crossways*, serial publication in the *Fortnightly Review*, June–December 1884

1885 *Diana of the Crossways*, first edition, Chapman and Hall (3 volumes); and 1-volume Collected Edition, Chapman and Hall (printed by Virtue)
The Ordeal of Richard Feverel, Evan Harrington, and *The Adventures of Harry Richmond*, Collected Edition, Chapman and Hall (1 volume of each, printed by Virtue)

1886 *Sandra Belloni, Vittoria, Rhoda Fleming, Beauchamp's Career, The Egoist*, Collected Edition, Chapman and Hall (1 volume of each, printed by Virtue)

1887 *Ballads and Poems of Tragic Life*, first edition, Macmillan and Co. (1 volume); American edition published by Roberts Bros. (1 volume)
The Shaving of Shagpat and *Farina*, Collected Edition, Chapman and Hall (1 volume, printed by Virtue)

1888 *The Pilgrim's Scrip*, first edition, Roberts Bros. (1 volume)
A Reading of Earth, first edition, Macmillan and Co. (1 volume); American edition published by Roberts Bros. (1 volume)

1889 *Jump-to-Glory Jane*, serial publication in the *Universal Review*, October 1889
Jump-to-Glory Jane, first edition, privately printed (1 volume)

1889 *Vittoria, Beauchamp's Career, The Egoist, The Shaving of Shagpat* and *Farina*, Collected Edition, Chapman and Hall (1 volume of each, printed by Clowes)

1890 *One of Our Conquerors*, serial publication in the *Fortnightly Review*, October 1890–May 1891
The Case of General Ople and Lady Camper, first edition, John W. Lovell

Co. (1 volume); Seaside Library Edition published by George Munro (1 volume)

The Tale of Chloe, first edition, John W. Lovell Co. (1 volume); re-issue from first edition by R.F. Fenno

Diana of the Crossways, Evan Harrington, The Ordeal of Richard Feverel, The Adventures of Harry Richmond, Sandra Belloni, Rhoda Fleming, Collected Edition, Chapman and Hall (1 volume of each, printed by Clowes)

1891 *One of Our Conquerors*, first edition, Chapman and Hall (3 volumes); Collected Edition, Chapman and Hall (1 volume, printed by Virtue)

The Case of General Ople and Lady Camper, Surprise Series, International Book Co. (1 volume)

Modern Love, American edition, Thomas B. Mosher (1 volume)

1892 *The Tragic Comedians*, Collected Edition, Ward, Lock & Bowden, (1 volume, contribution to Chapman and Hall's Collected edition, printed by Virtue); also second version, printed by Clowes.

Jump-to-Glory Jane, second edition, Swan Sonnenschein and Co. (1 volume)

1892 *Poems: the Empty Purse*, first edition, Macmillan and Co. (1 volume); American edition by Roberts Bros. (1 volume)

Modern Love, A Reprint, first edition, Macmillan and Co. (1 volume); American edition by Roberts Bros. (1 volume)

One of Our Conquerors, Collected Edition, Chapman and Hall (1 volume, printed by Clowes)

1893 *Lord Ormont and His Aminta*, serial publication in the *Pall Mall Magazine*, December 1893–July 1894

1894 *Lord Ormont and His Aminta*, first edition, Chapman and Hall (3 volumes)

The Tale of Chloe, The House on the Beach, The Case of General Ople and Lady Camper, Collected Edition, Ward Lock & Bowden (1-volume contribution to Chapman and Hall's Collected Edition, printed by Virtue)

Poems and Lyrics of the Joy of Earth, first edition, Macmillan and Co (1 volume)

Ballads and Poems of Tragic Life, re-issue of first edition, Macmillan and Co. (1 volume)

Diana of the Crossways, The Adventures of Harry Richmond, Colonial Issue of Collected Edition, Chapman and Hall (1 volume of each, printed by George Bell)

Modern Love A Reprint, Macmillan and Co. (1 volume)

1895 *The Amazing Marriage*, serial publication in *Scribner's Magazine*, January–December 1895

The Amazing Marriage, first edition, A. Constable and Co. (2 volumes);

American edition by Charles Scribner's Sons (2 volumes)

A Reading of Earth, second edition, Macmillan and Co. (1 volume)

1895 *Lord Ormont and His Aminta*, Collected Edition, Chapman and Hall, (1 volume, printed by Virtue)

Poems and Lyrics of the Joy of Earth, Macmillan and Co. (1 volume)

Evan Harrington, *The Ordeal of Richard Feverel*, *Rhoda Fleming*, *The Egoist*, *Lord Ormont and His Aminta*, Colonial Issue of Collected Edition, Chapman and Hall (1 volume of each, printed by George Bell)

Poems: The Empty Purse, Macmillan and Co. (1 volume)

Modern Love A Reprint, Macmillan and Co. (1 volume)

1896 *The Amazing Marriage*, second edition, A. Constable and Co. (2 volumes)

The Ordeal of Richard Feverel (Volumes I and II), *Evan Harrington* (Volumes III and IV), De Luxe Edition, Archibald Constable and Co.

1897 *Essay on Comedy*, first edition, Archibald Constable and Co. (1 volume); American edition by Charles Scribner's Sons (1 volume)

Selected Poems, first edition, Archibald Constable and Co. (1 volume); American edition by Charles Scribner's Sons (1 volume)

Ballads and Poems of Tragic Life, re-issue of first edition, Macmillan and Co (1 volume)

Sandra Belloni (Volumes V and VI), *Vittoria* (Volumes VII and VIII), *Rhoda Fleming* (Volumes IX and X), *The Adventures of Harry Richmond* (Volumes XI and XII), *Beauchamp's Career* (Volumes XIII and XIV), *The Egoist* (Volumes XV and XVI), *Diana of the Crossways* (Volumes XVII and XVIII), *One of Our Conquerors* (Volumes XIX and XX), *Lord Ormont and His Aminta* (Volumes XXI and XXII), *The Amazing Marriage* (Volumes XXIII and XXIV), De Luxe Edition, Archibald Constable and Co.

1897 *The Ordeal of Richard Feverel*, *Rhoda Fleming*, *Sandra Belloni*, *Vittoria*, *Diana of the Crossways*, *The Adventures of Harry Richmond*, *Beauchamp's Career*, *The Egoist*, Library Edition, Archibald Constable and Co. (each 1 volume)

1898 *Lord Ormont and His Aminta*, Collected Edition, Chapman and Hall (1 volume, printed by Clowes)

Essay on Comedy, second edition, Archibald Constable and Co.

Essays (Volume XXXII), De Luxe Edition, Archibald Constable and Co.

Selected Poems, re-issue of first edition, Archibald Constable and Co.

Odes in Contribution to the Song of French History, first edition, Archibald Constable and Co. (1 volume); American edition by Charles Scribner's Sons (1 volume)

Poems (Volumes XXIX–XXXI), De Luxe Edition, Archibald Constable and Co.

Nature Poems, first edition, Archibald Constable and Co. (1 volume).

Modern Love and Other Poems, American edition, Thomas B. Mosher.
The Shaving of Shagpat (Volume xxv), *The Tragic Comedians* (Volume xxvi), *The Tale of Chloe, The House on the Beach* (Volume xxvii), *Farina, The Case of General Ople and Lady Camper* (Volume xxviii), De Luxe Edition, Archibald Constable and Co.
Evan Harrington, The Tale of Chloe and Other Stories, The Shaving of Shagpat, One of Our Conquerors, The Amazing Marriage, Essay on Comedy, Poems, The Tragic Comedians, Library Edition, Archibald Constable and Co. (each 1 volume)

1899 *The Ordeal of Richard Feverel*, Pocket 'Revised Edition,' George Newnes
Lord Ormont and His Aminta, Library Edition, Archibald Constable and Co.

1900 *The Story of Bhanavar the Beautiful*, first edition, Archibald Constable and Co. Ltd.

1901 *A Reading of Life*, first edition, Archibald Constable and Co. Ltd.; American edition by Charles Scribner's Sons

1902 *The Ordeal of Richard Feverel, Beauchamp's Career, The Egoist, Evan Harrington, Diana of the Crossways, Sandra Belloni, Vittoria, Rhoda Fleming, The Adventures of Harry Richmond, One of Our Conquerors, Lord Ormont and His Aminta, The Amazing Marriage, The Shaving of Shagpat, The Tragic Comedians, Short Stories*, Pocket Edition, Archibald Constable and Co. Ltd. (each 1 volume)

1903 *Selected Poems*, re-issue, Archibald Constable and Co. Ltd.
Poems, Pocket Edition, Archibald Constable and Co. Ltd. (2 volumes)

1904 *Modern Love A Reprint*, American edition, Thomas B. Mosher

1906 *Meredith Pocket Book*, Archibald Constable and Co. Ltd.
Essay on Comedy, Pocket Edition, Archibald Constable and Co. Ltd.

1907 *Nature Poems*, second edition, Archibald Constable and Co. Ltd.

1908 *Tercentenary of Milton's Birth*, privately printed by Oxford University Press

1909 *Poems Written in Early Youth*, first edition, Constable and Co. (1 volume); American edition by Charles Scribner's Sons
Last Poems, first edition, Constable and Co. Ltd. (1 volume); American edition by Charles Scribner's Sons
Chillianwallah, first edition, privately printed (1 volume)
Twenty Poems, first edition, privately printed (1 volume)

1909 *Love in a Valley*, first American edition, R. Fletcher Seymour Co. (1 volume)
Modern Love A Reprint, Kennerly (1 volume)
The Shaving of Shagpat (Volume 1), *The Ordeal of Richard Feverel* (Volume

II), *Sandra Belloni* (Volumes III and IV), Memorial Edition, Constable and Co. Ltd.; and Memorial Edition, Charles Scribner's Sons

1910 *Celt and Saxon*, serial publication in the *Fortnightly Review*, January–August 1910; and in *The Forum* (New York), January–June 1910.

Celt and Saxon, first edition, Constable and Company (1 volume).

Selected Poems, re-issue, Constable and Company (1 volume)

Poems (Volume XXXIII), De Luxe Edition, Archibald Constable and Co.

Miscellaneous Prose (Volume XXXIV), De Luxe Edition, Archibald Constable and Co.

Rhoda Fleming (Volume V), *Evan Harrington* (Volume VI), *Vittoria* (Volumes VII and VIII), *The Adventures of Harry Richmond* (Volumes IX and X), *Beauchamp's Career* (Volumes XI and XII), *The Egoist* (Volumes XIII and XIV), *The Tragic Comedians* (Volume XV), *Diana of the Crossways* (Volume XVI), *One of Our Conquerors* (Volume XVII), *Lord Ormont and His Aminta* (Volume XVIII), *The Amazing Marriage* (Volume XIX), *Celt and Saxon* (Volume XX), *Short Stories* (Volumes XXI and XXII), *Miscellaneous Prose* (Volume XXIII), *Poems* (Volumes XXIV–XXVI), Memorial Edition, Constable and Co. Ltd. and Memorial Edition, Charles Scribner's Sons

1911 *Celt and Saxon* (Volume XXXV), De Luxe Edition, Archibald Constable and Co.

1911 *Bibliography and Readings* (Volume XXVII), Memorial Edition, Constable and Co. Ltd.

Alterations on Original Text and Bibliography (Volume XXVII), Memorial Edition, Charles Scribner's Sons

1912 *Poetical Works*, first edition, Constable and Co. Ltd.

The Letters of George Meredith Collected and Edited by his Son, first edition, Constable and Co. Ltd.

The Shaving of Shagpat (Volume I), *The Ordeal of Richard Feverel* (Volume II), *Sandra Belloni* (Volumes III and IV), *Rhoda Fleming* (Volume V), *Evan Harrington* (Volume VI), *Vittoria* (Volumes VII and VIII), *The Adventures of Harry Richmond* (Volumes IX and X), *Beauchamp's Career* (Volumes XI and XII), *The Egoist* (Volumes XIII and XIV), *The Tragic Comedians* (Volume XV), *Diana of the Crossways* (Volume XVI), *One of Our Conquerors* (Volume XVII), *Lord Ormont and His Aminta* (Volume XVIII), *The Amazing Marriage* (Volume XIX), *Celt and Saxon* (Volume XX), *Short Stories* (Volume XXI), *Poems* (Volumes XXII–XXIV), Surrey Edition, Times Book Club

1913 *Up to Midnight*, John W. Luce and Co. (Boston)

Letters from George Meredith to Edward Clodd and Clement K. Shorter, privately printed

1914 *Selected Poems*, re-issue, Constable and Co. (1 volume)

1919 *Letters from George Meredith to Richard Henry Horne*, privately printed

1922 *Letters from George Meredith to Algernon Charles Swinburne and Theodore Watts Dunton*, privately printed

1923 *The Letters of George Meredith to Alice Meynell*, The Nonesuch Press

1924 *Letters from George Meredith to Various Correspondents*, privately printed

1928 *The Contributions of George Meredith to the Monthly Observer*, Maurice Buxton-Forman, privately printed

1970 *The Letters of George Meredith*, ed. C.L. Cline, Clarendon Press

Index

This book

was designed by

ROBERT MACDONALD

under the direction of

ALLAN FLEMING

and was printed by

University

of Toronto

Press